Study Guide

for use with

Prepared by RANDALL OSBORNE
TEXAS STATE UNIVERSITY

SHIRLEY OGLETREE
TEXAS STATE UNIVERSITY

and PATRICIA BOECHLER
UNIVERSITY OF ALBERTA

NELSON EDUCATION

NELSON EDUCATION

Study Guide for use with Childhood and Adolescence: Voyages in Development
First Canadian Edition

by Randall Osborne, Shirley Ogletree, Patricia Boechler

Associate Vice President, Editorial Director:
Evelyn Veitch

Editor-in-Chief:
Anne Williams

Executive Editor:
Cara Yarzab

Executive Marketing Manager:
Lenore Taylor-Atkins

Developmental Editor:
Theresa Fitzgerald

Content Production Manager:
Christine Gilbert

Proofreader:
Cathy Witlox

Senior Manufacturing Coordinator:
Joanne McNeil

Design Director:
Ken Phipps

Managing Designer:
Katherine Strain

Printer:
Thomson West

Printed and bound in the United States of America
1 2 3 4 10 09 08

For more information contact Nelson Education Ltd., 1120 Birchmount Road, Toronto, Ontario, M1K 5G4. Or you can visit our Internet site at http://www.nelson.com

ISBN 978-0-17-647306-8

TABLE OF CONTENTS

CHAPTER 1

History, Theories, and Methods

Learning Objectives

By the end of this chapter, you should be able to generate well-thought-out responses to demonstrate your understanding of the following learning objectives (sample answer comments are included at the end of this chapter):

1. Explain what child development is.
2. Describe why it is important to study child development.
3. Discuss the history of child development. Have views about childhood and child development changed across time? If so, how?
4. Describe the major theories of child development.
5. Discuss the major controversies in the study of child development.
6. Describe how psychologists study child development.

Chapter Summary

What Is Child Development? Coming to Terms with Terms

Although we have used terms such as *child* all our lives, do we really know what those terms mean? In the strictest sense, a **child** is a person experiencing development from infancy to puberty. **Infancy** is defined as the first two years of life and **puberty** signals the development of reproductive capacity, which generally is seen as the transition from childhood to adulthood.

Development generally refers to the orderly appearance of characteristics over time. Although the most obvious changes are **physical,** children change (or develop) in **motor, cognitive, emotional,** and **social** ways as well. The terms **growth** and **development** are not the same. Growth refers to changes in size or quantity whereas **development** refers to qualitative changes. A child may grow in height and experience cognitive development.

Why Do We Study Child Development?

One of the most significant reasons for studying child development is to understand humans in general. We were all children. Many of us will have children. There is a strong desire to understand where we have come from. To understand why adults are the way they are, we must ask questions about the children they developed from. Studying child development can also assist us in understanding the occurrence of developmental problems such as **PKU, SIDS, Down syndrome,** and **autism.**

The Development of Child Development

Thoughts about child development have changed dramatically across time. Some early thinkers believed that children were born evil and needed to be severely punished. Children were viewed as property and treated as such. Still others considered children to be miniature adults that simply grew bigger. As you can imagine, one's views of child development would play a significant role in determining how children are treated. If one believes, for example, that children are miniature adults, then child labour would be considered appropriate.

John Locke, a famous philosopher, suggested that children are born a *tabula rasa,* a blank tablet. What does this imply about child development? First, it means that children are not born evil. They are born without prior knowledge or tendencies. Second, this "blankness" means the child develops as the result of experience. If the child has positive experiences, the child will develop into a "good" person.

Another important philosopher, Jean-Jacques Rousseau, believed that children were born good and simply needed freedom and support to express their natural impulses. If nurtured in this way, children would develop into positive, moral individuals. If one believes this, children should be encouraged to explore their world, should be given support to develop their talents, and should be assisted in developing positive qualities. If a child engages in negative behaviour, it is somehow caused by obstacles in the environment.

Theories of Child Development

Theories of child development consider questions such as "How do children learn?" and "What role do nature and nurture play in child development?" A key word in studying development is **maturation.** Maturation is the unfolding of genetically determined characteristics. All that is needed for maturation is the passage of time.

John Watson suggested that children develop and change not as a result of genetic patterns of maturation but as a result of learning. Development, then, is shaped by experience. If the child is reinforced for doing something, he or she will do it again. If the child is punished for doing something, he or she will not do it again. This way of considering child development is consistent with Locke's *tabula rasa.*

Contemporary theories of child development suggest that views of child development need to consider both genetics (**nature**) and environment (**nurture**) in trying to understand child development. Developmental psychologists seek to **describe, explain, predict,** and **influence** child development. Key areas of study include **heredity, perception, language, learning, cognition, emotion, socialization,** and **gender roles.**

Theories allow scientists to accomplish the goals of research, which are **description, prediction, control,** and **explanation.** Freud's theory of child development sought to explain how humans (children or adults) deal with conflicts, learn to follow rules, and develop a moral base. Erikson's theory looked at development across the lifespan and sought to explain how children and adults change in terms of social development. Both of these theories (as well as the theory of Piaget) are **stage** theories. Stage theories assume that development occurs in distinct stages that are the same for all persons. The development in one stage sets the tone for development in the next stage.

Freud felt that most of human development is influenced by **unconscious** forces that are aggressive and sexual in nature. The child struggles to come to terms with these feelings and does so through the working of three structures: **id, ego,** and **superego.** Id is biological and present at birth. Id is driven by the pleasure principle and follows the motto "I want what I want when I want it." Clearly, we could not survive long if all we were to do is strive to pleasure ourselves. Conflicts with reality prompt the development of ego, which attempts to satisfy id's urges but to do so safely. It is important to note that ego has no moral base and does not pass judgment on what id desires. In order to survive in a society in which others are also driven by pleasure, we develop **superego,** which operates according to morality. This moral base is given to us by our parents and is internalized.

Freud's view of child development looks at **psychosexual development** and seeks to understand how children develop identities, learn to understand their own sexual and aggressive tendencies, and develop into adults with particular personality characteristics and preferences.

Erikson's theory of **psychosocial development** is considered less pessimistic than Freud's and seeks to explain how humans develop as a result of "crisis" events in their lives. It is important to note that Erikson did not consider a **life crisis** to be bad. A crisis is simply a developmental challenge that, when dealt with and resolved positively, moves the person forward in a positive way to the next stage of development. In infancy, for example, the child must grapple with the quality of **trust vs. mistrust.** If the parents provide predictable and positive care, the child will come to trust the world. If the child trusts the world, he or she is in a good position to positively resolve the second developmental crisis of **autonomy vs. shame and doubt.** A child that feels autonomous will exercise self-control and strive to become increasingly independent.

Behaviouristic theories of child development used principles of **reinforcement** and **punishment** to understand how children change. **Classical conditioning** views looked at how new associations (or learning relationships) are formed. An infant, for example, will automatically turn his or her head in the direction of a touch on the cheek in order to nurse. If the mother says the infant's name, then touches the cheek and nurses the infant, the child will eventually learn to turn his or her head in the direction of the sound (the **stimulus**) of his or her name being said. In this example, the neutral stimulus—or the **conditioned stimulus** (the sound of his or her name)—comes to be associated with a stimulus that automatically evokes a response (the **unconditioned stimulus**) to the touch on the cheek, which **elicits** a predictable response (the **unconditioned response**). Eventually, the new stimulus (the sound of his or her name) will come to elicit the same response that used to be evoked by the touch on the cheek. When the child turns his or her head in the direction of the sound of his or her name being said, it is called a **conditioned response.**

As these patterns of conditioning were studied, it was discovered that they could explain how simple things, such as turning one's head, could be learned as a response to a variety of things (the sound of one's name or the command "look at me"). This pattern of learning, however, cannot explain how complex abilities (such as tying one's shoes or learning to solve math problems) are acquired. To explain these events, **operant conditioning** was used. Through the process of **shaping,** children learn complex behaviour patterns. Shaping involves the systematic reinforcement of steps in a desired behaviour. If I want to teach my son to tie his shoes, for example, I may first reward him for finding his shoes. Then I may reward him for getting them on his feet, then I may reward him for making the first cross-over of his shoelaces, and so on. Clearly, this will need to occur over time, and each step may need to be reinforced multiple times before he is ready to move on to the next step in the process. In this fashion, very complex behaviours can be learned.

Social cognitive theorists (such as Canadian-born Albert Bandura) have sought to understand how children learn things they have not been reinforced. All of us have probably had the experience of discovering that a young child knows some nasty words that have not been reinforced. In other words, through **observational learning** children can learn skills that lie latent until some time at which those skills are demonstrated. These theories look at the interplay between the child's behaviour, cognitive characteristics, and the environment. A child, for example, may demonstrate artistic talent. The parents might reinforce this, praise the child, place pictures on the refrigerator, etc. This may convince the child that he or she is "a good drawer," which encourages the child to draw more and try harder.

The **cognitive perspective** focuses on the development of the child's mental processes. Some of these theories focus on information processing. Others, like Jean Piaget's **cognitive-developmental theory**, focuses on how children form mental concepts about the world and learn to manipulate those concepts in order to have an impact on the external world. Piaget looked at the development of **schemes** or organized categories of information about the world. In addition, he looked at how children come to use symbols and the importance of using symbols for the development of language or mathematical ability.

According to Piaget, children learn to categorize (create internal **mental representations** of the external world) through the processes of **assimilation** and **accommodation.** A child might, for example, learn that a small furry creature is called a kitten. When the child sees a puppy, his or her first guess might be to call it a kitten. This is assimilation. The child attempts to categorize similar things into the same category. After all, the puppy is also small and furry. But the child will learn that the two creatures are different (one meows and the other barks) and will "accommodate" this information by creating a new scheme for "puppy." This process continues as the child learns about more animals and learns to separate their differences. A balance of these two processes that helps incorporate new knowledge is referred to as **equilibration.**

Piaget proposed four stages of cognitive development. The stage of infancy is referred to as **sensorimotor** development. Think of it this way, the child knows about and understands the world through senses and motor movement. The child may think, for example, that objects exist only if they can be experienced with the senses and may cease to exist if they move beyond (or out of) sensory awareness. The second stage of cognitive development is referred to as **preoperational** and focuses on the development of very basic symbols that allow for the development of language. The child still does not think with logic or in abstract terms. The third stage is called **concrete operations** and involves the systematic manipulation of symbols that allow the child to think with numbers. The final stage of cognitive development (which carries the child into adolescence and adulthood) is **formal operations** and involves logic, abstract reasoning and the ability to think beyond one's own person and to have concern and empathy for others.

Information processing theory is another cognitive approach. It differs from Piaget's theory in that it is not a stage theory. Rather, the brain is regarded as being similar to the hardware of a computer, and children, as they develop, learn to process information more efficiently.

The **biological perspective** looks at how development occurs and may be driven or influenced by biology. Some research shows that infants are "ready" to experience developmental advancements, and age and growth allow these advancements to unfold. Some of these advancements are referred to as **fixed action patterns** because the assumption is that they are built in and simply unfold as the child ages. The study of instinctive behaviours that are specific to a certain species is called **ethology.**

Ecological systems theory focuses on the relationships among a child (or adult) and all other aspects of the environment. The **microsystem** refers to those aspects of the environment (like parents, teachers, and siblings) with whom the child directly interacts, while the **macrosystem** includes beliefs, values, expectations, and lifestyles of the culture in which that child is developing. These macrosystems can vary widely as a function of culture, household income, educational expectations, and so on.

The **sociocultural perspective** views children as social beings influenced by the culture in which they live. This perspective assumes that we are influenced by both biological and sociological variables. A key theorist in this area was Lev Vygotsky, who suggested that children are greatly influenced by their social interactions within the home. Vygotsky viewed the child's development as adaptive to both the social and cultural environments in which he or she is being raised.

Vygotsky included in his theory a concept called **zone of proximal development.** In short, this term refers to those things the child can do with the assistance of others who are more skilled. A child with an older sibling, for example, may start to engage in behaviours earlier in development than a child without such assistance. Vygotsky also referred to **scaffolding,** in which the child "builds" toward certain abilities. One example would be learning to sound out words during the reading process.

Human diversity is of particular interest in the sociocultural perspective. Those developmental psychologists who emphasize societal and cultural factors are also often interested in differences among children based on **gender** and **ethnic group.**

Controversies in Child Development

Several controversies surround the study of child development. One has already been alluded to in this chapter. That is, the issue of **nature vs. nurture.** The issue here is how much of child development is influenced by genetic material (nature) and how much is determined by environmental influences (nurture). Another significant issue is one of **continuity vs. discontinuity.** Theories of continuity assume that child development is gradual and slow. Discontinuity theories look at development as occurring in major leaps in which the child experiences qualitative changes with time.

Another significant controversy involves the role the child may play in his or her own development. On one side of the issue are those who assume that children are passive recipients of the world. This is consistent with John Locke's view and the **tabula rasa.** Others (such as Rousseau) believe that children are born ready to experience the world and will become active participants in their own development.

How Do We Study Child Development?

The study of child development begins with questions. How do children learn? What determines the child's intelligence level? How do children learn to separate themselves from their parents and become independent? The key approach, of course, is the **scientific method.** This method includes having a **hypothesis,** which is defined as a "specific statement about behaviour that is tested through research." There are many ways in which scientists can gather data to attempt to answer questions about child development. One method employs what is known as the **correlational method.** This involves statistically determining the degree to which two events occur together. If I determine, for example, that a child cries more often when loud noises are present, I can say that these two events are **positively correlated.** With a positive correlation, whatever happens to one **variable** (it goes up or down) will be the same as what happens with the other (it will go up or down). With a **negative correlation,** whatever happens to one variable (it goes up or down) will be the opposite of what will happen to the other variable.

It should be noted that correlations do not tell us what causes things to happen. Perhaps wearing tight shoes is correlated with having headaches. We do not know from this correlation if wearing tight shoes causes one to have headaches or if having headaches causes one to tie one's shoes tightly. We simply know that these two events tend to co-occur in predictable ways.

The best method to use in studying human development (or in conducting any scientific research) is the **experimental** method. This method involves the systematic manipulation of variables (referred to as **independent variables**) and measuring the impact of those manipulations on outcomes that we also measure (referred to as **dependent variables**). If we have half of a group of children watch violent television and the other half watch nonviolent television, degree of violent television viewing (which we have manipulated) would be the independent variable. If we then measure amount of aggression in these children, that measurement represents our **dependent variable.** It is referred to as the dependent variable because we assume that its level (in this case, aggression) "depends" on whether they watched or did not watch the violent television (the independent variable).

Developmental psychologists are also particularly interested in studying how children change over time. Several methodologies are used. In **longitudinal** research, a cohort or group of children (or adults) of the same age are studied over a period of time. For example, the cognitive development of a group of infants could be tracked until these children are adults. As you can guess, this would be very expensive, and some of the participants might move or die, depleting the sample.

Another alternative is the **cross-sectional** research method, in which a number of different cohorts are studied at one point in time. For example, cognitive development could be studied in one-year-olds, in three-year-olds, in five-year-olds, etc. at one point in time. A problem with this method, though, is that differences may not be due to actual changes in the children over time but rather due to differences among cohorts; this is called a **cohort effect.** If we found that sixty-year-olds scored lower on an intelligence test than twenty-year-olds, we wouldn't know if the differences were due to the sixty-year-olds becoming less intelligent with age or differences among the groups, such as the twenty-year-olds being more likely to have gone to college.

Cross-sequential research includes aspects of both methods, following different-aged cohorts for a shorter period of time. If we wanted to study changes in intelligence during adolescence, we could compare ten-year-olds, fifteen-year-olds, and twenty-year-olds, following all three groups for five years.

Critical Thinking Exercises

Exercise 1

A member of a university department wants to study child development. You run a child development centre and want to help. Based on what you have learned in this chapter, how would you design a study to determine if extra cognitive stimulation (beyond what is normally available in your facility) improves language development in the infants in your facility? Be sure to include what is known about typical language development and cognitive development for the children that you serve. Their ages are six months to eighteen months.

Exercise 2

A parent has asked you about Piaget's theory of cognitive development. Based on what you have read in this chapter and learned in this course, what would you tell the parent to expect about the cognitive development of his or her child during the first year? Be sure to include a discussion of the following concepts in your response:

- schemes
- sensorimotor intelligence
- assimilation
- accommodation
- preoperations

Internet Activities

Activity 1

Choose one of the following terms and run an Internet search:

- Piaget
- Erikson
- Freud
- Vygotsky

Choose one of the sites that come up as a result of your search and read the information presented. After reading the information on the site, answer the following questions:

What content (points made) in the article matches what was stated in your textbook?

1. What content (points made) in the article was different from what was stated in your textbook?
2. What is the most important thing you learned by reading this article? Why?

Activity 2

Access the Internet and go to the following URL:
http://www.oikos.org/Piagethom.htm

Based on the information on this site and in your textbook, generate a defensible definition for each of the following:

- schemes
- assimilation
- accommodation
- adaptation
- self-reflection

Read the information provided on the site and compare the information to what you have learned from this chapter. In order to enhance your understanding, answer the following questions about the site:

1. What content (points made) on the site matches what was stated in your textbook?
2. What content (points made) on the site was different from what was stated in your textbook?
3. What is the most important thing you learned by reading this site? Why?

Activity 3

Your text discussed the classical conditioning approach to bedwetting. You can see what the Canadian Paediatric Society advises about bedwetting by going to the following URL:

http://www.cps.ca

Once you are at this website, go to the "search" space on the bottom left-hand side of the page and type in "bed-wetting." After reading an article on the site, answer the following questions:

1. What content (points made) on the site matches what was stated in your textbook?
2. What content (points made) on the site was different from what was stated in your textbook?
3. What is the most important thing you learned by reading this site? Why?

Power Preview: Learning Objectives Sample Answers

1. Explain what child development is.

Child development focuses on the time period from birth (infancy) to puberty (when the young person gains reproductive capacity). Although we typically think of child development as physical (e.g., the

child is getting bigger and gaining size and muscle mass), development occurs in cognitive, emotional, moral, and social areas as well.

2. Describe why it is important to study child development.

Studying child development helps us to answer questions we have about our own development. We, as adults, may ponder "why" we were born, "what" we are destined to be, and "how" we came to be the beings we have become. Studying child development allows us some insight into how to answer these questions. Studying child development allows us to address questions of gender differences in development as well as assist in efforts to predict which children will develop such illnesses as PKU or SIDS.

3. Discuss the history of child development. Have views about childhood and child development changed across time? If so, how?

Thoughts on child development have changed throughout history. Early thoughts envisioned children as evil and in need of strong discipline to be tamed. Others, such as the thoughts of John Locke, suggested that children are born blank slates and experience (what comes from one's environment) writes itself onto that blank slate. Still others, such as Freud, believed that children are born with inherent tendencies toward evil that are only circumvented by society and the development of the superego. Erikson felt that human development occurs through a series of distinct stages that are marked by the confrontation with, and successful resolution of, developmental crises in one's life. Very young children, for example, grapple with issues of trust that influence the relationships that will be developed and how that child approaches them. Early thoughts considered children to simply be small adults. Of course, these views resulted in children being placed into adult roles such as working in factories. The key point is that how one envisions the child influences what one demands from and expects from that child.

4. Describe the major theories of child development.

This question is partially answered by the response to question three. Behaviouristic theories of child development assume that children will repeat behaviours that have been reinforced and will cease engaging in behaviours for which they have been punished. Freudian psychoanalytic theory assumes that children are driven by aggressive and sexual urges and that development involves efforts to curb these impulses and live productively in society. Erikson's theory focuses on social development and the crises that occur in one's life that predict how one will enter the next stage of development. Cognitive theories focus on how the child is processing information, storing information, forming representations of the world, or learning to categorize the world.

5. Discuss the major controversies in the study of child development.

Controversies in the study of child development greatly influence what theories are developed. One dominant controversy, for example, is one of nature vs. nurture. This controversy asks the question "How much of child development is due to the unfolding of genetic influences (nature) and how much is due to the environment in which the child is developing (nurture). Although this has been a controversy for many years, almost all developmentalists now agree that it is a question of **how much** ***development is due to each and not*** **whether** ***development is due to one or the other. Another major controversy centres on how development "unfolds." The continuity approach assumes that genetics is predominantly a matter of maturation. In other words, development occurs through a series of discrete and genetically determined stages. Discontinuity approaches assume that development can be far more variable. Another point of contention centres on how active (or passive) a role the child takes in his or her own development.***

6. Describe how psychologists study child development.

How do we study something as unpredictable as the human child? Correlations allow us to determine

relationships between events. I might notice, for example, that my son cries, and when he does, I check his diaper and he is wet. Can I determine that his crying means the diaper is wet? No. The two events are correlated, but I cannot be certain that one causes the other. If, on the other hand, I were to conduct an experiment in which I place a wet diaper on my son and he always cries (and never cries when I place a dry diaper on him), I can be fairly confident that one event (wet diaper) causes the other event (crying). When we manipulate variables (like putting wet diapers on some babies and dry ones on others), those variables are called "independent" variables. When we measure some outcome (like measuring which infants cry and which do not), those variables are called "dependent" variables. We call them dependent because we assume that the level of those variables (how much crying occurs) "depends" on the independent variable (whether they were given wet or dry diapers).

Chapter Review

Multiple Choice

1. Infancy refers to:
   a. the first two years of life
   b. the period between early and middle childhood
   c. the period before a child can walk
   d. the first six months of life
2. The founder of American Behaviourism was:
   a. Jean Piaget
   b. B. F. Skinner
   c. Erik Erikson
   d. John Watson
3. In Freud's theory, id:
   a. operates according to the reality principle
   b. operates according to the pleasure principle
   c. operates according to the morality principle
   d. operates according to the endurance principle
4. According to Erik Erikson, we develop by:
   a. confronting and resolving our repressed aggressive and sexual urges
   b. confronting and resolving developmental crises in our lives
   c. gaining cognitive stages through experiences
   d. the unfolding of developmental stages that are genetic in nature
5. According to Erikson, what is the first stage in development?
   a. trust vs. mistrust
   b. sensorimotor
   c. autonomy vs. shame and doubt
   d. preoperational

6. Paul believes that he can influence his child most by altering reinforcement and punishments. He most likely follows which theory of development?
   a. psychosocial
   b. psychoanalytic
   c. cognitive
   d. behaviourism
7. Jamal laughs whenever he is tickled. Now his dad says, "I'm going to get you," then tickles him, and he laughs. Now, whenever his dad says "I'm going to get you," Jamal laughs. In this example, laughing to the phrase, "I'm going to get you" is:
   a. an unconditioned stimulus
   b. a conditioned response
   c. a conditioned stimulus
   d. an unconditioned response
8. Learning in which unconditioned stimuli become paired with conditioned stimuli is called:
   a. operant conditioning
   b. social learning
   c. classical conditioning
   d. habituation learning
9. A child learns by seeing, touching and tasting. Piaget called this:
   a. sensorimotor intelligence
   b. preoperational intelligence
   c. concrete operations
   d. formal operations
10. What is a scheme?
    a. a sneaky plan for doing something the parents won't like
    b. an organized category of information in memory
    c. an unconscious urge pushing for expression
    d. none of these
11. A child knows chairs have four legs. Now she sees a table and calls it a "chair." This child:
    a. is using the concept of accommodation
    b. is using the process individuation
    c. is using the process of differentiation
    d. is using the concept of assimilation
12. Which theory focuses on the evolution of humans within the animal kingdom?
    a. ethology
    b. maturation
    c. endocrinology
    d. ecology
13. You have the hypothesis that eating chocolate will improve memory. You have half your participants eat chocolate and the other half eat fruit, and then you measure memory. In this study, what is the independent variable?

a. accuracy of memory
b. the eating of fruit
c. the eating of chocolate
d. what food is eaten

14. Stage theories of human development:
    a. assume that human development is gradual and slow
    b. assume that human development differs greatly from person to person
    c. assume that human development is predictable and discrete
    d. assume that human development is driven by environment only

15. John Locke assumed:
    a. that children are born good
    b. that children are born evil
    c. that children are born without prior knowledge
    d. that children are born with all they need to know

Matching

Match each of the items from Column A with the corresponding item from Column B. There is only one correct answer per item. The correct answers are provided at the end of this chapter.

	Column A		Column B
1.	_______ tabula rasa	a.	development is gradual and even
2.	_______ stage theory	b.	operates according to reality principle
3.	_______ id	c.	psychosocial development
4.	_______ Freud	d.	blank tablet
5.	_______ independent variable	e.	development is discrete and distinct
6.	_______ dependent variable	f.	measured
7.	_______ continuity	g.	manipulated
8.	_______ Erikson	h.	from 2 to 5 years
9.	_______ early childhood	i.	psychosexual development
10.	_______ ego	j.	operates according to pleasure principle

True–False

1. The term *infancy* has Latin roots that mean "not speaking."

   TRUE or FALSE

2. The founder of American behaviourism was Arnold Gesell.

   TRUE or FALSE

3. Operant conditioning involves pairing a conditioned and unconditioned stimulus.

   TRUE or FALSE

4. Piaget's theory of cognitive development is a discontinuous or stage theory.
   TRUE or FALSE
5. Changing a schema or creating a new scheme is called "accommodation" in Piaget's theory.
   TRUE or FALSE
6. Urie Bronfenbrenner is associated with the ecological perspective.
   TRUE or FALSE
7. The exosystem refers to environmental changes over time.
   TRUE or FALSE
8. The best way to study a cause-and-effect relation is to use the correlational method.
   TRUE or FALSE
9. The dependent variable is the variable that is "treated" or "manipulated."
   TRUE or FALSE
10. Longitudinal research involves following one age cohort or group for an extended period of time.
    TRUE or FALSE

Solutions

Chapter Review

Multiple Choice

1. a (4)
2. d (8)
3. b (10)
4. b (13)
5. a (13)
6. d (17)
7. b (16)
8. c (15)
9. a (22)
10. b (20)
11. d (21)
12. a (24)
13. d (40)
14. c (10)
15. c (6)

Matching

1. d (6)
2. e (10)
3. i (10)
4. j (10) i
5. g (40)
6. f (40)
7. a (34)
8. c (12)
9. h (4)
10. b (10)

True–False

1. T (4)
2. F (8)
3. F (16)
4. T (21)
5. T (21)
6. T (24)
7. F (26)
8. F (39)
9. F (40)
10. T (41)

CHAPTER 2

Heredity and Conception

Learning Objectives

By the end of this chapter, you should be able to generate well-thought-out responses to demonstrate your understanding of the following learning objectives (sample answer comments are included at the end of this chapter):

1. Explain the difference between a gene and a chromosome.
2. Describe how sperm and egg cells are formed.
3. Why are couples who delay childbearing more likely to have twins?
4. Explain why identical twins are more likely than fraternal twins to share disorders such as schizophrenia and vulnerability to alcoholism.
5. Explain the following: If adopted children are more like their biological parents than their adoptive parents on a trait, such as eye colour or sociability, then heredity is likely to play a key role in the development of that trait.
6. Explain where conception normally occurs.
7. Describe why for every "successful" sperm cell, there are literally hundreds of millions of "failures."
8. Explain what is meant by a "test-tube baby."
9. Describe how a mother could have a baby that is biologically hers but yet not carried in her uterus.
10. Is it possible for parents to select the gender of a child? What would be the advantages/disadvantages?

Chapter Summary

The Influence of Heredity on Development: The Nature of Nature

Genetics is the study of **heredity,** how our characteristics or traits are passed down from our parents to us through our genes. While physical characteristics, such as the colour of our eyes and our height, are most clearly influenced by heredity, certain personality traits may also be partially genetically based. We have forty-six **chromosomes,** structures composed of **genes,** organized into twenty-three pairs that carry this genetic information. Genes are composed of **DNA** (**deoxyribonucleic acid**). Of these chromosome pairs, twenty-two are called **autosomes,** pairs that are similar and possess genetic information for the same traits, while the twenty-third pair is the **sex chromosomes,** either an X or Y chromosome. Females inherit an X chromosome from both their father and their mother while males inherit an X chromosome from their mother and a Y chromosome from their father.

Most of the cells in our bodies replicate in a process that produces another cell with the same forty-six chromosomes; this is called **mitosis.** However, the sex cells, formed by **meiosis,** contain only twenty-three chromosomes. When the egg and sperm are joined in the woman's fallopian tube, conception takes place, producing a new cell (a new potential person) now containing forty-six chromosomes. This single cell is called a **zygote.**

If this new cell replicates many times and eventually becomes a new infant, the baby will have traits inherited from both the mother and father. A trait is determined by a pair of genes, one gene coming from the father and one from the mother. The different forms of genes are called **alleles.** If the genes for a specific trait are the same, then the person is **homozygous** for the trait. However, if the alleles are different, the individual is **heterozygous** for that trait.

In the latter case, some alleles are **dominant** while others are **recessive.** For example, if a person inherits an allele for blue eyes from the mother and an allele for brown eyes from the father, the person will be heterozygous for eye colour, with the actual eye colour being brown. The gene for brown eyes is dominant while the gene for blue eyes is recessive. Moreover, the genotype is the person's actual genetic composition (heterozygous—one allele for blue eyes, one allele for brown eyes), but the phenotype is the actual trait that is expressed. Two people with brown eyes (the phenotype) could have different genotypes (heterozygous or homozygous). However, two individuals with blue eyes would have the same genotype (homozygous—two alleles for blue eyes) because blue eyes is a recessive trait.

Some kinds of disorders are caused by differences in the numbers of chromosomes. For example, **Down syndrome** is caused by an extra chromosome (twenty-first pair), as is **Klinefelter's syndrome** (extra sex chromosome—XXY). A girl with **Turner's syndrome** is missing an X chromosome and has only forty-five chromosomes.

Many kinds of genetic abnormalities are **recessive,** meaning that for a child to actually inherit the disorder, he or she would need to receive the recessive gene for that trait from both parents. Both of the parents would likely be **carriers** but not have the disease since they would have a **dominant** "normal" gene to offset the recessive gene. **Cystic fibrosis, sickle-cell anemia,** and **Tay-Sachs disease** are all examples of a recessive disorder. **Huntington's disease** is an example of a dominant genetic disorder in which one would need to have the gene from only one parent to actually have the disease. Parents, though, might not have known they had the disease when they were conceiving the baby because the onset of Huntington's disease frequently does not happen until midlife.

Some genetic abnormalities are recessive and **sex-linked,** meaning that they are carried on the X chromosome. This is the case with **hemophilia.** Since women have two X chromosomes but males have only one, women are more likely to be carriers of the disease while men are more likely to actually have hemophilia. Some forms of **muscular dystrophy** are also sex-linked.

Genetic counselling may be helpful for couples who are deciding whether or not to conceive. If a couple does conceive, the woman may choose to undergo several kinds of genetic testing. **Amniocentesis** involves removing amniotic fluid approximately during the fourteenth to sixteenth week of pregnancy. **Chorionic villus sampling** removes a bit of membrane that surrounds the fetus and amniotic sac. This procedure can be done as early as the ninth or tenth week of pregnancy. Tests run on the mother's blood, such as the **alpha-fetoprotein (AFP) assay,** can detect neural tube defects like **spina bifida. Ultrasound** is used in conjunction with amniocentesis and chorionic villus sampling as well as to check for normal development of limbs and size of the fetal head.

Heredity and the Environment: Nature versus Nurture

To differentiate the effects of heredity and the environment, scientists conduct studies that compare people of differing genetic relatedness. Of special interest are studies of identical/fraternal twins and adopted children. While **monozygotic** (MZ, identical) twins share 100% of their genes, **dizygotic** (DZ, fraternal) twins share only 50%. A researcher can compare how similar MZ twins are to how similar DZ twins are and estimate the importance of heredity for a particular trait. Of course, as explained in your text, perhaps MZ twins are treated more similarly than DZ twins. However, if they are reared in separate families (cases in which the twins are both adopted), one could probably assume that the environments for MZ and DZ twins would be different; any greater similarity for MZ twins would then be due to genetics.

Regarding adopted children, psychologists are interested in comparing how similar these children are to their biological parents, to the parents who adopted them, and to the other siblings in their adopted families. If adopted children are more similar to their biological parents than to the parents who adopted them, a strong case is made for the role of heredity on a trait.

Conception: Against All Odds

Conception occurs when an **ovum** and sperm cell unite. Women are born with all the immature ova, around 400,000, that they will ever have. Men, on the other hand, continually produce sperm once they reach sexual maturity. In fact, one typical ejaculation contains between 200 and 400 million sperm. Many of the sperm are lost along the way, due to gravity, acidity in the vagina, and having to swim against the tide of female fluid from the cervix.

Of those sperm who eventually reach the vicinity of the egg, only one can enter. The ovum is surrounded by the **zona pellucida,** a gelatinous layer that must be penetrated in fertilization. This layer hardens once it has been penetrated by one sperm. The chromosomes of the egg and sperm now combine to form the forty-six chromosomes that will potentially be in the cells of the new individual.

Some couples have problems conceiving. Contributing factors to male infertility include low sperm count, low sperm **motility** (ability to move), or irregularly shaped sperm. Certain infectious diseases or injuries to the testes can be possible reasons for these problems.

Infertility in women may be caused by failure to ovulate or blockages in the fallopian tubes. Stress and malnutrition may contribute to failure to ovulate; drugs have been developed that promote ovulation in women. Blockages in the fallopian tubes prevent the egg and sperm from meeting. Blockages can be caused by **pelvic inflammatory disease,** resulting from an untreated sexually transmitted disease, or from **endometriosis,** when the endometrial tissues lost during menstruation accumulate in the abdomen.

Techniques have been developed to help couples with infertility problems. If a man has low sperm count, sperm from multiple ejaculations can be frozen and injected into the woman's uterus during ovulation (**artificial insemination**). **In vitro fertilization** refers to conception taking place in a laboratory dish; this method may be used if the woman's fallopian tubes are blocked. **Donor IVF** is used to help a woman who needs a donor egg but whose uterus is healthy; after the fertilization of the egg in vitro, the egg is transplanted into the woman's uterus. A **surrogate mother** provides a uterus for bringing a baby to term.

The surrogate mother's ova could be fertilized through artificial insemination, or the biological mother's ova could be extracted, fertilized using the in vitro technique, and then implanted into the surrogate mother's uterus.

Since sperm containing a Y chromosome are smaller and swim faster than sperm containing an X chromosome, some experts have suggested methods that may increase a couple's chance of having a boy or a girl. Techniques to separate sperm carrying X genes from those carrying Y genes have been developed based on amount of genetic material, swimming rates (X-bearing sperm are heavier and slower), or differential electrical charges. Preimplantation genetic diagnosis involves fertilizing ova through the in vitro procedure, determining which embryos are of the desired sex, and then implanting one or more into the uterus. Post-conception procedures, such as abortion and infanticide, have been used in countries such as China and India.

Critical Thinking Exercises

Exercise 1

Overpopulation is a crucial issue in a world with limited resources. Should we institute a policy limiting the number of children a couple can have? For example, a couple might be limited to two children and then be asked to adopt. How might such a policy be encouraged? What would be the implications of imposing a fine on couples having "extra" children? How could couples be monetarily rewarded for having fewer children and adopting? What kind of ethical concerns might arise from such a policy?

____

____

____

____

Exercise 2

Write a paragraph comparing and contrasting Huntington's disease and sickle-cell disease. Include the following terms in your discussion:

- recessive
- dominant
- heterozygous
- homozygous
- carriers
- prenatal testing

Internet Activities

Activity 1

Should human cloning be permitted? Access the Internet and go to the following URL: http://www.bioethics.com

Read the information on the site, paying special attention to material on the following:

- cloning
- gene therapy
- frozen human embryos
- stem cell research

Once you have read the material, answer the following questions in relation to that material:

1. What content (points made) in the article did you find most informative? Why?
2. What content (points made) in the article do you think are most relevant to you, your life, and/or your career? How?
3. What is the most important thing you learned by reading this article? Why?

Activity 2

Explore the website of the Society of Obstetricians and Gynaecologists of Canada at this URL:

http://sogc.medical.org/index_e.asp

Once you are at this website, go to the "search" space on the left and type in "amniocentesis" or "prenatal diagnosis." After reading information on the site, answer the following questions:

1. What content (points made) in the article matches what was stated in your textbook?
2. What content (points made) in the article was different from what was stated in your textbook?
3. What is the most important thing you learned by reading this article? Why?

Activity 3

According to your text, about one Canadian couple in six or seven has fertility problems. Consider that down the road you might be one of these couples; either you or your spouse may have problems related to conceiving.

Research one of the following topics on the Internet and review two websites that come up from your search:

- pelvic inflammatory disease
- endometriosis
- male infertility

After looking at two of the websites, write a summary including the following points:

1. Explain how this condition contributes to infertility.
2. What might a couple do in response to this kind of infertility?
3. What is the most important thing you learned from exploring these websites? Why?

Print copies of the material from the website to attach to your paper.

Observing Children and Adolescents CD-ROM Activity

Play the video "Prenatal Assessment." Imagine that a couple is seeking advice from you regarding whether or not they should have amniocentesis. What advice would you give them? Based on information from the video, address the following issues in your advice:

- Risk factors associated with amniocentesis
- Chances of having an infant with an abnormality that could be detected through amniocentesis
- Other diagnostic procedures that could be used and information learned from those procedures

Power Preview: Learning Objectives Sample Answers

1. Explain the difference between a gene and a chromosome.

A gene consists of segments of DNA, deoxyribonucleic acid. A number of genes strung together make up the chromosomes. All human cells (except for sperm and egg cells) contain 30,000 to 40,000 genes, which together form forty-six chromosomes.

2. Describe how sperm and egg cells are formed.

Egg cells (ova) and sperm are formed through the process of meiosis (reduction division). Initially, the forty-six chromosomes in the cell are arranged into twenty-three pairs. The cell then divides, with one chromosome from each pair becoming part of the nucleus of a new cell. The two resulting cells both have twenty-three chromosomes.

3. Why are couples who delay childbearing more likely to have twins?

As women grow older, they tend to ovulate less regularly. As part of this change, women are more likely to release multiple eggs, thus increasing the chance of both eggs being fertilized and implanting in the uterus.

4. Explain why identical twins are more likely than fraternal twins to share disorders such as schizophrenia and vulnerability to alcoholism.

Monozygotic or identical twins share 100% of their genes, whereas fraternal or dizygotic twins share only 50%. Any trait that has a genetic component is more likely to be found in both identical twins, compared to fraternal twins, if it is found in one. Studying the concordance rates (or both twins having a trait) for identical compared to fraternal twins is one method used to estimate the relative genetic contribution to a particular trait. Schizophrenia and vulnerability to alcoholism both have a genetic component.

5. Explain the following: If adopted children are more like their biological parents than their adoptive parents in a trait, such as eye colour or sociability, then heredity is likely to play a key role in the development of that trait.

If studies of adopted children find that they are more like their biological parents in a given trait, the argument can be made that heredity must be an important factor. If, in spite of being reared by their adoptive parents, they are more like their biological parents, then heredity must make an important contribution to that trait. While we can more easily agree with this statement on a characteristic such as eye colour that is clearly genetically determined, it is also true for other traits such as sociability.

6. Explain where conception normally occurs biologically.

Conception usually occurs in the fallopian tube. The egg is released from the ovary and then enters the fallopian tube, where it is united with a sperm.

7. Describe why for every "successful" sperm cell, there are literally hundreds of millions of "failures."

One ejaculation typically contains 200 to 400 million sperm, but many of these are lost along the way. Gravity may cause millions to flow from the woman's vagina if she gets up following intercourse. Acid in the vagina also kills many more sperm, and swimming against the "current" of fluid moving down from the cervix may also result in the loss of sperm. One estimate is that only 1 in 1,000 sperm will ever come close to the ovum.

8. Explain what is meant by a "test-tube baby."

A "test-tube baby" is one whose fertilization takes place outside of the mother's body. Another name for this is in vitro fertilization; the union of the egg and sperm occurs in a laboratory dish. The fertilized egg is then placed into the woman's uterus.

9. Describe how a mother could have a baby that is biologically hers yet is not carried in her uterus.

If a woman has had her uterus removed but still has ovaries, she could have her ova extracted, fertilized through in vitro fertilization, and then implanted in a surrogate mother's uterus.

10. Is it possible for parents to select the gender of a child? What would be the advantages/disadvantages?

Techniques are being developed that can separate sperm based on differences between X-bearing and Y-bearing sperm. These sperm differ in weight, in how fast the sperm swim, and in electrical charge. In vitro fertilization with preimplantation diagnosis is also an alternative. An advantage would be, for parents who have several children of one sex and wish to have a child of the other sex, increasing the probability of a child of the desired sex. However, in many societies males are valued more than females. If parents are able to choose the sex of their child, there might be a shortage of girls in such societies.

Chapter Review

Multiple Choice

1. When a human cell replicates and the resulting cells have forty-six chromosomes, the process is called:
   a. reduplication
   b. regeneration
   c. meiosis
   d. mitosis
2. Which of the following is most likely to cause infertility in women?
   a. pelvic inflammatory disease
   b. appendicitis
   c. herpes
   d. a previous abortion
3. PKU is best characterized as:
   a. an inherited sex-linked disorder
   b. an inherited dominant gene disorder
   c. an inherited recessive gene disorder
   d. a chromosomal disorder
4. Curly hair is a dominant trait while straight hair is recessive. If Mary and her husband, Ron, both have curly hair, their children could have:
   a. straight hair or curly hair
   b. only straight hair
   c. only curly hair
   d. no hair at all
5. Turner's syndrome is a:
   a. chromosomal disorder involving an autosome
   b. disorder involving an extra chromosome
   c. a chromosomal disorder involving an autosome and an extra chromosome
   d. none of the above
6. Neural tube defects can be detected using:
   a. an alpha-fetoprotein assay
   b. an x-ray
   c. an ultrasound
   d. none of the above
7. Down syndrome is caused by:
   a. an extra X chromosome
   b. an extra Y chromosome
   c. only one sex chromosome
   d. an extra twenty-first chromosome

8. Although both amniocentesis and chorionic villus sampling facilitate prenatal testing for genetic disorders, __________ permits this testing to be done somewhat earlier in the pregnancy.
   a. chorionic villus sampling
   b. amniocentesis
   c. either; both can be done at approximately the same age
   d. neither; these procedures do not screen for prenatal disorders

9. When the alleles in a gene pair are the same, the individual is said to be __________ for that trait.
   a. recessive
   b. dominant
   c. heterozygous
   d. homozygous

10. Tay-Sachs disease is most likely to affect an infant of __________ ancestry.
    a. European American–French origin
    b. African American–South African origin
    c. Hispanic American–Central American origin
    d. Jewish American–Eastern European origin

11. Conception takes place in the:
    a. uterus or womb
    b. ovary
    c. fallopian tube
    d. vagina

12. Sperm and egg cells are produced through __________ and contain __________ chromosomes.
    a. mitosis; forty-six
    b. meiosis; forty-six
    c. mitosis; twenty-three
    d. meiosis; twenty-three

13. Which of the following statements is NOT true regarding monozygotic/dizygotic twins?
    a. Monozygotic twins are often called identical twins
    b. Dizygotic twins are often called fraternal twins
    c. Dizygotic twins share 75% of the same chromosomes and are therefore more alike than other siblings except for monozygotic twins
    d. A woman whose mother is a fraternal twin has an increased likelihood of having twins

14. An individual who has the phenotype of blue eyes could have which of the following genotypes?
    a. one gene for brown eyes, one for blue eyes
    b. two genes for brown eyes
    c. two genes for blue eyes
    d. one gene for brown eyes and one for blue eyes OR two genes for blue eyes

15. Regarding sex-linked genetic disorders:
    a. women are more likely to be carriers while men are more likely to have the disorder
    b. women are more likely to be carriers and to have the disorder
    c. men are more likely to be carriers while women are more likely to have the disorder
    d. men are more likely to be carriers and to have the disorder

Matching

Match each of the items from Column A with the corresponding item from Column B. There is only one correct answer per item. The correct answers are provided at the end of this chapter.

	Column A		Column B
1. ______	polygenic trait	a.	two alleles that are the same
2. ______	Down syndrome	b.	determined by more than one gene pair
3. ______	chorionic villus sampling	c.	the expression of a gene pair
4. ______	meiosis	d.	how sex cells (eggs, sperm) are formed
5. ______	phenotype	e.	the joining of a sperm and egg
6. ______	conception	f.	a sex-linked disorder
7. ______	endometriosis	g.	a prenatal testing procedure
8. ______	homozygous	h.	identical twin
9. ______	monozygotic	i.	a possible cause of infertility
10. ______	hemophilia	j.	caused by an extra 21st chromosome

True–False

1. Homozygous refers to having two alleles, or gene forms, for a given characteristic that are different from each other.

   TRUE or FALSE

2. New sperm cells are produced in the male body through the process of meiosis.

   TRUE or FALSE

3. Huntington's disease is caused by two recessive genes, one inherited from each parent.

   TRUE or FALSE

4. PKU is an example of a sex-linked genetic disorder.

   TRUE or FALSE

5. Amniocentesis is usually performed earlier than chorionic villus sampling.

   TRUE or FALSE

6. Monozygotic twins are more genetically similar than dizygotic twins.

   TRUE or FALSE

7. The father's sperm determines the sex of the baby.

   TRUE or FALSE

8. In vitro fertilization refers to uniting the sperm and egg (fertilization) in a laboratory dish.
   TRUE or FALSE
9. Pelvic inflammatory disease is one possible cause of infertility in women.
   TRUE or FALSE

Solutions

Chapter Review

Multiple Choice

1. d (53)
2. a (73)
3. c (61)
4. a (55)
5. d (61)
6. a (66)
7. d (57)
8. a (65)
9. d (55)
10. d (62)
11. c (70)
12. d (54)
13. c (55)
14. c (56)
15. a (62)

Matching

1. b (53)
2. j (57)
3. g (65)
4. d (54)
5. c (67)
6. e (70)
7. i (73)
8. a (55)
9. h (55)
10. f (62)

True–False

1. F (55)
2. T (54)
3. F (61)
4. F (61)
5. F (65)
6. T (55)
7. T (54)
8. T (74)
9. T (73)

CHAPTER **3**

Prenatal Development

Learning Objectives

By the end of this chapter, you should be able to generate well-thought-out responses to demonstrate your understanding of the following learning objectives (sample answer comments are included at the end of this chapter):

1. Describe what it means to say that the "most rapid and dramatic human developments are 'out of sight' or occur before birth."
2. Explain why a newly fertilized egg cell must survive for more than a week without nourishment from the mother.
3. Discuss how early the heart starts beating. How large is the embryo when the heart starts beating?
4. Why do some parents play classical music and point the speakers toward their abdomens during pregnancy?
5. Is it true that embryos and fetuses take what they need from their mothers? Why or why not?
6. Do pregnant women need to be concerned about their diets? Why or why not?
7. What disease-causing germs can cross the placental barrier and infect the embryo and fetus?
8. Is it safe for a pregnant woman to have a couple of glasses of wine in the evening? Why or why not?
9. Is it safe for a pregnant woman to smoke? Why or why not?
10. What is the ideal age for carrying and bearing a child?

Chapter Summary

This chapter focuses on the events that transpire from conception to birth. By the end of the chapter, you should be able to describe to someone how the developing child is conceived and the developmental changes that occur from conception to birth. Research, for example, shows that **neonates** can hear about eight months after conception and will move in response to particular sounds (such as the mother's voice).

The Germinal Stage: Wanderings

Prenatal development is divided into three stages. The earliest stage, called the **germinal** stage, lasts two weeks after conception. A few days into the germinal stage, the dividing cell mass takes the form of a fluid-filled ball of cells called a **blastocyst.** The **trophoblast** is the outer part of the blastocyst from which the amniotic sac, placenta, and umbilical cord develop. The inner part of the blastocyst has two distinct layers of cells that form a thickened mass of cells called the **embryonic disk** or **ectoderm.** These cells will become the embryo and eventually the fetus.

During this stage, the fertilized egg cell travels to the uterus and attaches to the uterine wall. The key features of this stage are a rapid dividing of cells, the beginning of cell differentiation, and the development of the umbilical cord and the placenta. The **umbilical cord** will serve as a pathway for nutrients to be passed from the mother to the developing child and for wastes to be transferred from the developing child to the mother for disposal. The **placenta** serves as a filtration system that will keep many (but not all) harmful chemicals and viruses from being transferred from the mother to the child.

The Embryonic Stage

The second stage of prenatal development is called the **embryonic** stage, which lasts from the implantation of the zygote to the uterine wall until the eighth week of development. The embryo develops within the **amniotic sac,** a clear membrane filled with **amniotic fluid** that cushions the growing embryo. Key features of this stage of development include (1) development of the nervous system (from the **neural tube**), (2) development of key organs such as the pancreas and liver (from the **endoderm**), (3) development of the circulatory systems (from the **mesoderm**), and (4) sexual differentiation. Development follows two general trends: **cephalocaudal,** meaning "head to tail" and **proximodistal,** meaning "near to far."

The Fetal Stage

The third stage of prenatal development is referred to as the **fetal** stage. This period lasts from about the eighth week after conception until birth. During this stage, the developing child will begin moving and responding to external stimulation. In addition, this period is marked by rapid and substantial growth of the developing child.

Intriguing studies (such as one conducted by DeCasper and Fife in 1980) have shown that the fetus responds to external stimulation, that the fetus can hear, and that newborns show preferences for things they have heard while in the uterus. This amazing discovery suggests that children can, at some level, remember what they heard while in utero.

Environmental Influences on Prenatal Development

During all stages of prenatal development, the developing child is vulnerable to the effects of external agents, called **teratogens,** which include drugs, alcohol, environmental pollutants, and pathogens such as the **rubella** virus. The effect these agents may have on the developing child depends on (1) the extent of the exposure, (2) the type of agent, and (3) the time period at which the developing child is exposed to the agent. The best advice, of course, is to avoid as many of these agents as possible for the duration of the pregnancy.

Other "environmental" influences on the developing child include nutrition. Research shows that malnutrition in the mother can have serious and, sometimes, potentially long-term effects on the child.

Toxemia, a life-threatening disease characterized by high blood pressure during pregnancy, has been linked to malnutrition. Obese mothers have a higher risk of **stillbirth** while mothers who are overly slender run the risk of having a **premature** baby.

Teratogens do not include just environmental influences or items that the mother ingests. They can also be produced by the mother's own body. **Rh incompatibility,** for example, is an illness that results when the mother produces Rh-positive antibodies (because she is Rh-negative) and is carrying an Rh-positive fetus. The resulting incompatibility can cause anemia, mental deficiencies, or even death to the fetus.

One key idea to take away from this chapter is balance. Too much or too little of things can be dangerous to the developing child. Mothers who are underweight run risks, as do mothers who are obese. Vitamins are a good thing and are especially important if the mother's nutrition is otherwise poor. At the same time, excessive intake of vitamins (such as A and D) have been associated with central nervous system damage. Other treatments intended to address health issues in pregnancy have caused problems. **Thalidomide** was taken for insomnia and nausea in the 1960s but was found to cause missing or malformed limbs in babies whose mothers had taken it. **Progestin** is a hormone used to maintain pregnancy that can cause masculinization of the fetus. **DES** (diethylstilbestrol), used for that purpose, is linked to reproductive cancers in the children of women who took it.

Maternal ingestion of drugs such as marijuana and cocaine has also been shown to have negative effects on children. Although the effects can only be directly tested in animal research, longitudinal studies of children born to mothers who have used these drugs have documented significant effects. Marijuana use during pregnancy, for example, is associated with attention deficits in children. Cocaine use during pregnancy is related to hyperactivity and attention problems as well.

Maternal ingestion of alcohol may lead to **fetal alcohol syndrome** (**FAS**). This syndrome is characterized by distinct facial features (such as widely spaced eyes, a flattened nose, and underdeveloped jaw). It is uncertain how much alcohol will lead to this disorder so, again, the best advice for anyone who is pregnant or might become pregnant is to avoid alcohol consumption. There are interesting racial and ethnic differences in vulnerability to FAS. In addition, FAS is associated with a variety of cognitive impairments as well as with problems in coordination and in the cardiovascular system. FAS is included among the **fetal alcohol spectrum disorders,** a larger group of problems related to alcohol use by pregnant mothers.

It should be noted that the impact of substances is not solely the responsibility of the mother. Research shows that alcohol and drug consumption on the part of the father can also affect the conceived child. Part of this effect may be due to the fact that ingestion of some chemicals can cause deformities in the sperm of the father. Additionally, this appears to be true for men who smoke.

Pregnant women are encouraged to also be aware of environmental toxins that may be less recognizable such as **lead** and **mercury.** Children living in towns in Yugoslavia with smelters, which emit lead fumes, scored lower on intelligence tests than did children living in towns without smelters. Harmful effects of mercury on the developing fetus were noted in Japan when some pregnant women ate fish from a polluted bay; babies were born with severe neurological problems and profoundly retarded.

The mother's state of mind can also effect the fetal environment. As the text suggests, emotions such as stress may be psychological feeling states, but they also have physiological components. When a person is under stress, the endocrine system will release hormones such as **adrenaline.** This will stimulate the mother's heart, respiratory, and other systems. This heightened arousal can also affect the fetus because hormones can pass through the placental barrier and increase activity in the developing child.

Although this chapter presents information that may make it seem as if there is little chance of giving birth to a child that *is* healthy, it also presents information on what can be done to minimize the risks. The best advice is to keep in mind that, for the most part, whatever the mother ingests, the baby ingests: The better the mother's nutrition, the better the baby's nutrition; if the mother ingests alcohol, so does the developing child. Much of the risk can be offset with appropriate nutrition and by monitoring what is ingested.

Critical Thinking Exercises

Exercise 1

You are running a clinic for expectant mothers in a very poor neighbourhood. One of the mothers has asked for your advice on what she can do to increase her chances of having a healthy baby. She cannot afford to eat a very good diet. Given this information, and based on what you have learned in this chapter, what advice would you give her? Be sure to include information from the chapter to support your advice.

Exercise 2

You have been asked to design a prenatal care program for a local community centre. Based on what you have learned in this chapter, what four programs would you implement and why? Assume that you have enough resources to implement the programs that you design.

Internet Activity

Access the Internet and go to the following URL:

http://www.modimes.org

Read the material on the site, being sure to search for information on the following:

- teratogen
- fetal alcohol syndrome
- toxemia

Assume that you are a nurse giving prenatal information and advice to an expectant mother. Based on what you have learned from this site:

1. How would you describe three conditions described on this site to this expectant mother?
2. What advice would you provide to this mother to minimize the possibility of these conditions affecting her unborn child? Why are you giving this advice?
3. What is the most important thing you learned by reviewing this site? Why?

Power Preview: Learning Objectives Sample Answers

1. Describe what it means to say that the "most rapid and dramatic human developments are 'out of sight' or occur before birth."

Essentially this means that so much of the development of the child occurs between the time of conception and the time of birth. Although we cannot "see" the developing child, the external environment can have a profound and, perhaps, lasting effect on that developing child. Because the mother cannot control the prenatal environment completely, her best advice is to assume that whatever happens to her body happens to that of the developing child.

2. Explain why a newly fertilized egg cell must survive for more than a week without nourishment from the mother.

Once the egg is fertilized, it must make its way to the uterus and attach to the uterine wall. Until this happens, the placenta and umbilical cord cannot protect and nourish the developing child. After conception, the developing child must survive off the yolk sac that forms after conception. Once the developing child is attached to the uterine wall, nourishment will come from the mother.

3. Discuss how early the heart starts beating. How large is the embryo when the heart starts beating?

During the third week after conception, the heart begins to beat. At this point, the organism is only one-fourth of an inch long and weighs less than one ounce. The implication is that the heart will continue to beat from this point until the developing person dies. For most people, this will be around 80 years!

4. Why do some parents play classical music and point the speakers toward their abdomens during pregnancy?

Research shows that fetuses can respond to sound waves by the thirteenth week following conception. This means that the developing child can hear music or the sound of voices. One study found that unborn children who "heard" a certain Dr. Seuss story in utero demonstrated a preference for that story (by sucking on a pacifier) and for the mother's voice to read that story. This research reveals several things. First, it reveals that learning does take place in utero. Second, it reveals that newborns have preferences.

5. Is it true that embryos and fetuses take what they need from their mothers? Why or why not?

No. If this were true then mothers would not have to worry so much about prenatal nutrition. In fact, the child gets what it can from the mother—both good and bad. If the mother is malnourished, so is the child. If the mother drinks alcohol, so does the child. The best advice is to assume that whatever the mother ingests, the child ingests.

6. Do pregnant women need to be concerned about their diets? Why or why not?

Yes. Research shows that maternal nutrition (quality and amount) can have profound effects on the developing child. Obesity, for example, is associated with an increased risk of stillbirth. Maternal malnutrition has been linked to deficits in cognitive development. These deficits, however, may be overcome by supportive and enriched daycare programs.

7. What disease-causing germs can cross the placental barrier and infect the embryo and fetus?

One example is rubella, also known as German measles. Another example is HIV. It is not known how HIV crosses the placenta nor why, in many cases, it does not, but the disease can create significant problems for the unborn child. The placenta filters many impurities, including those that might otherwise be transferred from the mother.

8. Is it safe for a pregnant woman to have a couple of glasses of wine in the evening? Why or why not?

No. The research is not clear. When the research cannot pinpoint the amount of alcohol that may lead to fetal alcohol syndrome (FAS), the safest bet is to consume no alcohol.

9. Is it safe for a pregnant woman to smoke? Why or why not?

No. There is a more direct relationship (research-wise)between smoking and the development of the child. Smoking, of course, affects the mother's lungs. At the same time, that oxygen deprivation will have an impact on the developing child. Babies born to mothers who smoke tend to be smaller, more often are stillborn, and, as children, are more likely to have behavioural and cognitive problems.

10. What is the ideal age for carrying and bearing a child?

From a biological standpoint, the twenties may be a woman's ideal age for bearing children. Among women who are younger, there is a higher incidence of infant mortality and low birth weight while older mothers (over age thirty) are at greater risk of having a child with Down syndrome.

Chapter Review

Multiple Choice

1. Which of the following is another term for *newborn?*
   a. embryo
   b. fetus
   c. neonate
   d. zygote

2. Cephalocaudal development means:
   a. near to far
   b. from the inside out
   c. from simple to complex
   d. head to tail
3. The liver and pancreas form the:
   a. endoderm
   b. ectoderm
   c. mesoderm
   d. indoderm
4. Which of the following is true about hearing in the unborn?
   a. children cannot hear until they are born
   b. as early as the thirteenth week following conception, the fetus responds to sounds
   c. the unborn respond to movements but not sound waves
   d. none of these is accurate
5. What determines the eventual sex of the child?
   a. the presence of female sex hormones
   b. the genetic contribution from the mother
   c. the presence of estrogen
   d. the genetic contribution from the father
6. What structure keeps the circulatory systems of the mother and developing child separate?
   a. placenta
   b. umbilical cord
   c. amniotic sac
   d. uterine wall
7. A teratogen is:
   a. a test that is done to test for fetal Rh incompatibility
   b. a natural substance the mother produces that may harm the fetus
   c. a chemical produced by the placenta to protect the child
   d. a substance that can cross to the child and potentially cause harm
8. Which of the following is true about fetal movements?
   a. fetal movements may correspond to external activity
   b. fetal activity may be related to activity levels of the child after birth
   c. movements may decrease as the child gets larger
   d. all of these are true of fetal movements
9. Maternal obesity is linked to:
   a. prematurity
   b. cognitive deficiencies
   c. stunted growth
   d. stillbirth

10. If you want to increase your ingestion of vitamin E, what might you eat?
    a. fish
    b. milk
    c. whole grains
    d. liver
11. Does it matter when, during pregnancy, a mother is exposed to toxins?
    a. yes, but only if the child is already at risk
    b. yes, but degree of harm may depend on phase of pregnancy
    c. no, they are always harmful
    d. no, the mother's system always compensates for the potential damage
12. Which of the following is true about maternal HIV?
    a. the virus is filtered by the fetus and cannot infect the unborn child
    b. it can be transferred to the child through breast feeding
    c. it is blocked from the fetus by the placenta
    d. a mother with HIV will always give birth to a child with HIV
13. Toxemia is:
    a. characterized by high blood pressure during pregnancy
    b. a sexually transmitted disease that can cause birth defects
    c. more common in younger rather than older pregnant mothers
    d. caused by abnormal sperm from the father
14. Which of the following is true of vitamins?
    a. they can be an important part of prenatal nutrition
    b. they may offset some of the problems of maternal malnutrition
    c. excessive amounts may be harmful to the developing child
    d. all of these are true of vitamins
15. How many drinks of alcohol are necessary before fetal alcohol syndrome develops?
    a. at least two per day
    b. the amount is unknown
    c. the mother must be an alcoholic
    d. it depends on the age of the mother

Matching

Match the each of the items from Column A with the corresponding item from Column B. There is only one correct answer per item.

	Column A		Column B
1. ______	neonate	a.	first two weeks after conception
2. ______	embryonic stage	b.	female genetic code
3. ______	placenta	c.	transfers food between mother and child
4. ______	teratogen	d.	associated with stillbirths
5. ______	XX	e.	associated with preterm deliveries
6. ______	obesity	f.	third to eighth week of development
7. ______	low maternal weight	g.	male genetic code
8. ______	germinal stage	h.	filters material transferred to child
9. ______	XY	i.	newborn
10. ______	umbilical cord	j.	alcohol

True–False

1. The germinal stage ends with the completion of implantation of the zygote in the uterine wall.

   TRUE or FALSE

2. The trophoblast is the outer part of the blastocyte.

   TRUE or FALSE

3. The mesoderm develops into the nervous system, nails, teeth, hair, the sensory organs, and the outer skin layer.

   TRUE or FALSE

4. Neurons in the developing embryo/fetus do not begin to fire until the middle of the fifth month.

   TRUE or FALSE

5. The Wolffian ducts are internal reproductive structures in the female embryo.

   TRUE or FALSE

6. The majority of babies whose mothers are infected with HIV are born already infected with HIV.

   TRUE or FALSE

7. A pregnant woman usually first becomes aware of fetal movement in the middle of the fourth month.

   TRUE or FALSE

8. The developing heart is most vulnerable to teratogens from the third to fifth weeks following conception.

   TRUE or FALSE

9. Thalidomide, marketed in Germany and England, resulted in babies being born with limb defects.

   TRUE or FALSE

10. A problem related to researching the effects of drugs, particularly illegal drugs, on unborn children is the selection factor.

    TRUE or FALSE

Solutions

Chapter Review

Multiple Choice

1. c (84)
2. d (86)
3. a (96)
4. b (93)
5. d (89)
6. a (85)
7. d (98)
8. d (96)
9. d (97)
10. c (97)
11. b (99)
12. b (99)
13. a (99)
14. d (101)
15. b (105)

Matching

1. i (84)
2. f (86)
3. h (91)
4. j (98)
5. b (89)
6. d (97)
7. e (97)
8. a (84)
9. g (89)
10. c (85)

True–False

1. T (84)
2. T (85)
3. F (87)
4. F (89)
5. F (89)
6. F (99)
7. T (96)
8. T (99)
9. T (101)
10. T (103)

CHAPTER **4**

Birth and the Newborn Baby: In the New World

Learning Objectives

By the end of this chapter, you should be able to generate well-thought-out responses to demonstrate your understanding of the following learning objectives (sample answer comments are included at the end of this chapter):

1. Explain what is meant by the phrase "the fetus may actually signal the mother when it is 'ready' to be born."
2. Describe the three stages of childbirth. What are the significant characteristics of each?
3. Compare and contrast the various methods of childbirth. Provide at least one advantage and one disadvantage to each method choice.
4. Describe the most common birth problems. What are the most common causes for each? What can be done (if anything) to minimize the chance of each occurring?
5. Describe the postpartum period. Why are postpartum "blue" feelings common? Can this problem become severe? If so, how would one know?
6. Describe the characteristics of neonates. What do newborns look like? How well developed are their senses? What are major (name at least three) reflexes they demonstrate? Discuss why they might demonstrate these.

Chapter Summary

Countdown...

Although most of the time it is fairly obvious when a woman is in the advanced stages of pregnancy, it is not always so clear when the birth becomes an impending event. There are, for example, **Braxton-Hicks contractions,** sometimes called false labour contractions. These are considered to be relatively painless and some women have reported experiencing them as early as the sixth month into the pregnancy. They are called false because they do not signal that the birth is about to occur although sometimes mothers confuse them and may make an undue trip to the hospital.

About 24 hours or so before the labour process begins, the mucus tissue that had plugged the cervix and protected the child from external infection gets dislodged, and the **amniotic sac** may burst. Remember that this sac was fluid filled and proved a protective environment for the developing child. Most of the time, the amniotic sac will not burst until the end of the first stage of labour. About one in ten women, however, will experience this event prior to the first stage of labour. In any case, it is a signal of the upcoming birth process that, all things going well, will result in the birth of a healthy baby.

Although surprising to many, the actual initiation of labour appears to be triggered by the fetus and not the mother. Hormones are secreted from the adrenal and pituitary glands of the fetus. These hormones stimulate the uterus and the placenta to secrete **prostaglandins** that excite the muscles of the uterus and cause labour contractions to begin. Later during labour, **oxytocin,** a hormone from the pituitary, is released, and the contractions become strong enough to expel the baby.

The Stages of Childbirth

Childbirth is divided into three stages. Each of these stages is marked by significant events. The first stage of childbirth, of course, prepares both mother and baby for the birthing process. The cervix will become **effaced** and **dilated** so that the baby can pass through it. For women delivering their first babies, the first stage typically lasts about half a day but may range from several hours to more than twenty-four hours.

Sometimes the mother will be "prepped" for the delivery by shaving her pubic hair so that an **episiotomy,** an incision between the birth canal and the vagina, can be performed later. Although considered to be a measure that can prevent tearing during delivery, critics claim that it is performed significantly more often than necessary and reflects more how the doctor was trained and his or her preferences than actual need. During this stage, a **fetal monitor** may be used to measure the fetal heart rate. If an abnormal heart rate is detected, delivery can be sped up with **forceps** or a **vacuum extraction tube.**

In the second stage of childbirth, the baby first appears at the opening of the birth canal and is clearly ready to join the world. The labour contractions propel the baby along the birth canal in a process that can last from just a few minutes to a few hours. Mucus is removed from the baby's mouth to prepare it for breathing. The umbilical cord will be clamped once the baby is breathing on its own and the majority of the birthing process has been completed.

The third and final stage of the birthing process can also last from a few minutes to an hour or more. After separating from the uterine wall, the placenta and fetal membranes are expelled through the vagina; the uterus starts to shrink in size.

Methods of Childbirth

Many controversies surround methods of childbirth or birthing choices. Should the mother deliver the baby at home with the assistance of a **midwife?** Should the delivery take place in a delivery room without the presence of the father? Should a **doula** (female companion) be used in the delivery room? Should **anesthetics** or **tranquillizers** be used? We have all of these questions because the answers to them could potentially affect the quality of the delivery experience for the mother and the health of the child being born.

General anesthetics may affect the newborn's sleeping and waking cycles as well as social responsiveness and attention in the baby's first six weeks. **Local anesthetics**, including epidural or spinal blocks, have more minor effects on the newborn's activity level.

Issues of **natural childbirth** differ from issues of prepared childbirth. One of the more popular methods for prepared childbirth, for example, is the **Lamaze method.** This method focuses on breathing and relaxation during each contraction. Women using the Lamaze method report less pain and, especially if a partner is present, ask for less medication.

Caesarean section is another important although sometimes controversial delivery method. With this method, surgery is used to remove the baby through the abdomen rather than through vaginal delivery. This method is most often used if it is believed that the baby is too large for vaginal delivery, if there are concerns related to transmission of HIV or genital herpes, if the baby appears to be in distress (perhaps as identified by fetal monitoring), or if the baby is a **breech presentation.**

Some birthing facilities use LDRP rooms, in which labour, delivery, recovery, and postpartum periods of birthing take place in the same room. These may resemble very nice hotel suites, but they also have the medical equipment needed for a typical birth; usually emergency facilities are close, just down the hall.

Birth Problems

Although most infants are born with relative "ease," there can be significant complications. These complications can range from oxygen deprivation (either **anoxia**—"without oxygen" or **hypoxia**—"under oxygen") to preterm and low-birth-weight infants. Each of these problems can create unique problems during the birth process and for the infant following birth.

Oxygen deprivation has been associated with a multitude of problems. The nature and severity of the symptoms depends, in large part, on the nature and severity of the deprivation. Prenatal (prior to birth) oxygen deprivation, for example, may impair development of the nervous system. Oxygen deprivation during delivery has been associated with a variety of problems ranging from cerebral palsy to early-onset schizophrenia.

It is important to understand that oxygen deprivation can be caused by a variety of factors such as maternal diabetes or pressure against the umbilical cord during delivery. Fetal monitoring can be used to detect anoxia before it causes damage, and this sometimes will warrant the use of a C-section for a more rapid delivery of a fetus in distress.

Some infants are born **preterm** (prior to thirty-seven weeks of gestation). These babies tend to have low birth weights, which have been associated with several developmental challenges in childhood, such as neurological and cognitive deficits. Preterm infants often have fine, downy hair called **lanugo** and a white substance on their skin called **vernix.** Mothers who smoke, use drugs, or receive poor prenatal nutrition are at increased risk of giving birth to **small-for-date babies**—that is, babies who are not premature but still have low birth weight; these babies are even more at risk than preterm babies for long-term complications. A significant challenge to preterm infants is lung development. The muscles of the preterm infant may not be well developed enough to sustain breathing. In addition, the walls of the air sacs in the preterm babies' lungs may tend to stick together because they don't yet produce the lubricating substance needed. This collection of symptoms is referred to as **respiratory distress syndrome.** Preterm infants are often put in **incubators** in the hospital to control the temperature around them and protect them from disease.

Preterm infants are also at risk for poorer postnatal treatment by parents. Part of this may be brought on by feelings of guilt or frustration on the part of the mother, fear that interacting with the child will hurt because the child is so small and frail-looking, or the child's irritability and unsociability.

The Postpartum Period

One significant characteristic of the postpartum period is a significant risk for the "blues" or even depression. The most common form of postnatal blues is referred to as **baby blues.** Between 50 and 80 percent of women experience baby blues. These feelings are characterized by sadness, crying, and irritability. It is strongly suspected that the hormonal changes following pregnancy and the mother's adjustment to the changes in her daily life may trigger these blues.

A more severe form of postpartum blues is referred to as **postpartum depression** (**PPD**). This may occur in as many as one woman out of five and can last for several weeks or months following delivery. PPD is characterized by extreme sadness, feelings of worthlessness, changes in sleep and appetite patterns, and other symptoms. PPD may also be brought on by a drop-off in estrogen and stressors such as marital problems. In addition, women who experienced depression prior to pregnancy are more likely to experience PPD following pregnancy than women who have not.

Lastly, there is an extreme form of postpartum blues/depression that involves "psychotic features" that may affect one woman out of 1,000. In these cases, the woman experiences breaks with reality. Symptoms may include delusions and "command hallucinations," which may in some instances lead to the infant being harmed.

Bonding is a significant experience that may occur between the infant and the mother (and the father but perhaps at a lesser extent) during the hours, weeks, and months following delivery. Some research shows that the bonding experience soon after delivery may have some long-term benefits on the parent–child relationship. Perhaps this is because it allows the relationship to get "off on the right foot."

Characteristics of Neonates

Newborns may not look as "beautiful" as you think. Their skin is thin, and the veins can be clearly seen, giving them a blue hue. The head may be oddly shaped because of the pressure of squeezing through the birth canal. Although this can be disconcerting to new parents, the skull of the newborn is purposefully soft for this reason and will assume a regular shape and solidify after birth.

As soon as possible following the birth, the neonate's overall level of health is assessed using the **Apgar scale.** This scale assesses the infant for (1) colour, (2) pulse, (3) grimace, (4) muscle tone, and (5) rate of breathing. A score of seven or above is usually considered to be a sign that the infant is not in danger.

The **Brazelton Neonatal Behavioural Assessment Scale** measures the neonate's **reflexes** and behaviour patterns and indicates the infant's level of **neural** functioning. Newborns show many reflexes that prepare them to respond to the external environment. This ability to respond, of course, enhances the chances that the newborn will do things such as turn the head to nurse (the **rooting reflex**), suck, **grasp**, and startle to sudden changes in movements or sounds (the **Moro reflex**).

Neonates also have sensory capabilities that allow them to respond to their external environment. Hearing is well developed prior to birth. Although **visual acuity** is perhaps only 20/600, neonates can see and **track** objects that are about as far away as the mother's face during feeding. Neonates show little **visual accommodation** (adjusted focus to objects at different distances), nor do they exhibit **convergence** (coordinating both eyes to look at a very close object). Understanding how neonates see colour is difficult because we have no way of knowing if they are responding only to a specific characteristic of a colour (**intensity, hue,** or **saturation**). At birth, the **cones** of the retina, which detect colour, are not as well developed as the **rods,** which detect light input.

In addition, newborns can distinguish between different smells (showing preference for the odour of their own mother's breast milk) and show preferences for certain tastes (such as sweets). They also have the ability to respond to sounds of different **amplitude** and **pitch.**

Newborns sleep about sixteen hours per day, but they do not typically sleep for longer than four hours at a time. These four-hour cycles are followed by about one hour of wakefulness in which feeding will typically occur. In addition, newborns spend significantly more of their sleep time in **REM** (rapid eye movement) sleep than older children and adults. Perhaps this is because REM sleep is associated with neural development that would be occurring at a very rapid pace during the early years of brain development.

Finally, a few words must be said about **Sudden Infant Death Syndrome** (**SIDS**). This unexplained syndrome results in the death of some infants. Although little is known about the cause, each week three babies die of SIDS in Canada. Some have speculated that it has to do with a variety of risk factors including (1) the age of the infant (related to lung development), (2) sleeping on the stomach, (3) preterm and low birth weight, (4) gender (it is more common among male infants), (5) economic status (it occurs more often in lower-income families), (6) race (it occurs more often among African American babies), (7) age of mother (it is more likely to occur to children of teenage mothers), and (8) maternal habits, such as smoking during or after pregnancy or narcotic use during pregnancy. It has been suggested that **apnea,** intermittent periods when the baby stops breathing during sleep, may be related to SIDS.

Critical Thinking Exercises

Exercise 1

A friend of yours is considering her birthing options. She knows you are taking this course and wants to ask you a few questions. First, she wants to know what you think about the use of medications to ease the pain of childbirth. Second, she wants to know what you think about using natural childbirth methods (like birthing at home using a midwife) instead of going to the hospital. Based on what you have learned from this chapter, provide her with the advantages and disadvantages of choosing to medicate or not medicate and choosing home birth versus having the child at the hospital.

____

____

____

____

____

____

Exercise 2

Your friend has now had her baby, and it is a healthy girl. She has noticed certain "habits" that the baby does, like turning her head in the direction of a touch on her cheek or grasping the mother's finger when she places it against her palm. "How does she know how to do this?" the new mother asks. Using your knowledge of infant reflexes, explain each of these and discuss why the baby might do these. Also discuss why most of these reflexes disappear as the child gets older.

____

____

____

____

____

____

Internet Activities

Activity 1

Access the Internet and go to the following URL:

http://www.sidscanada.org

Once you have accessed the site, read all the material you can find on Sudden Infant Death Syndrome (SIDS). In order to enhance your understanding, answer the following questions about the material on the site:

1. What content (points made) on the site did you find most informative? Why?
2. What content (points made) on the site do you think are most relevant to you, your life, and/or your career? How?
3. If the topic can be considered controversial (people disagree about it), did this site present both the pros and cons on the issue? If so, how? If not, why not?
4. What is the most important thing you learned by reading the material on this site? Why?

Activity 2

Choose one of the following terms and run an Internet search:

1. Infant mortality
2. Prematurity
3. Infant senses

Choose one of the sites that come up as a result of your search and read the information presented. Assume that you are a nurse giving prenatal information and advice to an expectant mother. Based on what you have learned from this article, answer the following.

1. How accurately do you feel this site portrays information about your topic? Why?

2. Were there any critical pieces of information missing that you feel should have been provided? If so, what were they? If not, what were the most critical pieces conveyed?
3. What is the most important thing you learned by reading the information on this site? Why?

Observing Children and Adolescents CD-ROM Activity

Watch the birth video and read the material on page 9 of *Observing Children and Adolescents.* Then answer the following questions:

1. What was your reaction to watching Carter's birth? What aspects of the birth were you expecting? Which were surprising?
2. What information did you learn about a typical newborn's appearance?
3. Describe how the newborn's health is assessed.

Power Preview: Learning Objectives Sample Answers

1. Explain what is meant by the phrase "the fetus may actually signal the mother when it is 'ready' to be born."

Research shows that labour may be initiated by hormones secreted by the adrenal and pituitary glands of the fetus. Apparently these hormones trigger the secretion of prostaglandins, or hormones, by the uterus and placenta that then initiate the labour sequence. Later in the labour process, oxytocin will be secreted, which will initiate the stronger labour contractions needed to move the baby down the birth canal and, eventually, to be born.

2. Describe the three stages of childbirth. What are the significant characteristics of each?

The first stage of childbirth is more of a preparatory stage in which uterine contractions cause the cervix to become effaced and dilated to a point where birthing the child becomes possible (about 10 cm). This stage can last a few hours to twenty-four hours or more for first delivery. Fetal monitoring may be used during the first stage to monitor the health of the baby (in particular, his or her heart rate). The most important characteristics of this stage are the dilation of the cervix and the contractions that will move the baby down the birth canal. In the second stage, the baby will actually be born. Strong contractions move the baby down the birth canal and eventually the baby's head will crown—meaning it is about ready to emerge from the birth canal and be born. It is at this point that an episiotomy might be performed, although the use of this procedure is somewhat controversial. The significant characteristic of this stage is the actual birth of the baby. The final stage results in the passage of the placenta and the fetal membranes.

3. Compare and contrast the various methods of childbirth. Provide at least one advantage and one disadvantage to each method choice.

In North America, the most common contemporary birthing choice is the hospital. This, however, has not always been the case. Until this century, childbirth took place in the home, often in the company of a midwife. Although some consider home childbirth to be more natural and, perhaps, comforting to the mother, the hospital has the advantage of full medical facilities should complications arise during the delivery. Some women choose to have a "doula" present. This female companion's role is to provide

continuous emotional support. Other birthing options include the use of medications. Although some women prefer to avoid (or at least minimize) the pain of delivery, some studies have shown that the medications may affect the fetus and newborn for an extended period of time after birth. Local anesthetics can minimize risks associated with medicating the fetus should this choice be made.

4. Describe the most common birth problems. What are the most common causes for each? What can be done (if anything) to minimize the chance of each occurring?

Perhaps the most problematic birth problem is oxygen deprivation. This can occur prenatally due to maternal smoking or the fetus's pressing against the umbilical cord. Typically, however, this will occur as a complication of the delivery process. Fetal monitors may be used to watch for the signs of oxygen deprivation, and an emergency C-section may be done in such cases. Maternal illnesses such as diabetes or even accidents can cause such deprivation. Maternal health, then, should be monitored closely. The second significant problem is prematurity. Infants born at or prior to thirty-seven weeks of gestation are considered preterm or premature. Underdeveloped lungs are only one of the problems. In such cases, premature infants may be given oxygen until their lungs are strong enough to work on their own. Prematurity and low birth weight, especially very low birth weight, are associated with motor, neurological, and cognitive deficits in early childhood. It has been shown that providing the child with a caring and stimulating environment with lots of affection may help to counter many of these potential cognitive and intellectual challenges.

5. Describe the postpartum period. Why are postpartum "blue" feelings common? Can this problem become severe? If so, how would one know?

The postpartum period is often characterized by feelings of sadness, tearfulness, and irritability. In fact, these feelings occur in 50 to 80 percent of all new mothers. It is suspected that changes in hormonal levels (in particular, estrogen), combined with dramatic changes in daily life, may contribute to these feelings. About 10 to 20 percent of all mothers may experience a more severe form of postpartum blues called postpartum depression. With PPD, feelings of despair and worthlessness, along with physical symptoms such as changes in sleep and appetite patterns, may occur with the aforementioned symptoms. Life stresses (financial issues, marital problems, having a sick baby, etc.) and prepregnancy depression are predictors of this more serious form of blues. About one out of 1,000 women will suffer a very severe form of these blues with psychotic features. Psychosis means a break from reality and is characterized by hallucinations and delusions. Some mothers in this state may physically abuse their infants. The range and severity of symptoms will signal which form of the illness is being experienced.

6. Describe the characteristics of neonates. What do newborns look like? How well developed are their senses? What are the major (name at least three) reflexes they demonstrate? Discuss why they might demonstrate these.

Neonates are not particularly attractive beings (a matter of opinion, of course). Their heads may be cone-shaped from the force of the birthing process. In addition, their skin may appear blue because it is thin and the veins are close to the surface. Some infants, especially if they are premature, are born covered with a fine downy hair called "lanugo" or even an oily white substance called "vernix." Newborns have a well-developed sense of hearing even before they are born. Their vision is about 20/600, which is perfect for seeing things about seven to nine inches away (about the distance of the mother's face during feeding). Newborns can show preferences for sounds in the range of the human voice and can also show taste preferences for things that are sweet or their own mothers' milk. The most important reflexes are probably the "rooting reflex" (in which the infant turns in the direction of a touch on its cheek), the "sucking reflex" (in which the newborn begins suckling motions if something touches its mouth), and the Moro reflex (in which the infant shows a startle response to sudden shifts in how it is being held or to sudden noises). These reflexes prepare the infant for survival. The rooting

reflex allows the child to find the nipple during feeding. The sucking reflex ensures that he or she will know what to do with it once it is found. Being startled by sudden movements or sounds also has survival value as it prepares the infant to respond to changes in its environment.

Chapter Review

Multiple Choice

1. A Braxton-Hicks contraction:
   a. signals that birth is imminent
   b. happens after birth to deliver the placenta
   c. may tone the muscles that will be used in delivery
   d. tend only to happen to young mothers
2. Why might vitamin K be given to a newborn?
   a. to add to the development of the immune system
   b. to ensure that the baby's blood will clot normally
   c. to replace minerals from the amniotic fluid the infant has floated in
   d. to assist with the development of the eye muscles
3. The Lamaze method is associated with:
   a. underwater birthing
   b. use of acupuncture
   c. use of tranquillizers rather than anesthetics
   d. use of relaxation and breathing exercises
4. Anoxia is:
   a. a form of oxygen deprivation before or after birth
   b. a maternal infection associated with early-onset schizophrenia in children
   c. a genetic illness in which diabetes is transferred from mother to child
   d. a physical abnormality common to preterm infants
5. A newborn is categorized as low-birth-weight when he or she weighs:
   a. between 3,500 and 4,000 grams
   b. between 3,000 and 3,499 grams
   c. between 2,500 and 2,999 grams
   d. under 2,500 grams
6. Preterm infants are vulnerable to:
   a. respiratory distress syndrome
   b. later cognitive deficits
   c. poorer treatment by parents
   d. all of these

7. What percentage of new mothers in Canada will suffer some form of postpartum blues?
   a. 50–80
   b. 10–30
   c. 20–40
   d. 80–95
8. Approximately how many women experience "psychotic features" with postpartum depression after giving birth?
   a. approximately 1 in 4 or 5
   b. approximately 1 in 10 or 20
   c. approximately 1 in 50 or 100
   d. approximately 1 in 1,000
9. Which of the following is NOT assessed using the Apgar scale?
   a. eye tracking
   b. general appearance or colour
   c. heart rate
   d. muscle tone
10. You suddenly shift the baby's position, and she arches her back, flings her arms and legs out, and then brings them back toward her chest in a hugging motion. You have just witnessed:
    a. the Palmar reflex
    b. the Tonic-neck reflex
    c. the Moro reflex
    d. the Babinski reflex
11. What is the typical visual acuity of the newborn?
    a. 20/200
    b. 20/600
    c. 500/20
    d. 200/20
12. Which statement is NOT true regarding newborns' hearing capacity?
    a. neonates respond more to high-pitched than low-pitched sounds
    b. neonates are soothed by sounds higher in amplitude and pitch
    c. neonates seem to prefer their own mothers' voices to voices of other women
    d. neonates will often turn their heads in the direction of a shaking rattle
13. Which part of the eye is responsible for colour vision?
    a. rods
    b. cornea
    c. iris
    d. cones

14. You puff air in the infant's eye and he blinks. Then you sound a tone, puff the air and the infant blinks. Now when you sound the tone, the infant blinks. What kind of learning has taken place?
    a. this is not learning; it is simply a reflex
    b. habituation learning
    c. classical conditioning
    d. operant learning
15. What is true regarding REM sleep?
    a. infants spend less time in REM sleep than adults do
    b. REM sleep is a period during which the brain is relatively inactive
    c. REM sleep may serve to provide needed stimulation to the brain
    d. preterm infants spend less time in REM sleep than babies who are full-term

Matching

Match each of the items from column A with the corresponding item from column B. There is only one correct answer per item.

1.	_______	REM sleep	a.	strengthen contraction for birthing
2.	_______	SIDS	b.	intermittent suspension of breathing
3.	_______	oxytocin	c.	four
4.	_______	tonic-neck reflex	d.	fine, downy hair covering newborn
5.	_______	prostaglandins	e.	associated with sleeping on stomach
6.	_______	lanugo	f.	seven
7.	_______	stages of REM Sleep	g.	cause labour contractions
8.	_______	hopeful Apgar score	h.	oily, white substance covering newborn
9.	_______	vernix	i.	active EEG patterns
10.	_______	apnea	j.	fencing position

True–False

1. For most women, the amniotic sac bursting and a warm gush of water coming from the vagina signals the beginning of labour.

   TRUE or FALSE

2. Women in labour are typically told to go to a birthing centre or hospital when contractions are four or five minutes apart.

   TRUE or FALSE

3. Transition in labour refers to the period between the second and third stages of labour.

   TRUE or FALSE

4. Sweden is the safest country in the world for a woman to deliver her baby.

   TRUE or FALSE

5. Respiratory distress syndrome includes a number of breathing problems; preterm babies are particularly at risk for this syndrome.

   TRUE or FALSE

6. In a multicultural country like Canada, issues of maternal depression are also related to a lack of culturally relevant support systems

   TRUE or FALSE

7. Small-for-date babies are both premature and underweight.

   TRUE or FALSE

8. A persistent (lasting longer than the first year) Babinski reflex may be an indicator of problems with the lower spinal cord.

   TRUE or FALSE

9. Infants have the ability to discriminate colours at birth.

   TRUE or FALSE

10. Infants are most at risk for dying of SIDS in the first several weeks following birth.

    TRUE or FALSE

Solutions

Chapter Review

Multiple Choice

1. c (118)
2. b (122)
3. d (124)
4. a (128)
5. d (129)
6. d (129)
7. a (135)
8. d (136)
9. a (138)
10. c (140)
11. b (142)
12. b (144)
13. d (144)
14. c (146)
15. c (148)

Matching

1. i (148)
2. e (152)
3. a (119)
4. j (141)
5. g (119)
6. d (130)
7. c (148)
8. f (138)
9. h (130)
10. b (152)

True–False

1. F (118)
2. T (119)
3. F (120)
4. T (132)
5. T (131)
6. T (135)
7. F (129)
8. T (141)
9. F (144)
10. F (152)

CHAPTER 5

Infancy: Physical Development

Learning Objectives

By the end of this chapter, you should be able to generate well-thought-out responses to demonstrate your understanding of the following learning objectives (sample answer comments are included at the end of this chapter):

1. Describe the processes of physical growth and development during infancy.
2. Explain how the brain and nervous system develop during infancy.
3. Discuss the roles that genetics and experience play in motor development.
4. Describe sensory and perceptual development in infancy.

Chapter Summary

Physical Growth and Development

Despite the fact that infants progress physically at somewhat different rates, the patterns of physical development are remarkably consistent. A child must, for example, be able to crawl or creep before he or she can stand and walk. Because of patterns of cephalocaudal development, the child's head and torso will develop physically before the arms and legs. Children can sit up and crawl before they can walk. In addition, the principle of proximodistal development tells us that, physically, the child will mature from the torso outward. Given that the spinal cord is the central axis for the rest of the body, it makes sense that this area (including the torso) would develop first so that all other development can build from it.

Another important concept in physical growth and development is one of **differentiation.** This refers to the tendency for infant (and childhood) behaviours and physical reactions to become more specific and distinct as the child develops. As an example, imagine that you tickle an infant's foot. Before differentiation, the child may squeal, jerk its leg, and engage in overall body movements. As the child's nervous system differentiates, the reaction becomes more targeted and specific. The child might, for example, still squeal and withdraw the leg, but may not show the overall bodily reaction of earlier infancy.

Infant growth in height and weight are substantial. The infant's height, for example, will increase by 50% during the first year, and the child is likely to triple his or her birth weight during that same year. Contrary to previous views, however, growth is not a steady and slow process. Research shows that infants do not grow 90 to 95 percent of the time. Instead, growth is marked by many "spurts."

Some infants will show an unusual pattern referred to as **failure to thrive.** With this pattern, the infant may refuse to eat. As a result of inappropriate amounts of nutrition, these children do not show typical weight and height gains. This problem has also been linked to behavioural and emotional problems. Although the exact cause of **FTT** is unclear**,** many researchers believe it is caused, at least in strong part, by deficiencies in caregiver–child relationships.

Many children who fall behind developmentally for a variety of reasons do nonetheless return to relatively normal patterns of development. Once a problem (such as poor nutrition) is alleviated, many children show accelerated patterns of growth that assist the child in "catching up" with other children. This tendency is referred to as **canalization.**

In terms of infant nutrition, there are several pieces of advice. These include (1) build up to a variety of foods—try one at a time to assess preference as well as potential allergies, (2) pay attention to the child's appetite—when he or she is hungry, he or she will eat, (3) don't restrict fat and cholesterol too much—the child's physical needs are different from those of the grown-up, (4) be careful with high-fibre foods—most infants have no trouble being "regular," (5) avoid items with sugar and salt as much as possible, and (6) encourage foods with high iron content—infants need more iron (percentage-wise) than adults.

There continues to be a controversy as to whether mothers should breast-feed. Although this is clearly a personal choice, research shows that there is no better substitute for digestibility, immune system protection, and meeting the changing nutritional needs of the infant. On the other hand, breast milk may transmit HIV to the infant if the mother is infected and may provide inadequate nutrition if the mother is malnourished. Also, if the mother drinks alcohol or uses drugs, these substances may be passed to the baby through the breast milk.

Development of the Brain and Nervous System

The primary mover and shaker in the nervous system is the **neuron.** A neuron is a cell that is specialized to receive and transmit messages from one part of the body to another. Neurons are able to complete this communication function because of how they are constructed. The **dendrites** (branchlike fibres) of the neuron receive incoming signals, usually from other neurons. These signals are sent to the **cell body** for processing. The cell body can be considered a decision maker because it is the part of the neuron that "decides" if the information it is receiving is important enough to send on. The cell body completes this function by means of a threshold. If the threshold (a minimum amount of stimulation needed) is reached or exceeded, the cell body will send that electrical message on via the **axon.** Axons are often coated with a **myelin sheath**—a fatty substance that serves to insulate the neuron and make the conducting of signals more efficient. Problems with **myelination** are associated with significant illnesses such as **multiple sclerosis.** If the electrical signal reaches the end of the axon, chemical messengers known as **neurotransmitters** are released and may make their way to the dendrites of other neurons to continue the process. **Nerves** are bundles of axons from many neurons.

Brain development occurs at a remarkable rate in the neonate. By the child's first birthday, the brain will have reached about 70 percent of its adult weight. Significant brain structures that are developing include the **medulla** (involved in basic functions such as heartbeat and respiration), the **cerebrum** (a layer of neurons covering the human brain that allow for thought, imagination, and language), and the **cerebellum** (which helps the child maintain balance and coordinate muscles so that walking becomes possible). Surprisingly enough, the infant brain actually has more neural connections than the adult brain. In an example of "**use it or lose it,**" those connections that are activated by experience will be maintained; those that are not will be pruned.

Motor Development: How Moving

Infant motor development is predictable in the sense that it follows both **cephalocaudal** (head to tail) and **proximodistal** (from the centre outward) patterns of development. Infants, for example, can lift their heads and control their torsos before they can engage in coordinated arm or leg movements. Fine motor skills like grasping progress from a clumsy grasp with all fingers against the palm (**ulnar grasp**) to a **pincer grasp,** which uses the thumb and index finger. Genetics and experience play a role in these developmental processes. Infants who are deprived of experience (such as Hopi children strapped to cradle boards for the first year of life) may experience rapid acceleration in development once the obstacle thwarting development has been removed. This process, called **canalization,** illustrates the relationship between genetics and experience. Genetics provide a **reaction range** in which the infant can develop. Experience, then, may influence how rapidly the child develops within that range.

Sensory and Perceptual Development

Sensation refers to the stimulation the sensory organs pick up from the environment and send to the brain, whereas **perception** refers to the process by which the brain interprets and creates meaning from that input. How do infants learn to integrate and make sense of the many pieces of sensory information they are receiving from the world? Although adults may take the ability to organize, perceive, and make sense of the world for granted, imagine this task as a newborn knowing nothing of the world. One important task is deciding what sensory information to pay attention to and what to ignore. Newborns' vision restricts their ability to gather visual information. Although a newborn's visual acuity is poor, by the time an infant is six months of age, acuity is 20/50. Adult levels of acuity are reached by the time the child is three to five years old.

Although an infant's vision is fine for feeding and looking at the person holding him or her, it does not allow for much exploration beyond that. But vision is a muscular sense, and the infant's eye muscles will quickly develop. Visual acuity will then develop rapidly.

Infants prefer visual images that resemble the human face. Following eight hours of mother–infant contact, spaced over four days, a neonate can distinguish his or her mother's face from that of other women. By the time infants are crawling, they demonstrate **depth perception.** With this skill, the infant is able to discriminate flat surfaces from drop-offs, thereby keeping him or her from crawling off edges. Other perceptual abilities developing in the infant include an understanding of **perceptual constancy** (perceiving an object as the same even though the sensations produced are different under various circumstances—such as a closed door and an open door), **size constancy** (a tendency to perceive the object as the same size even though the image on the retina may be smaller due to distance), and **shape constancy** (a tendency to perceive an object as the same even when viewed from dramatically different angles).

Although newborns can turn their heads toward a sound, the ability to localize a sound improves until the infant approaches adult levels of locating the direction of a sound, usually by 18 months. Scientists use **habituation,** becoming used to or bored with a stimulus, to learn if babies can distinguish sounds. As early as one month of age, babies can differentiate sounds that are very similar, such as "bah" and "pah."

Amazingly, infants are capable of hearing all the sounds (sounds that you and I cannot hear) of all languages, but during the second half of the first year, they lose the ability to discriminate sounds that they do not hear in the language being spoken around them.

Psychologists have debated whether or not infants/children play an active role or a passive role in the development of their perceptual abilities. While a newborn may be more "mechanical" or "passive," having inborn mechanisms that guide what they perceive, as the child grows older, perception becomes more intentional, systematic, and selective.

Critical Thinking Exercises

Exercise 1

You have read a research study in which rats were exposed to an "amusement park" with ladders, platforms, and other things on which to climb and explore. In comparison to rats not raised in this environment, the amusement park rats developed heavier brains. Research shows this difference in brain weight is due to (at least in part) a greater number of dendrites and axons. Based on this, how would you apply this concept to raising a child?

____

____

____

____

____

____

Exercise 2

A friend of yours says, "Why bother with stimulating the child? Genetics determine how they develop, not experience." Based on the concepts of **canalization** and **reaction range,** explain to your friend why this viewpoint might be inaccurate. Be sure to describe the concepts and give detailed enough examples that your friend can understand what you are talking about and why he or she should change his or her mind.

____

____

____

____

____

____

Internet Activities

Activity 1

Choose one of the following terms and run an Internet search:

- Breast feeding
- Nature vs. nurture
- Depth perception

Choose one of the sites that come up as a result of your search and read the information presented. Assume that you are a nurse giving prenatal information and advice to an expectant mother. Based on what you have learned from this article:

1. How accurately do you feel this site portrays information about your topic? Why?
2. Were there any critical pieces of information missing that you feel should have been provided? If so, what were they? If not, what were the most critical pieces conveyed?
3. What is the most important thing you learned by reading the information on this site? Why?

Activity 2

Access the Internet and go to the following URL:

http://www.hc-sc.gc.ca/fn-an/food-guide-aliment/choose-choix/advice-conseil/child-enfant/index_e.html

Imagine that you are a social worker who is responsible for educating new mothers and fathers about early childhood nutrition. Based on the information on this site, how would you answer the following questions from these parents:

1. Should I be careful not to overfeed my child so that he or she does not develop a weight problem? Why or why not?
2. Is it true that young children need less fat and protein than older children? If this is not true, what is the right balance for my young child?

Below is the URL of AboutKidsHealth from the Toronto Sick Children's Hospital. Go to the website and in the search box on the upper right-hand side of the page, type in "Failure to thrive":

http://www.aboutkidshealth.ca/Default.aspx

Read some of the articles and answer these two questions:

1. How would someone know if a child is exhibiting "failure to thrive"?
2. If a child does have "failure to thrive," what can be done about it?

Observing Children and Adolescents CD-ROM Activity

Watch "The Newborn: Sensation and Perception" (Module 1, Section 1) and read the material on page 14 of *Observing Children and Adolescents.* Then answer the following questions:

1. What was your reaction to watching Carter with his mother and father? What stimuli did Carter seem most interested in? How far from his mother's face was Carter being held?
2. What does a newborn (Carter) or very young infant (Aiden—one week old) hear? What kind of auditory stimuli are most interesting to them?
3. Describe how perceptual preferences were being measured in Giuseppina, the two-month-old infant. What visual stimuli most interest two-month olds?

Power Preview: Learning Objectives Sample Answers

1. Describe the processes of physical growth and development during infancy.

During the first year of life, the infant will increase in height by about 50 percent and will triple his or her birth weight. Slowly, the child's body will "catch up" with the head in terms of percentage of body proportion. Children receiving adequate nutrition are likely to demonstrate the following sequence of physical development: (1) rolling over, (2) sitting up, (3) crawling, (4) creeping, (5) standing, (6) walking by holding onto objects, and (7) walking unassisted. Infants who are thwarted in their development due to illness or some other obstacle, tend to accelerate in their development once that obstacle is removed. This tendency is referred to as canalization.

2. Explain how the brain and nervous system develop during infancy.

One of the most significant changes is the development and refinement of neural connections in the brain. The infant brain contains significantly more neural connections than the adult brain. This could reflect the fact that the infant is prepared to learn virtually anything. Those neural connections that are used are maintained while those that are not used are pruned. Another significant event is the development of myelin (a fatty substance that coats the neuron—in particular, the axon). Myelin serves as an insulator and allows for the neurons to conduct messages with greater efficiency. In terms of brain development, some of the most striking changes may occur as the cerebellum matures. The cerebellum allows for coordinated motor movements and is an essential player as the child learns to move about the world and eventually begin walking and running.

3. Discuss the roles that genetics and environment play in motor development.

The old idea of nature vs. nurture does not seem to adequately apply to human development. Instead, researchers discuss "reaction range." This concept refers to the relationship between the infant's genetic potential and the environment or experience. In other words, genetics provides a range within which the child can develop. Environment and experience, however, may strongly influence where within that range the child will develop. A child in an enriched and stimulating environment, for example, may come closer to reaching her genetic potential for intelligence than a child raised in an impoverished and under-stimulated environment.

4. Describe sensory and perceptual development in infancy.

Infants quickly show preferences for humanlike visual and auditory sensations. Infants will, for example, spend more time looking at a picture of a human face than other objects. Infants' ability to localize sounds improves rapidly until it approximates adult levels at eighteen months; infants' sound sensitivity also increases during the first few months. Although infants only a few months of age can discriminate slight differences in sounds, the ability to make distinctions based on the loudness and pitch of sounds increases during children's preschool years. Through experience, infants learn perceptual constancies that allow them to recognize objects despite changes in the shape or size of the images that fall on the retina. Additionally, infants develop an understanding of depth and demonstrate depth

perception before they begin to crawl. This ability, of course, is essential to keep them from crawling off edges and getting hurt.

Chapter Review

Multiple Choice

1. Cephalocaudal development means:
   a. from the top down
   b. from the centre outward
   c. returning to normal development
   d. getting developmentally off track
2. Proximodistal development means:
   a. from the top down
   b. from the centre outward
   c. returning to normal development
   d. getting developmentally off track
3. Which of the following correctly describes perceptual development?
   a. as the infant grows older, perception becomes less intentional and more mechanical
   b. perceptual search becomes less systematic over time
   c. as children grow older, attention becomes more selective
   d. irrelevant information is harder to ignore as the child grows older
4. An infant grows:
   a. virtually nonstop during the first year
   b. about 90% of the time
   c. about 50% of the time
   d. about 10% of the time
5. Nadia eats fitfully and often refuses to eat. She may suffer from:
   a. failure to thrive
   b. SIDS
   c. damage to the cerebellum
   d. medulla damage
6. Jared was kept in his crib and not allowed to move or explore until he was eighteen months old. Despite this, once allowed to move about, he learned to crawl and then walk almost as quickly as children not restricted in this way. This demonstrates:
   a. the power of cephalocaudal development
   b. a tendency called canalization
   c. that crawling and walking are independent of experience
   d. this is not possible

7. In terms of diet, which of the following is true?
   a. children prefer salty and bitter foods
   b. infants do not prefer sugary foods as many adults assume
   c. infants need more fat and cholesterol than adults do
   d. infants do not know when they are hungry or full
8. Breast milk:
   a. is easily digestible
   b. may prevent childhood cancer
   c. contains antibodies that protect the infant
   d. all of these can be said about breast milk
9. The dendrites of a neuron:
   a. process information
   b. protect the neuron by coating it
   c. receive signals from other neurons
   d. send chemical messengers to communicate with other neurons
10. The cell body of the neuron:
    a. processes information
    b. protects the neuron by coating it
    c. receives signals from other neurons
    d. sends chemical messengers to communicate with other neurons
11. Multiple sclerosis involves:
    a. replacement of myelin with a fibrous tissue
    b. damage to the cerebrum
    c. an overly active medulla
    d. destruction of the neurotransmitters normally involved in neural communication
12. Infant brains:
    a. have significantly fewer brain structures than the adult brain
    b. weigh about 70% of their adult weight
    c. simply get bigger as the child grows
    d. have significantly more neural connections than the adult brain
13. If we show an object to an infant until he or she stops looking at it, then switch the object, and the infant becomes attentive again, what do we know?
    a. that the infant can distinguish between the two objects
    b. that the infant prefers things that are new or different
    c. that a habituation research technique has been used
    d. we know all of these things
14. Infants prefer to look at:
    a. brightly coloured, odd-shaped objects
    b. a black and white bulls-eye pattern
    c. the features of the human face
    d. infants have no visual preferences; they are all learned

15. Infants prefer sounds:
    a. that fall within the range of the human voice
    b. that are out of range of what most adults can hear
    c. that are very deep and full of bass
    d. that are mechanical and nonrhythmic

Matching

Match each of the items from column A with the corresponding item from column B. There is only one correct answer per item.

	A		B
1. _______	habituation	a.	tendency to return to normal development
2. _______	ulnar grasp	b.	involved in motor control
3. _______	canalization	c.	receives signals from other neurons
4. _______	pincer grasp	d.	organizing sensations in meaningful ways
5. _______	medulla	e.	what is genetically possible
6. _______	dendrite	f.	involved in heartbeat and breathing
7. _______	perception	g.	involved in transmitting messages
8. _______	axon	h.	grasping present by 3 to 4 months
9. _______	cerebellum	i.	becoming bored with or used to a stimulus
10. _______	reaction range	j.	grasping not present until at least 9 months

True–False

1. Cephalocaudal development means that development occurs earlier in the lower body parts than in the upper body parts, including the head.

   TRUE or FALSE

2. Infants double in height and triple their weight during the first year of life.

   TRUE or FALSE

3. Failure to thrive may be related to problems in physical, cognitive, emotional, and behavioural development.

   TRUE or FALSE

4. The Canadian Paediatric Society recommends exclusive breast feeding for the first six months of life.

   TRUE or FALSE

5. HIV has not been detected in breast milk.

   TRUE or FALSE

6. Myelinization of neurons that are used in hearing begins before birth, around the sixth month after conception.

   TRUE or FALSE

7. Children's visual acuity at birth is 20/50.

   TRUE or FALSE

8. Robert Fantz found that by eight to twelve weeks, infants preferred straight lines to curved lines.

   TRUE or FALSE

9. The visual cliff was used by Gibson and Walk to measure depth perception in infants.

   TRUE or FALSE

10. According to Eleanor Gibson, infants' perception becomes more intentional and less automatic as they mature.

    TRUE or FALSE

Solutions

Chapter Review

Multiple Choice

1. a (162)
2. b (162)
3. c (180)
4. d (162)
5. a (165)
6. b (166)
7. c (167)
8. d (169)
9. c (171)
10. a (171)
11. a (171)
12. d (174)
13. d (188)
14. c (181)
15. a (188)

Matching

1. i (188)
2. h (176)
3. a (166)
4. j (176)
5. f (172)
6. c (171)
7. d (180)
8. g (171)
9. b (173)
10. e (180)

True–False

1. F (162)
2. T (161)
3. T (166)
4. T (169)
5. F (170)
6. T (174)
7. F (180)
8. F (181)
9. T (182)
10. T (191)

CHAPTER 6

Infancy: Cognitive Development

Learning Objectives

By the end of this chapter, you should be able to generate well-thought-out responses to demonstrate your understanding of the following learning objectives (sample answer comments are included at the end of this chapter):

1. Describe the kinds of cognitive developments that occur prior to the use of language and how researchers assess them.
2. Explain why "out of sight" is also apparently "out of mind" for two-month-old infants. For example, when toys are placed behind a screen, these infants act as if they no longer exist.
3. Why did Carolyn Rovee-Collier and her colleagues tie one end of a ribbon to an infant's ankle and the other end to a brightly coloured mobile?
4. Describe imitation in a one-hour-old infant.
5. Explain how intelligence might be measured in infants and at what ages researchers can begin to measure intelligence.
6. Describe evidence that crying is a primitive form of language.
7. Discuss babbling from a cross-cultural perspective.
8. Describe pros and cons of correcting children's language errors.
9. Explain parental behaviours that promote a child's language development.
10. Discuss "prewiring" of children to listen to language in such a way that they come to understand rules of grammar.

Chapter Summary

Cognitive Development: Jean Piaget

Jean Piaget, after carefully observing his own and other children, formulated a theory describing how children mentally represent the world. He believed that children continually **assimilate** (incorporate new events into their existing representations or **schemes**) and **accommodate** (change their existing representations to take into account new information from the world).

Piaget believed that cognitive development took place in stages, and that children thought about the world in different ways using different processes in different stages. The first of Piaget's stages is the **sensorimotor stage,** which usually spans the first two years of life. Initially, infants respond to events in the world with reflexes such as sucking and grasping but with maturation and experience develop purposeful actions.

The sensorimotor stage is divided into six **substages.** The first substage, simple reflexes, lasts for the first month after birth. From about one to four months, the infant is in the second substage, **primary circular reactions,** in which the infant tries to repeat (circular) actions that are focused on his own body (primary). In the third substage, from four to eight months, the infant develops **secondary circular reactions;** the infant now is interested in trying to repeat actions that involve objects in the environment. The fourth substage is called the coordination of secondary schemes substage. In this substage, the infant is combining and coordinating secondary circular reactions. For example, a child who picks up a ball and throws it is combining two schemes. In the fifth substage, from twelve to eighteen months, the child becomes an active experimenter, varying his or her actions, now called **tertiary circular reactions,** to explore their various effects. Finally, in the sixth substage, which covers the ages of eighteen to twenty-four months, infants show the beginnings of internal representation and symbolic thought.

According to Piaget, infants initially do not cognitively represent objects and do not understand that things continue to exist if they are not looking at or interacting with them. **Object permanence** is the infant's understanding that people and objects continue to exist even when the infant is not looking at them. Piaget found that at six months of age, the infant would not look for an object that had been covered with a blanket unless part of the object was visible.

While Piaget's theory provides good descriptions of infant behaviours, many psychologists have disagreed with some of Piaget's claims. First, some developmental psychologists believe that development is more gradual, that it does not involve stages or abrupt shifts in development. Second, some studies have provided data suggesting that Piaget may have underestimated the competencies of young infants. For example, Piaget believed that **deferred imitation,** imitation of a behaviour that occurred at a prior time, would not occur until about eighteen months, but one study found that nine-month-old infants imitated novel actions made by adults twenty-four hours earlier.

Information Processing

The information processing approach is not a stage approach; psychologists advocating this point of view believe that developmental changes take place much more gradually. This approach focuses on how children process information from the environment. Infant memory is one of the areas studied to try to understand cognitive development.

Amazingly, newborn infants demonstrated a memory for their mother's voice when she'd read a story to them during the last weeks of pregnancy. They sucked at a certain rate to hear their mother read the same story they'd heard prenatally. Older infants show other kinds of memory. For example, in one study two-month-olds were able to remember how to make a mobile move, even with a three-day delay.

Imitation is another capacity that newborns have. Infants ranging in age from less than an hour to seventy-one hours old have been found to imitate adults opening their mouths or sticking out their tongues. Some studies, though, have not found this imitative behaviour in children older than two weeks. Perhaps it is a reflexive behaviour that drops out shortly after birth and reappears later as a more purposeful behaviour.

Individual Differences in Intelligence among Infants

Psychologists interested in intelligence testing have been interested in differences among individuals. Tests used to measure intelligence in infants are very different than those used for adults, which often include vocabulary items and requests for explanations about how two concepts are similar. The Bayley Scale of Infant Development was one of the first widely used tests of infant development and includes a variety of items.

One of the problems with infant intelligence tests has been their poor predictive power for later school achievement and intelligence test scores. Perhaps the kinds of test items are too different from those used in later intelligence tests.

A more recent effort to link infant cognitive ability to later intelligence has focused on **visual recognition memory,** which is the ability to differentiate previously viewed stimuli from new stimuli. This can be assessed by measuring how long infants look at a new picture versus one previously seen. Infants who scored higher on infant visual recognition memory tests scored higher on intelligence tests given several years later.

Language Development

Prelinguistic (before language) vocalizations include crying, **cooing,** and **babbling.** Crying is, of course, present at birth; cooing begins during the second month and is usually vowel-like sounds often associated with positive feelings. Babbling starts around six to nine months and is usually a combination of consonants and vowels. By ten to twelve months, babies tend to repeat syllables, which is referred to as **echolalia.**

Somewhere during the first year, children say their first word and, toward the end of the first year, are using patterns of **intonation** that resemble adult speech. Children may have a vocabulary of 50 words by about eighteen months. A child's **receptive vocabulary** refers to the words that he or she understands whereas the **expressive vocabulary** refer to the words the child says. Children typically understand many more words than they can say.

Some children show a **referential language style,** often using language to label things in their environment, while others use an **expressive language style,** in which more of the focus of language is on interactions with others.

When children are first learning the meaning of a word, **overextensions,** applying the word to similar objects, are common. For example, children may use the word "car" to apply to trucks and buses as well as cars.

As children begin to speak in "sentences," they use **telegraphic speech** in which only the most essential words are included. "Mommy home" might mean "Mommy has come home." **Holophrases,** using a word to express a longer meaning, are similar. A child pointing and saying "milk" could mean "Give me some milk." The average number of morphemes that children use in sentences (**the mean length of utterance—MLU**) gives us a method for characterizing their level of speech.

If you've tried to learn a second language as an adult, you know how difficult it is to master vocabulary, pronunciation, and rules for combining words (**syntax**). How do children so quickly acquire language? According to learning theory, imitation of more proficient speakers (**models**) and reinforcement play crucial roles in learning a language. **Extinction** and **shaping** play roles in language acquisition just as in the acquisition of other behaviours. On the other hand, the nativist view promotes the importance of innate factors in the acquisition of language.

Psycholinguistic theory explains language acquisition as an interaction between an innate tendency for acquiring language and the environment. Chomsky referred to an inborn **language acquisition device,** an innate "prewiring" in humans, that facilitates language acquisition. Chomsky believed that a universal grammar is present in all languages and that in acquiring a language, children acquire transformations that allow them to go from the **deep structure,** or underlying meaning, to the **surface structure,** or expression of that meaning. Eighteen months to puberty is a **sensitive period** for children to acquire language because of brain plasticity. This is not specific to spoken language, as deaf children using **American Sign Language (ASL)** have demonstrated this sensitive period as well.

With brain research, we now know that several structures are very important for language acquisition. Broca's area and Wernicke's area are thought to be crucial; damage to either area can result in language deficits. **Broca's aphasia** refers to difficulty with expressive language, speaking, while **Wernicke's aphasia** refers to problems with receptive language, understanding what others are saying.

Critical Thinking Exercises

Exercise 1

Your text discusses the stimulation parents provide their children. Do you think parents should buy special toys, videotapes, CDs, and flashcards to provide extra stimulation during infancy? What might advantages be? Disadvantages? What would you do as a parent?

Exercise 2

How do children acquire language? Compare Skinner's learning approach to Chomsky's psycholinguistic approach. Include the following terms in your discussion:

- imitation
- reinforcement
- shaping
- language acquisition device
- universal grammar
- deep structure
- surface structure

____

____

____

____

____

____

Internet Activity

What kind of things can parents do to help infants/children acquire language? Is it beneficial for children to learn a second language as well? Access the Internet and go to the following URL:

http://www.ecs.soton.ac.uk/~harnad/Papers/Py104/pinker.langacq.html

As you read through the material, consider the following terms:

- language acquisition
- second language
- sensitive period

After looking at this website, write a summary including the following points:

1. Describe how parents might help a child acquire a first or second language.
2. What benefits or problems might be associated with a child acquiring a second language?
3. What is the most important thing you learned from exploring this website? Why?

Print copies of the material from the website to attach to your paper.

Observing Children and Adolescents CD-ROM Activity

Watch the "Piaget's Sensorimotor Stage" video (Module 1, Section 3) and read the material on pages 36 and 37 of *Observing Children and Adolescents.* Then answer the following questions:

1. What was your reaction to watching the movements of the infants in the video? Were the movements what you expected, or were you surprised?
2. Describe how infants advance from initial reflexive movements during the sensorimotor stage. Include examples from the video of three of these five kinds of actions: reflexes, primary circular reactions, secondary circular reactions, coordination of secondary schemes, and tertiary circular reactions.
3. What is object permanence? Describe differences in how two-month-old Giuseppina reacted when an object was hidden and how several older infants reacted.

Power Preview: Learning Objectives Sample Answers

1. Describe the kinds of cognitive developments that occur prior to the use of language and how researchers assess them.

Infants show a number of remarkable abilities. They are able to recognize a story their mother read to them prenatally, and will suck a nipple at a specified rate to hear the story. Infants in their first year show the ability to recognize visual stimuli. This is demonstrated by comparing looking times for old and new stimuli. Object permanence also develops during the first year. Piaget watched infants' attempts to search for hidden objects; others have compared the amount of time infants look at possible versus impossible events.

2. Explain why "out of sight" is also apparently "out of mind" for two-month-old infants. For example, when toys are placed behind a screen, these infants act as if they no longer exist.

Piaget argued that young infants lack object permanence, the understanding that things continue to exist when one is not looking at them. He thought that even eight- to twelve-month-olds make mistakes in object permanence. Other researchers (Baillargeon & colleagues) believe that at least some aspects of object permanence are present in infants as young as two or three months.

3. Why did Carolyn Rovee-Collier and her colleagues tie one end of a ribbon to an infant's ankle and the other end to a brightly coloured mobile?

Rovee-Collier and colleagues were studying infants' memories. The infants learned that they could make the mobile move by kicking and, after this discovery, increased their kicking rate. Two-month-olds demonstrated some memory for this experience even with delays as long as three days while three-month-olds demonstrated memory for this knowledge for a week or more.

4. Describe imitation in a one-hour-old infant.

Infants less than an hour old up to seventy-one hours old demonstrate imitation of mouth movements. When adults open or close their mouths or stick out their tongues, infants mimic these actions. This may be a reflexive behaviour that drops out after infants are about two weeks old; more intentional imitation returns later during infancy.

5. Explain how intelligence might be measured in infants and at what ages researchers can begin to measure intelligence.

The Bayley Scales of Infant Development can be used even with one-month-old infants with items such as the infant's ability to adjust his or her position slightly when lifted to an adult's shoulder. The Bayley Scales contain mental-scale and motor-scale items. The Bayley Scales may help screen infants with developmental problems, but the assessment may not correspond very well to later measures of intelligence. Visual recognition memory may correspond more clearly to later intelligence tests.

6. Describe evidence that crying is a primitive form of language.

Although technically crying is not language since the infant's cries aren't representing events or objects, crying is the neonate's only way of verbally communicating. Cooing and babbling start later during the first year.

7. Discuss babbling from a cross-cultural perspective.

Infants from different countries, hearing a variety of languages, babble the same sounds. In other words, infants in Canada initially babble the sounds found in Spanish, German, and African languages even if they could not have heard those sounds in the language spoken around them. Gradually, the sounds that infants do not hear spoken around them are dropped from the infant's maturing babbling.

8. Describe pros and cons of correcting children's language errors.

According to Skinner and learning theory, shaping, gradually correcting language until it approximates adult speech, is important in language acquisition. However, some data do not support this point of view. For example, parents tend to reinforce for truth-value rather than grammatical correctness. Also, even if parents do not correct grammar, children eventually acquire the grammar they hear spoken around them. According to Chomsky, sufficient exposure to the language, rather than shaping, is what is crucial in language acquisition. If children are not ready to acquire a grammatical rule, correction may not make a difference.

9. Explain parental behaviours that promote a child's language development.

These adult behaviours can promote language acquisition: using simpler, repetitive verbalizations, asking questions to actively engage the child, responding to the child's language, noticing what a child is observing adjoining them, using gestures to supplement verbal communication, and talking often with a child. According to the psycholinguistic theory, children have an innate readiness to acquire language and, with sufficient exposure, will develop vocabulary and language at their own rate.

10. Discuss "prewiring" of children to listen to language in such a way that they come to understand rules of grammar.

Chomsky believed that infants come "prewired" with a language acquisition device; all that is needed is hearing others speak the language. According to Chomsky, the commonalities (babbling similarities, orderliness of acquisition of syntax) imply a universal grammar. Children in all languages acquire transformations that allow them to go from a deep structure or underlying meaning to the surface structure or actual spoken words.

Chapter Review

Multiple Choice

1. Piaget's stage for infant development is called the:
   a. preoperational stage
   b. concrete operation stage
   c. sensorimotor stage
   d. formal operations stage

2. In this substage, the child's repetitive actions focus on his own body:
   a. primary circular reactions
   b. secondary circular reactions
   c. tertiary circular reactions
   d. quadratic circular reactions
3. Alana is about fifteen months of age and is experimenting with her food while sitting in her high chair. She notices how a pea rolls when she throws it on the floor and how apple sauce splats when she throws it on the floor. She is likely in which substage of cognitive development?
   a. primary circular reactions
   b. secondary circular reactions
   c. tertiary circular reactions
   d. quadratic circular reactions
4. Which of the following is NOT an accurate criticism of Piaget's theory?
   a. cognitive development may not occur in stages
   b. deferred imitation has been found earlier than what Piaget predicted
   c. Piaget may have underestimated the ages at which infants and children could perform tasks
   d. other observers of infant behaviour have been unable to find the kinds of actions Piaget observed
5. The infant's understanding that something continues to exist even when the infant cannot see it is called:
   a. object validation
   b. object verification
   c. object permanence
   d. object accommodation
6. According to information processing theory:
   a. cognitive development occurs in distinct stages
   b. understanding infant memory is not important
   c. infants show no capacity for imitation until six months of age
   d. the focus is on how children process environmental information
7. Imitation in infants:
   a. has rarely been observed
   b. is possible even in neonates
   c. begins to occur around six months of age
   d. is unimportant in cognitive development
8. Which of the following is an example of an infant intelligence test?
   a. the Bayley Scales of Infant Development
   b. the Jordan Mental Maturity Measurement
   c. the Brogden Test of Infant Intelligence
   d. there is no infant intelligence test since it is impossible to measure intelligence in infants

9. What has been found to moderately correspond to intelligence tests during childhood?
   a. motor milestones such as sitting up, standing, and walking
   b. age at which babbling first occurs
   c. visual recognition memory
   d. age at which deferred imitation occurs
10. Which of the following is true regarding cooing?
   a. cooing is present at birth
   b. cooing is usually a combination of vowels and consonants
   c. cooing is usually associated with pleasant emotions
   d. cooing does not occur unless parents first "coo" to infants
11. Regarding receptive and expressive language:
   a. expressive language precedes receptive language and refers to the understanding of language
   b. receptive language precedes expressive language and refers to the understanding of language
   c. expressive language is acquired only with great effort on the part of the parents
   d. receptive language is acquired only with great effort on the part of the parents
12. This term is used to refer to a single-word utterance that expresses a more complex meaning:
   a. uniphrase
   b. combophrase
   c. telephrase
   d. holophrase
13. Shaping is important according to this theory of language acquisition:
   a. learning theory
   b. nativist theory
   c. psycholinguistic theory
   d. cognitive theory
14. Who is associated with a language acquisition device?
   a. Skinner
   b. Piaget
   c. Chomsky
   d. Bromberg
15. Which of the following is true regarding the case of Genie?
   a. Genie did not acquire any language capacity whatsoever
   b. Genie's case provided no support for a sensitive period of language acquisition
   c. Genie developed "normal" language fluency
   d. Genie's language development was largely telegraphic

Matching

Match each of the items from Column A with the corresponding item from Column B. There is only one correct answer per item.

Column A		Column B
1. ______	visual recognition memory	a. a single word with a complex meaning
2. ______	deep structure	b. before language
3. ______	primary circular reactions	c. differentiation between new/old stimuli
4. ______	holophrase	d. "prewiring" for language acquisition
5. ______	babbling	e. the underlying meaning of language
6. ______	syntax	f. spoken words
7. ______	language acquisition device	g. objects exist when not looked at
8. ______	object permanence	h. rules for combining words
9. ______	prelinguistic	i. consonant and vowel sounds
10. ______	expressive language	j. repetitive actions focused on the body

True–False

1. Piaget's cognitive theory divides the sensorimotor stage into six substages.

   TRUE or FALSE

2. Changing one's scheme because of environmental events is called accommodation.

   TRUE or FALSE

3. The A-not-B error is an error infants make related to deferred imitation.

   TRUE or FALSE

4. According to Renee Baillargeon, infants develop knowledge of object permanence later than what Piaget predicted.

   TRUE or FALSE

5. Infants only three months old remembered how to make a mobile move even after a delay of a week or more.

   TRUE or FALSE

6. Babbling typically precedes cooing during the first year of infancy.

   TRUE or FALSE

7. An example of overextension would be an infant's calling a strange woman "mommy."

   TRUE or FALSE

8. Chomsky, in explaining language acquisition, emphasized the processes of imitation and reinforcement rather than innate capabilities of the infant.

   TRUE or FALSE

9. "Motherese," although commonly used by women with children, is not recommended as a way to promote the child's language acquisition.

   TRUE or FALSE

10. Wernicke's aphasia refers to deficits related to understanding language.
    TRUE or FALSE

Solutions

Chapter Review

Multiple Choice

1. c (200)
2. a (203)
3. c (204)
4. d (208)
5. c (205)
6. d (210)
7. b (211)
8. a (212)
9. c (214)
10. c (216)
11. b (218)
12. d (222)
13. a (224)
14. c (226)
15. d (229)

Matching

1. c (214)
2. e (226)
3. j (203)
4. a (222)
5. i (217)
6. h (222)
7. d (226)
8. g (205)
9. b (216)
10. f (217)

True–False

1. T (200)
2. T (200)
3. F (208)
4. F (205)
5. T (211)
6. F (217)
7. T (221)
8. F (226)
9. F (228)
10. T (227)

CHAPTER 7

Infancy: Social and Personality Development

Learning Objectives

By the end of this chapter, you should be able to generate well-thought-out responses to demonstrate your understanding of the following learning objectives (sample answer comments are included at the end of this chapter):

1. Explain how the infant's willingness to leave the mother to explore the environment is a sign of attachment.
2. Why does the number of diapers a father changes per week predict how strongly infants are attached to him?
3. Is there a relation between feeding and attachment to a parent?
4. Discuss the existence of a critical period for the attachment bonds between a child and his or her parents.
5. Why have child abusers frequently been the victims of child abuse themselves?
6. Explain why autistic children are alone, even when they are surrounded by people who are doing their best to get through to them.
7. Discuss pros and cons of placing a child in daycare when daycare children have been found to be more aggressive than children who stay home.
8. Discuss the normalcy of fear of strangers in infants and what "normal" means.
9. Describe how infants "check out" others when faced with a novel situation.
10. Describe how children come to realize they "exist."
11. Explain the kinds of "temperamental" children.
12. Describe early differences in toy preferences for boys and girls.

Chapter Summary

Attachment: Bonds That Endure

Attachment refers to emotional ties between two individuals or animals and may enhance the likelihood of survival of a baby human or animal. Babies who lose contact with an object of attachment may experience **separation anxiety.**

How is attachment measured? Mary Ainsworth developed the **Strange Situation Method** to assess attachment. An infant is taken into the laboratory by a parent, and the infant is observed through a one-way mirror while a series of parent–child separations and reunions occur.

Based on the Strange Situation Method, Ainsworth and her colleagues described three patterns of attachment. The babies who are **securely attached** are slightly upset by parents' departure, are easily comforted by their parents upon reunion, and are confident in their exploration of the environment. Ainsworth described two categories of insecure attachment. **Avoidant attachment** is characterized by the least distress when separated from parents and the child's ignoring the parent in reunion episodes, whereas **ambivalent/resistant attachment** is characteristic of babies who are the most upset when parents leave and show mixed emotions (wanting to be near but also rejecting behaviours) during reunions. A third insecure attachment category, **disorganized–disoriented attachment,** which involves babies appearing confused and disoriented, has most recently been proposed.

Babies who are securely attached tend to be more sociable, relate better to other children, and are more likely to use their mothers as a secure base to explore their surroundings. Positive outcomes as these children grow older may be related to both the secure attachment during infancy and the continued positive parent–child interaction as the child grows older.

Mothers of infants who are securely attached tend to be more reliable, predictable, and sensitive in their care-giving. Providing aid to mothers who are economically stressed has been found to result in more secure attachment in children compared to mothers and infants not receiving such support. The type of attachment relationship may also be related to the infants' temperament, with infants who are more irritable and negative being more likely to be classified as insecurely attached.

Fathers' behaviour also relates to the development of attachment relationships. In one study, the number of diapers a father changed was found to relate to strength of attachment, perhaps indicating the father's involvement in child-care. Fathers who are involved with their children are just as capable of providing high-quality care as mothers. Past research has indicated that fathers, when compared to mothers, have been more likely to play with their children than provide child-care such as feeding and bathing.

Ainsworth has described the following phases of attachment: (1) the **initial-preattachment phase,** lasting until about three months of age, in which the infant shows little signs of preference for the parent, (2) the **attachment-in-the-making phase,** which occurs from about three to four months to about six months, with the infant showing some preference for the parent, and (3) the **clear-cut attachment phase,** which begins around six to seven months and includes intensified reactions to the parent. Separation anxiety is more likely to occur during this stage.

How do we explain the acquisition of attachment? The cognitive theory emphasizes the development of object permanence while the behavioural theory emphasizes the reinforcement of the infant's attachment behaviours and the association of the parents with a baby's needs' being met. According to psychoanalytic theory, proper satisfaction of the baby's oral needs is crucial in development. Harlow studied attachment in infant monkeys with surrogate wire and cloth "mothers." Even if the baby monkeys were fed from the wire mesh "mother," they became attached to the cloth "mother," providing evidence that **contact comfort** with the terry cloth mother was more important in the development of the attachment than meeting the monkeys' oral needs.

The ethological theory of attachment focuses on the survival value of attachment behaviours. Attachment behaviours may be genetically based **fixed action patterns.** The baby's crying or smiling may result in care-giving that increases the baby's chances of living. A critical period is also hypothesized; if the attachment relationship does not occur early in life, it may not occur at all. **Imprinting,** as demonstrated by Konrad Lorenz, involves a baby gosling's following the first moving object it sees during a very limited time, or **critical period.** A potential critical period for humans, though, may be extended; children who are adopted at later ages still develop attachment bonds with their parents.

When Attachment Fails

What happens in instances in which children are neglected or abused? Harlow's infant monkey research found that those monkeys reared without contact with other monkeys developed a variety of problems in relating to other monkeys; female monkeys reared in these isolated conditions tended to neglect and abuse their own babies. Institutionalized children who are provided little social interaction also tend to be socially withdrawn and depressed. Intellectual development of such children may also be affected. Moreover, several studies by Yarrow suggest that after three months of age, for optimal development, children may need a stable primary caregiver.

Children who are abused by their parents tend to show a wide range of problems and are more likely to have had an insecure attachment relationship with their parents. Sexually abused children are also more likely to experience psychological problems as they mature. Parents who neglect and abuse their children are likely to have been abused themselves. Children who observe their parents being angry and violent are less likely to learn more appropriate techniques to deal with anger; seeing anger in one's own home may lead to acceptance of family violence as appropriate and normal.

Techniques to help prevent abuse include strengthening parenting skills, especially among high-risk groups; presenting information regarding abuse; and providing more support to families. Publicity regarding child abuse may help by increasing public awareness of the problem.

Autism spectrum disorders typically involve impaired communication skills, repetitive behaviours, and social interaction deficits. Attachment relationships are usually problematic for children with autism, who frequently experience major difficulties in the development of language. Stereotypical behaviour, such as rocking, is characteristic of these children; children with autism may also inflict harm upon themselves. Genetic and neurological factors may play a key role in the development of autism. Treatment tends to be based on operant conditioning principles, although the use of certain drugs is also being explored.

Daycare

The majority of mothers in North America, even with children who are not yet one, are employed. In many cases, children may be taken to daycare. The quality of group daycare varies tremendously; one factor to consider is the ratio of adult care-givers to children, especially for infants and toddlers.

Does daycare affect children's attachment to their parents? Belsky reported higher rates of insecure attachment for children whose mothers were employed, but others have pointed out the Strange Situation measure may not be as valid for children who experience daily separations from their mothers. It's also important to remember that the majority of infants whose mothers are employed are still securely attached to the mother.

Effects of daycare on children may be both positive and negative. While some studies have found children in daycare to be more aggressive and less compliant, other research suggests that daycare children are more self-confident, independent, and affectionate. High-quality daycare has also been related to cognitive benefits, particularly for children from poorer families.

Emotional Development

Emotions have cognitive and physiological as well as situational components. According to Katherine Bridges, newborns experience only the emotion of diffuse excitement; other emotions are differentiated over time. Sroufe points out that cognitive development may be necessary before some emotions become differentiated; jealousy, for example, may be dependent upon the infant's understanding of object permanence.

On the other hand, Carrol Izard believes that infants innately have discrete emotions. These emotions, though, may still appear in an orderly progression. Using a scoring system based on facial movements, Izard reported that two-month-old infants exhibited emotions such as sadness and anger. Emotional states may also be linked to attachment status with ambivalent/resistant infants at fourteen months responding more fearfully and being more distressed than other infants.

Frequently, **fear of strangers** develops in children at about six to nine months of age. Children are less likely to be upset if they are being held by their mothers and are in familiar surroundings. They are most likely to become upset when strangers touch them.

Social referencing refers to looking to others for guidance in strange or novel situations. By six months of age, children will observe facial expressions as well as listen for tones of voice for information regarding how to respond in new situations. If a mother looks worried versus friendly in the presence of a stranger, infants respond differently. The ability to control one's emotions is called **emotional regulation.** Looking away or sucking their thumbs may be ways infants use to help regulate emotions at a very early age. Several studies have suggested a link between secure attachment and positive regulation of emotions.

Personality Development

The **self-concept,** or sense of self, emerges gradually during infancy. One of the techniques used to study infants' sense of self has been to watch their reactions to observing themselves in a mirror after a dab of rouge is placed on the nose. When infants are eighteen months, they begin to show self-recognition by touching their own noses rather than reaching for the baby in the mirror. According to psychoanalyst Margaret Mahler, the process of **separation-individuation,** developing a sense of self that is separate from the mother, extends from approximately five months to three years.

Thomas and Chess studied the development of **temperament:** a style of reacting that includes characteristics such as activity level, mood quality, adaptability, and approach or withdrawal to new situations. These researchers differentiated three styles of temperament, **easy, difficult,** and **slow-to-warm-**

up. While the easy child approaches and adapts easily to new situations, the difficult baby is more likely to be fussy and respond negatively to new situations. The slow-to-warm-up infant may initially seem more like the difficult infant, but he or she adjusts to new situations somewhat more readily. Some of the children in the initial study were too inconsistent to be classified into any of these three temperament categories. Some evidence has been found for moderate stability of temperament from infancy into later childhood.

While there may be a biological basis for initial temperament differences among infants, the "**goodness of fit**" of the environment also plays an important role in the continuing development of the child. If parents of a child with a difficult temperament respond patiently rather than by withdrawing, positive outcomes are likely for the child.

Gender role socialization is found in all cultures and begins very early. While girl and boy babies are similar in many ways, adults respond to them differently depending upon the infant's sex. If adults believe a baby is a boy, they are more likely to offer "him" boy toys than if they believe the same baby is a girl. Parents, especially fathers, are more likely to encourage their sons to engage in rough-and-tumble play. Parents are more likely to talk to and smile at girls. Differences have also been found in room furnishings and infant clothing.

Critical Thinking Exercises

Exercise 1

Kate and John, parents of a one-year-old, find that both of them need to be employed to make ends meet. What are characteristics of a good daycare? What negative and positive effects might daycare have on their child?

Exercise 2

Ryan, a new father, wants to develop a secure attachment relationship with his son. Based on the research with infants and both mothers and fathers, what recommendations would you have for Ryan in developing that relationship? Do you think that he is likely to develop such a relationship? Why or why not?

Internet Activity

The following URL takes you to a Statistics Canada research paper that gives information about how Canadians are accessing and using daycare. Review some of the information in the paper and summarize some of the most interesting trends in daycare.

http://www.statcan.ca/english/research/89-599-MIE/89-599-MIE2006003.pdf

Answer the questions posed below:

1. How many children are in child-care programs in Canada?
2. What ages are these children?
3. Are they in child-care programs full-time or part-time?
4. What kinds of facilities (daycare, dayhomes, school programs) are available to children of working parents?

Observing Children and Adolescents CD-ROM Activity

Watch the "Temperament" video (Module 1, Section 3) and read the material on pages 46 and 47 of *Observing Children and Adolescents.* Then answer the following questions:

1. Four-month-old Abby's mother described her as being very happy. What did you notice about Abby as you watched the video? Which temperament type do you think she might be? Why?
2. What were characteristics of several other infants on the video that did not seem as happy as Abby? What might parents of slow-to-warm-up or difficult babies expect from their infants?
3. Have you ever heard your parents describe you as an infant? If so, which temperament type do you think you were? Do you believe that there are inborn differences among babies in temperament? Why or why not?

Power Preview: Learning Objectives Sample Answers

1. Explain how the infant's willingness to leave the mother to explore the environment is a sign of attachment.

Babies who are securely attached to their mothers are confident enough to be able to explore the environment around them. This doesn't mean they forget about the mother, however. These infants may use social referencing, glancing back at the mother to see if she is smiling and encouraging their

exploration rather than looking anxious or worried. Babies also may bring toys to the mother to show her.

2. Why does the number of diapers a father changes per week predict how strongly infants are attached to him?

Diapers changed are a likely indication of how involved the father is with the infant. The more diapers changed, the more involved he is. A father with little contact with an infant is not likely to either change diapers or have his infant strongly attached to him.

3. Is there a relation between feeding and attachment to a parent?

Just as diaper changing may signal involvement, so may feeding. However, the connection is not as direct as might have been predicted from psychoanalytic theory (oral stage). Harry Harlow's research with infant rhesus monkeys reared with cloth or wire surrogate mothers indicated that contact comfort was more important than being fed. Regardless of which surrogate mother fed the infant monkeys, they became attached to the cloth surrogate (contact comfort).

4. Discuss the existence of a critical period for the attachment bonds between a child and his or her parents.

Lorenz's research with imprinting in goslings supports a critical period in the development of the following response and "attachment" behaviours in goslings. However, the extent that these findings can be generalized to human infants is questionable since infants become attached to adopted parents who are not present at the birth of the children. There is some research, though, that suggests adoption is less problematic if it takes place before the infant is three months old. Mary Ainsworth suggests that the attachment relationship begins to form at three months of age.

5. Why have child abusers frequently been the victims of child abuse themselves?

Child abusers are modelling the behaviour that they observed in their parents. Perhaps they have been less likely to learn other ways to deal with anger. Also, exposure to violence in one's own home may "normalize" this behaviour; the parent may likely see nothing amiss with treating children abusively.

6. Explain why autistic children are alone, even when they are surrounded by people who are doing their best to get through to them.

Children who are autistic do not seem very interested in people. They do not maintain eye contact as do most other children, even with their primary caregivers. Also, communication and language are very problematic for autistic children. If they do not acquire language, developing relationships is much more difficult.

7. Discuss pros and cons of placing a child in daycare when daycare children have been found to be more aggressive than children who stay home.

Effects of daycare on children may be both positive and negative. While some studies find that children in daycare are more aggressive and less compliant, other research suggests that daycare children tend to be more self-confident, independent, and affectionate. Children in a high-quality daycare have performed higher on language/cognitive skills tests than children who remained at home.

8. Discuss the normalcy of fear of strangers in infants and what "normal" means.

Normal ***is hard to define. What may be considered normal in one society may be considered "abnormal" in another. We do know that many children in our society show fear of strangers in the second half of the first year. As the child is developing a strong attachment relationship with his or her parent(s), other adults may become scarier to the child, especially if the adult tries to touch him or her.***

9. Describe how infants "check out" others when faced with a novel situation.

Infants use social referencing, glancing at or even listening for tone of voice in parents, to know how to react to a new situation. If parents are smiling and reassuring, the infant is likely to respond with confidence. If parents act worried or fearful, infants respond accordingly.

10. Describe how children come to realize they "exist."

Watching infants' responses to looking at themselves in a mirror is one way to study their self-concept. In one study, a dab of rouge was placed on babies' noses. At around eighteen months, babies began to reach for their own noses, rather than reaching for the baby in the mirror. Infants younger than this age reached for the mirror, perhaps indicating that they have no awareness that they are looking at themselves.

11. Explain the kinds of "temperamental" children.

Thomas and Chess studied very young infants and categorized them into three types of temperaments: the easy baby that adapted well and developed regular rhythms, the difficult baby that reacted negatively to new situations, and the slow-to-warm-up baby that fell somewhere between the first two categories. About 35 percent of the infants were not consistent enough in their behaviours to be placed in one of these categories.

12. Describe early differences in toy preferences for boys and girls.

Even though male and female infants are similar in many ways, the adults around them react to them differently. This may be related to the toy preferences that begin to develop by twelve to eighteen months. Even at this very young age, boys prefer toys like trucks and tools while girls tend to prefer dolls and dishes.

Chapter Review

Multiple Choice

1. What is a method that has been used to measure infant attachment?
    a. the Rouge test
    b. the Strange Situation
    c. the Goodness of Fit categorization
    d. the Thomson Holistic Procedure

2. Which is not a pattern of attachment described by Mary Ainsworth?
    a. secure attachment
    b. avoidant attachment
    c. ambivalent/resistant attachment
    d. antagonistic attachment

3. Which of the following is true?
   a. no connection has been found between secure attachment in mothers and secure attachment in infants
   b. providing support to mothers who experience economic stress does not increase the likelihood of secure attachments in infants
   c. mothers who are sensitive and predictable in their care-giving are more likely to have securely attached infants
   d. attachment in siblings is no more similar than in children from different families
4. Which statement is NOT true regarding father–infant relationships?
   a. the more diapers a father changes, the stronger the attachment with the infant
   b. fathers, compared to mothers, spend less time on child-care tasks and tend to play more with the child
   c. father–infant attachment is not related to how affectionate the father–infant interaction is
   d. fathers can be as competent and capable as mothers in their interactions with their infants
5. Which is NOT one of the phases described by Ainsworth and her colleagues?
   a. attachment-in-the-making phase
   b. mutually-responsive-attachment phase
   c. initial-preattachment phase
   d. clear-cut-attachment phase
6. According to this theory of attachment, the development of object permanence is important:
   a. psychoanalytic theory
   b. ethological theory
   c. behavioural theory
   d. cognitive theory
7. Harry Harlow's research with infant monkeys reared with surrogate mothers:
   a. provided support for the importance of the infant's oral satisfaction
   b. indicated that fear of strangers develops at about the same time in human infants and rhesus monkey infants
   c. found evidence that contact comfort is very important in the development of attachment
   d. provided evidence that infant monkeys could become attached only to "real" mothers, not surrogate mothers
8. Fixed action patterns are associated with which view of attachment?
   a. ethological
   b. psychoanalytic
   c. cognitive
   d. behaviourist

9. Which statement is NOT true regarding social deprivation and attachment?
   a. Harlow found that female monkeys who had been separated from other monkeys as infants were likely to abuse and neglect their own infants
   b. as long as their physical needs were being met, institutionalized children developed normally, much like other children
   c. children who were adopted after they were six months old were more likely to have problems relating to other people at age ten
   d. children who were adopted by three months of age did not have moderate or severe problems in social responsiveness and in attachment to their new mother
10. The National Clearinghouse on Family Violence created guidelines in 2006 on how to deal with suspected child abuse. Which of the following was NOT one of its recommendations?
    a. keep the child from returning to the abusive or neglectful situation
    b. interview the child and try to get as many details as possible
    c. reassure the child that it was right to disclose what was happening to him or her
    d. consider immediate medical assessment/treatment of physical problems
11. Over time, infants and children develop more emotional and behavioural control. Which of the following is evident in infants?
    a. development of early impulse control
    b. development of self-soothing and self-stimulating strategies
    c. use of social referencing to judge own actions
    d. ability to regulate some activities by imitating others
12. Regarding daycare and development, which of the following is NOT true?
    a. the likelihood of insecure attachment is much greater in infants placed in daycare than in those cared for in the home.
    b. children who attend daycare may be more likely to be aggressive and noncompliant than children who spend little time in daycare
    c. for children from low-income families, going to daycare is related to better performance during elementary school
    d. daycare children are more affectionate, outgoing, and self-confident than home-reared babies
13. Regarding emotional development, Katherine Bridges proposed that:
    a. newborns experience four physiological emotional states
    b. newborns are incapable of experiencing any emotions
    c. newborns have one emotion—diffuse excitement
    d. newborns have the same range of emotions as adults
14. Infants' looking at the facial expressions of their primary caregivers when placed in a new situation is referred to as:
    a. cognitive glancing
    b. fear of strangers
    c. situational dependency
    d. social referencing

15. Separation–individuation is associated with which view of the development of the self-concept?
    a. behavioural
    b. psychoanalytic
    c. ethological
    d. cognitive

Matching

Match each of the items from Column A with the corresponding item from Column B. There is only one correct answer per item.

Column A		Column B
1. ______	slow-to-warm-up	a. attachment phase beginning at 6 to 7 months
2. ______	imprinting	b. "normal" fear peaks at 9 to 12 months
3. ______	Mary Ainsworth	c. survival value of attachment behaviours
4. ______	ethological theory	d. typified by "dazed," confused behaviour
5. ______	clear-cut attachment	e. the Strange Situation Method
6. ______	Harry Harlow	f. glancing at parent in novel situation
7. ______	fear of strangers	g. following behaviour in goslings
8. ______	separation–individuation	h. type of temperament
9. ______	disorganized–disoriented attachment	i. separation/independence from mother
10. ______	social referencing	j. studied monkey attachment

True–False

1. John Bowlby is associated with the ethological view of attachment.

   TRUE or FALSE

2. The majority of infants in daycare are insecurely attached to their mothers.

   TRUE or FALSE

3. Infants who are categorized as having avoidant attachment are more likely to cry when their mothers leave the room than infants in other attachment categories.

   TRUE or FALSE

4. Thomas and Chess described three temperament types: easy, difficult, and slow-to-warm up.

   TRUE or FALSE

5. Fathers, compared to mothers, are more likely to meet basic child-care needs rather than being playmates with the child.

   TRUE or FALSE

6. Contact comfort is more important in the development of attachment in baby rhesus monkeys than being fed.

   TRUE or FALSE

7. The earliest phase of attachment is called attachment-in-the-making.
   TRUE or FALSE
8. The mirror technique has been used to assess self-concept in infants.
   TRUE or FALSE
9. According to Izard, newborns have only one emotion—diffuse excitement.
   TRUE or FALSE
10. Parents talk more to infant daughters than to infant sons.
    TRUE or FALSE

Solutions

Chapter Review

Multiple Choice

1. b (237)
2. d (237)
3. c (239)
4. c (242)
5. b (243)
6. d (244)
7. c (245)
8. a (245)
9. b (249)
10. b (256)
11. b (259)
12. a (271)
13. c (258)
14. d (261)
15. b (264)

Matching

1. h (265)
2. g (246)
3. e (237)
4. c (245)
5. a (243)
6. j (245)
7. b (243)
8. i (264)
9. d (237)
10. f (261)

True–False

1. T(245)
2. F(271)
3. F(237)
4. T(265)
5. F(241)
6. T(245)
7. F(243)
8. T(264)
9. F(258)
10. T(269)

CHAPTER **8**

Early Childhood: Physical Development

Learning Objectives

By the end of this chapter, you should be able to generate well-thought-out responses to demonstrate your understanding of the following learning objectives (sample answer comments are included at the end of this chapter):

1. Describe brain development during the preschool years.
2. Describe what changes take place in motor development during the preschool years.
3. Explain the nutritional needs of the preschool-age child.
4. Describe the significant health and illness risks for children during the preschool years.
5. Describe the sleep patterns and potential sleep disorders common to early childhood.
6. Explain what is meant by "elimination disorders." How common are these in early childhood? What might cause these disorders?

Chapter Summary

Growth Patterns

During the early childhood years, growth rates slow down in comparison to infancy but still occur at a quick pace. The average early childhood child, for example, gains four to six pounds per year and grows two to three inches during those same years.

The most amazing growth, however, continues to occur in the brain. By age five, the brain will have reached 90 percent of its adult weight even though the total body weight of the five-year-old is only about one-third of adult weight. **Myelination** (development of a fatty tissue covering neuron fibres) of neural pathways allows for more sophisticated actions to occur. This is seen in enhanced balance and coordination. Additionally, the child shows improvements in the ability to attend to (pay attention to) and process visual information. The speed of visual processing also improves throughout childhood.

Although much has been made of being **right-brained** or **left-brained,** this way of thinking tends to obscure the fact that many abilities require sophisticated communication and collaboration between the two hemispheres of the brain. This communication between hemispheres is made possible by the **corpus**

callosum, a bundle of nerve fibres that physically connect the two hemispheres.

Although many parts of the brain do have specialized functions, thereby allowing our behaviour to be more complex, such specialization increases the risk of permanent damage should the brain be injured. The brain also shows **plasticity,** meaning it can compensate for injuries. Someone who has suffered a stroke and has lost the ability to speak, for example, may be able to learn to speak again as other brain areas may take up the functions for the damaged area. This plasticity is less prevalent as the child gets older and becomes an adult. Nonetheless, there still may be some plasticity even in the adult brain. Plasticity is possible due to **sprouting** (the growth of new dendrites) and **redundancy** (meaning multiple brain areas may serve the same function—like having a backup system).

Motor Development

The maturing nervous system of children during the preschool years brings on significant advancements in motor skills. As the nervous system matures, children are able to engage in more precise and coordinated movements. Motor skills include **gross motor skills,** those that include large muscle groups used in locomotion. By the age of three, for example, children can balance on one foot. Although adults may take this skill for granted, it is not an easy feat to accomplish. The opportunity to play with other children and observe their behaviour appears to be more important in facilitating motor development than instructions from adults.

One significant form of physical and social activity is **rough-and-tumble** play. This form of play consists of chasing, wrestling, running, making faces, etc. Although this kind of play may appear to be aggressive, it is not. Rough-and-tumble play is not engaged in with the purpose of hurting another child but represents important social interactions that facilitate the development of both physical and social skills.

Children vary considerably in terms of **activity level.** To some degree, physically active children are more likely to have physically active parents. This can be explained by a variety of factors such as (1) role-modelling of activity by the parents, (2) sharing of activities within the family (such as taking the family to play tennis), and (3) the fact that activity level also appears to have a genetic component.

During the preschool years, children also demonstrate improvements in **fine motor skills.** In comparison to gross motor skills, however, fine motor skills develop more gradually. This, of course, is another example of the **proximodistal** (from the centre outward) pattern of human development. Control of the arms and legs (gross motor groups) will develop sooner than control over fingers and toes (fine motor groups).

Children's drawings also reflect improvements in motor skills. In addition, they reflect the burgeoning cognitive skills of the child. According to research, children progress through four stages as they move from scribbles to the drawing of actual pictures. These stages are (1) placement, (2) shape, (3) design, and (4) pictorial. Children's early drawings tend to symbolize broad categories rather than very specific objects. A child might, for example, draw the same drawing twice, at one point calling it a car and the next time calling it a school bus.

Handedness emerges early in childhood, perhaps as early as two months. From four to eleven months, children show an increasing preference for right-handedness by reaching for and grasping objects with the right hand. Although estimates vary, approximately 10 percent of the population is left-handed. Being left-handed has been connected to both negative (language problems and psychological disorders) and positive outcomes (excelling in math and several sports like baseball). While handedness likely has a genetic component, monozygotic twins often differ in handedness; perhaps they are "mirror opposites" in some ways. Other species, including parrots and chimpanzees, also demonstrate handedness.

Nutrition

The nutritional needs of children change slightly during the preschool years. Children in this age range need more calories than they did as toddlers (1,800 from ages four to six vs. 1,300 from ages one to three). However, since preschool-age children are not growing as fast as they did in previous years, they need to consume fewer calories per pound of body weight than younger children.

Related to nutrition is the issue of eating behaviour. Because the child's growth has slowed, there may be a subsequent drop in appetite. Children may also develop definite preferences for certain food. Parents are encouraged to be aware of the eating behaviour they model for their children, limiting sweet and salty foods and nurturing vegetable preferences. Rather than bribing a child to eat a new food, one expert suggests repeatedly encouraging a child to try a small amount of a food over a few weeks, which may lead to the child's liking the food.

Health and Illness

Although people may believe that few children in Canada die annually, that assumption may not meet with fact. However, childhood deaths have dropped dramatically with immunizations against **rubella, measles, tetanus, mumps, whooping cough, diphtheria,** and **polio.** Developing countries, however, experience 2 million deaths annually just due to diarrhea. **Accidents** cause more childhood deaths in Canada than the next top two killers combined. Approximately 10,000 children under the age of 12 are injured in automobile collisions every year in Canada.

Sleep

Most preschoolers need about ten hours of sleep each night. Children at this age may use a **transitional object** such as a teddy bear to help them feel more comfortable sleeping by themselves. Several kinds of sleep disorders can occur in young children, including nightmares and sleep terrors. **Nightmares** (bad dreams), which occur during REM sleep, are more likely to occur in the morning hours since periods of REM sleep lengthen as the night progresses. **Sleep terrors,** which may be more severe, occur during deep sleep rather than REM sleep.

Children are also more likely to sleepwalk than adults. Like sleep terrors, sleepwalking, or **somnambulism,** tends to occur during deep sleep. Contrary to popular myth, there appear to be no dangers in waking a sleepwalker. It is suspected that sleepwalking may reflect the immaturity of the nervous system. If this is true, we would expect sleepwalking to diminish as the child gets older. Such is the case.

Elimination Disorders

As children develop muscular control, they can also learn to control the timing of visits to the restroom. Even after toilet training is accomplished, many children will have nighttime accidents for up to a year. Children who do not become toilet trained within a reasonable time frame may suffer from **enuresis** (failure to control the bladder) or **encopresis** (failure to control the bowels). Although there may be physical explanations for some cases of elimination disorders, generally they have been linked to stressful situations.

Critical Thinking Exercises

Exercise 1

Parents have asked you what you have learned in this course about eating patterns in preschool-age children. They are concerned by the fact that their daughter will eat only chicken nuggets and won't even look at a green vegetable. Based on what you have learned from this chapter, what advice would you give them? Be sure to provide advice about child nutrition and how they might be able to get their daughter to try new foods.

____

____

____

____

____

____

Exercise 2

Another couple you know has a son who is experiencing nighttime bed-wetting and soiling. They are very concerned that there might be something wrong with him medically. Based on what you have learned in this chapter, what suggestions do you have that these parents might try to work with their child to reduce and, eventually, eliminate these problems? Why are you making these suggestions? What advice would you give about ways these parents should NOT try to deal with these problems? Why are you giving this advice?

____

____

____

____

____

____

Internet Activities

Activity 1

Access the Internet and go to the following URL:

http://www.aafp.org/afp/20010115/277.html

As you read the material on the site, pay close attention to material about each of the following:

- enuresis
- sleep terrors
- nightmares

In order to enhance your understanding, answer the following questions about the website material:

1. What content (points made) on the website did you find most informative? Why?
2. What content (points made) on the website do you think is most relevant to you, your life, and/or your career? How?
3. Based on the content of this website, what three pieces of advice would you give to parents of preschool children? Why?
4. What is the most important thing you learned by reviewing this website? Why?

Activity 2

Choose one of the following terms and run an Internet search:

- Brain plasticity
- Left-handed
- Childhood disease

Choose one of the sites that come up as a result of your search and read the information presented. Assume that you are a child development specialist giving information and advice to parents of preschool-age children. Based on what you have learned from this article or site:

1. How accurately do you feel this site portrays information about your topic? Why?
2. Were there any critical pieces of information missing that you feel should have been provided? If so, what were they? If not, what were the most critical pieces conveyed?
3. What is the most important thing you learned by reading the information on this site? Why?

Observing Children and Adolescents CD-ROM Activity

Watch the "Gross Motor" and "Fine Motor" videos (Module 2, Section 1) and read the material on pages 64 and 65 in *Observing Children and Adolescents.* Then answer the following questions:

1. Describe the gross motor skills a three-and-a-half-year-old child such as Olivia would have.

2. How does twenty-month-old Tess draw? What changes would you expect in Tess's drawing skills in the next several years?
3. What aspect of the videos surprised you the most, or what did you find the most interesting about early childhood physical development?

Power Preview: Learning Objectives Sample Answers

1. Describe brain development during the preschool years.

The following typify brain development during the preschool years: (1) significant increases in brain weight—presumably due to increased myelination of neural pathways and the corpus callosum, (2) continued brain plasticity due to "sprouting" of new dendrites and "redundancy" (meaning similar functions may be found in two or more locations of the brain), and (3) completion of the myelination of neural pathways that link the cerebellum to the cerebral cortex, which facilitates the development of fine motor skills.

2. Describe what changes take place in motor development during the preschool years.

Again, this is a time of marked change. The child will demonstrate increasing command over gross motor skills (those involving large muscle groups) such as being able to stand on one foot or easily navigate stairs. Although advancements will be made in fine motor skills (those involving small muscle groups and sophisticated coordination of movement), these advances are more gradual than those of gross motor skills. Advances in fine motor skills allow the child to begin to draw recognizable objects. It is also during these years that handedness will become quite obvious as the child begins to write.

3. Explain the nutritional needs of the preschool-age child.

Children in this age range continue to have increased caloric needs. The typical four- to six-year-old, for example, needs 1,800 calories per day in comparison to the average one- to three-year-old, who requires 1,300. It should be noted, however, that because of the increased size of the preschool child, he or she actually needs fewer calories per pound of body weight than a younger child. The child continues to need a diet higher in fat and cholesterol than the older child or adult.

4. What are the significant health and illness risks for children during the preschool years?

Although immunizations have dramatically reduced the number of childhood deaths due to serious diseases in Canada, such diseases continue to be a problem for children living in developing countries or in low-income environments. Over 2 million children, for example, die of diarrhea annually in developing countries. In Canada, accidents cause more childhood deaths than the next two most frequent causes combined.

5. Describe the sleep patterns and potential sleep disorders common to early childhood.

Most children in this age range will sleep about ten hours per night. It is not unusual for these children to take a "transitional object" (such as a stuffed animal or some other toy) to bed with them. It has been suggested that these transitional objects assist the child in gaining more independence and separation from the parents. The child may experience nightmares during periods of REM sleep; since periods of REM sleep lengthen as the night progresses, children are more likely to experience nightmares in the morning hours. Sleep terrors, which are *not* ***simply intense nightmares, may occur during the deepest stages of sleep and can be very anxiety-provoking for the child.***

6. Explain what is meant by "elimination disorders." How common are these in early childhood? What might cause these disorders?

Generally there are considered to be two elimination disorders. Enuresis is a failure to maintain bladder control past the age at which children "normally" can maintain such control. Loss of contro is more likely to happen at night and is more common in boys (7 percent) than girls (3 percent). Encopresis, soiling, involves loss of bowel control. This is more likely to occur during the day, with about 1 to 2 percent of seven- and eight-year-olds experiencing encopresis. Behavioural methods may be effective in treating these. The key is not to pressure the child as stress may actually make the problem worse. Some devices (such as bed-wetting alarms) may be employed. They are designed to wake the child and assist him or her in recognizing the feelings that signal that elimination is needed. Over time, the child should learn to wake in response to these feelings, and the problems should disappear.

Chapter Review

Multiple Choice

1. The growth in brain weight during the preschool years appears to be due primarily to:
   a. increased myelination of neurons
   b. significant growth in the size of the frontal lobe
   c. large increases in the size of the cerebellum
   d. there is not significant growth in brain weight during these years
2. The bundle of nerve fibres that connect the two hemispheres of the brain are called:
   a. the limbic system
   b. the medulla
   c. the cerebrum
   d. the corpus callosum
3. Brain plasticity is possible due to:
   a. development of new neural tissue
   b. brain plasticity is not possible
   c. sprouting of new dendrites
   d. formation of new brain structures
4. In comparison to gross motor skills, fine motor skills:
   a. develop more rapidly during the preschool years
   b. do not develop at all during the preschool years
   c. are more completely developed prior to the preschool years
   d. develop gradually
5. What percentage of people will become right-handed?
   a. it varies greatly from culture to culture
   b. around 90 percent
   c. 50 percent if they are not forced to use the right hand
   d. it varies greatly between the genders

6. What appears to be true regarding the causes of handedness?
   a. handedness may have a genetic component although monozygotic twins often differ in handedness
   b. handedness is determined solely by genetics; hence monozygotic twins never differ in handedness
   c. handedness is determined solely by pressure from society and parents
   d. handedness is a function of the development of the cerebellum
7. How many calories per day does the average four- to six-year-old need?
   a. 1,300
   b. 1,500
   c. 1,800
   d. 2,000
8. In terms of food preferences, preschool-age children:
   a. do not have preferences
   b. will generally not try anything new
   c. may need repeated exposures to new foods to get them "used" to them
   d. show strong preferences for sweets, which decreases over time
9. What is the leading cause of death of children in Canada?
   a. cancer
   b. accidents
   c. diarrhea
   d. rubella
10. Which of the following is one of the leading causes of death of children in developing countries?
    a. cancer
    b. meningitis
    c. diarrhea
    d. jaundice
11. What is a "transitional object"?
    a. a preferred toy that may help the child to increase independence from the parents
    b. a pretend object or person the child uses to increase imagination
    c. an item that assists the child in facing and confronting his or her fears
    d. none of these
12. Somnambulism is a technical term for:
    a. nightmares
    b. sleep terrors
    c. sleep apnea
    d. sleepwalking
13. When is a sleep terror likely to occur?
    a. when first falling asleep
    b. during deep sleep
    c. during REM sleep
    d. during dream sleep

14. What is enuresis?
    a. failure to control the bladder beyond a "normal" age for doing so
    b. a sleep disorder involving intense bouts of fear
    c. lack of control of the bowels
    d. a technical term for sleepwalking
15. What is encopresis?
    a. failure to control the bladder beyond a "normal" age for doing so
    b. a sleep disorder involving intense bouts of fear
    c. lack of control of the bowels
    d. a technical term for sleepwalking

Matching

Match each of the items from column A with the corresponding item from column B. There is only one correct answer per item.

	A	B
1. _______	left-brain	a. drawing a picture
2. _______	rough-and-tumble play	b. deep sleep
3. _______	gross motor skill	c. emotions
4. _______	major illness if treated	d. REM sleep
5. _______	sleep terrors	e. taking something from another child
6. _______	right-brain	f. diarrhea
7. _______	aggression	g. standing on one leg
8. _______	minor illness if treated	h. mumps
9. _______	nightmares	i. logic
10. _______	fine motor skill	j. wrestling with another child

True–False

1. The brain reaches 90 percent of its adult weight by the time the child is five.

   TRUE or FALSE
2. Fine motor skills develop earlier than gross motor skills.

   TRUE or FALSE
3. Children tend to go through four stages in their drawing: placement, shape, design, and pictorial.

   TRUE or FALSE
4. Monozygotic (identical) twins may differ in handedness (left- or right-handed).

   TRUE or FALSE
5. On average, children in Canada between one and three experience about eight or nine illnesses per year.

   TRUE or FALSE

6. Sleep terrors, unlike nightmares, occur during REM sleep.

   TRUE or FALSE

7. Accidents are responsible for nearly half the deaths of children one to four years of age.

   TRUE or FALSE

8. Enuresis tends to be most common when parents try too early to toilet train a child.

   TRUE or FALSE

9. Sleep terrors tend to occur late in the night, when periods of deep sleep are shortest.

   TRUE or FALSE

10. Oral rehydration therapy, giving children a salt and sugar solution, could prevent many deaths in developing countries.

    TRUE or FALSE

Solutions

Chapter Review

Multiple Choice

1. a (282)
2. d (284)
3. c (284)
4. d (285)
5. b (291)
6. a (292)
7. c (293)
8. c (293)
9. b (301)
10. c (300)
11. a (304)
12. d (306)
13. b (305)
14. a (308)
15. c (309)

Matching

1. i (284)
2. j (287)
3. g (285)
4. h (298)
5. b (305)
6. c (284)
7. e (287)
8. f (295)
9. d (305)
10. a (288)

True–False

1. T (282)
2. F (288)
3. T (284)
4. T (292)
5. T (295)
6. F (305)
7. T (301)
8. T (308)
9. F (305)
10. T (303)

CHAPTER 9

Early Childhood: Cognitive Development

Learning Objectives

By the end of this chapter, you should be able to generate well-thought-out responses to demonstrate your understanding of the following learning objectives (sample answer comments are included at the end of this chapter):

1. Discuss whether or not children's having imaginary playmates is a sign of loneliness or psychological problems.
2. Describe how a preschooler's logic is different than your own.
3. Explain why two-year-olds assume their parents know everything that is happening to them, even when the parents are not present.
4. Describe why three-year-olds might believe that it gets dark outside so that they can go to sleep.
5. Why might "Because Mommy wants me to?" be a perfectly good explanation—for a three-year-old.
6. Discuss why a typical four-year-old might believe that dreams are real.
7. Explain how children's levels of intelligence, not just their knowledge, are influenced by early learning experiences.
8. Describe the advantages provided in school later on by a highly academic preschool education.
9. Explain why preschoolers often cannot differentiate between commercials and the TV programs themselves.
10. Describe memory for past events in one- and two-year-olds.
11. Describe three-year-old children's use of rehearsal, even without their being taught to do so.
12. Why does a three-year-old girl say, "We singed it all up" to explain that she and her mother finished singing a song?
13. Explain why "Daddy goed away" rather than "Daddy went away" is really a sign that three-year-olds understand rules of grammar.

Chapter Summary

Jean Piaget's Preoperational Stage

The **preoperational stage,** Piaget's second major stage of cognitive development, lasts from about two to seven years of age. The development of symbolic thought is a primary achievement of this stage. Language is one very important form of symbolic thought; pictures and **symbolic play,** play involving "make-believe" or pretending, are also forms of symbolic or representational thinking. While children as young as twelve or thirteen months may pretend to do familiar activities related to themselves, their pretend play becomes more complex and focused on other objects as they grow older. One form of pretend play is with imaginary friends. While imaginary friends are more common in firstborn and only children, one estimate is that 65 percent of preschoolers have imaginary playmates. Children with imaginary friends typically do not neglect the "real world"; rather they are described as having more friends, being more cooperative, less aggressive, and also may be more advanced in language development.

Preschoolers typically think very differently than do adults. Piaget believed that children at this age lack **operations,** flexible mental acts that transform or change objects. Rather, the world of the preschooler is **egocentric,** focused on his or her own way of perceiving the world and often failing to understand that others' perceptions are different. Piaget demonstrated this with the three-mountains test. Young children believe that a child or doll viewing the three mountains from a different side still see the same thing that they themselves do.

Children in the preoperational stage may also explain things that happen in the natural world as centred around themselves. Children may believe that the sun shines so they can see what they are doing or to keep them warm. Piaget used the term **precausal** to describe this kind of thinking; children do not yet understand natural causes of events so, instead, tie the cause to themselves.

Other kinds of preoperational thinking include **transductive reasoning,** linking unrelated events together; **animism,** the belief that inanimate objects are alive; and **artificialism,** believing that natural events are constructed by humans. Preschool children also tend to believe that dreams are real, that they happen outside the body and are not constructed in the head. They believe that others could also see the dream if they were there.

Preoperational thought is also characterized by the failure to conserve. **Conservation** is the understanding that quantity remains the same after simple transformations, such as squashing a ball of clay or pouring water from a short glass into a tall glass. Children whose thinking is preoperational demonstrate **centration,** becoming stuck or centred on one dimension (such as height of a glass) of a two-dimensional problem (ignoring the width of the glass). They also do not conserve because of **irreversibility,** failing to realize that the action, such as pouring the water from a short glass into a tall glass, can be reversed, pouring the water back into the original glass, and thus demonstrating that quantity remained the same.

Preschool children also have difficulty with **class inclusion,** the understanding that groups of objects can belong to higher-level classifications. As explained in your text, if children are shown four pictures of cats and six pictures of dogs and then were asked if there are more dogs or more animals, the preschooler will answer more dogs.

More recent research on Piaget's preoperational stage has provided some evidence that Piaget may have underestimated the abilities of the preschool child. Characteristics or demands of a particular task may result in children's failure on some tasks. Even though three-year-olds do not correctly give the perspective of another on the three-mountains task, they succeed with less demanding perspective-taking problems. For example, if a doll is placed behind a screen, the children understand that the doll cannot "see" the mountain scene. Regarding conservation, perhaps researchers asking whether or not the amount of water is the same and then directing children to watch the water being poured primes them to expect a change.

Language Development: Why "Daddy Goed Away"

Children make amazing strides in language development during the preschool years. Children very rapidly learn new words. **Fast-mapping** refers to children quickly attaching the label or word to the corresponding concept; they may have built-in constraints that guide them in this process such as assuming that a word refers to a whole object rather than to part of an object. The **contrast assumption** refers to an object's having only one name so an unknown word must then refer to a new object.

Children's acquisition of grammar is rapid and orderly. During the preschool period, children demonstrate **overregularization,** following rules of grammar even in cases that adult users consider exceptions. For example, a child may add an "ed" or an "s" inappropriately to irregular verbs and nouns, incorrectly saying "goed" and "mans." One study demonstrated that children are clearly learning rules of grammar by showing them first a picture of one "wug" and then showing a picture of two and asking children to finish the sentence "There are two _____." Of course, "wugs" was the response even though no child could have heard this word previously. The practical social-setting knowledge regarding language is called **pragmatics.** Children learn to vary their speech according to whether they are talking to teachers or playmates and what word choices are appropriate in different situations.

The relation between cognition and language is important and complex. According to Piaget, cognitive development leads to the development of language; children become capable of symbolic thought and then acquire language. Others have argued that language can influence cognitive development. The interactionist perspective would be that language and thought both influence each other. Vygotsky believed that initially language and cognition were separate but that they began to merge during the second year. **Inner speech,** one of Vygotsky's concepts, is an example. Although the young preschool child may speak his or her own thoughts out loud, the words become internalized as the child grows older. The initial spoken words, often used to describe the child's own actions, may help the child learn to regulate his or her behaviour.

Theory of Mind: What Is the Mind? How Does It Work?

Theory of mind refers to the common understanding adults have of the mind and how it works. We are aware, for example, that we gather knowledge through our eyes, ears, and other senses, and we are also aware of the distinction between our internal, created world and the external world. While Piaget believed that the preschooler did not have a "theory of mind," more recent research has provided evidence that even preschool children have some abilities in this area.

In one study, children were shown a videotape about a girl, Cathy, who found a bag containing some crayons. While Cathy was gone from the room, a clown replaced the crayons with rocks. Children were then asked to predict if Cathy would think that there were crayons or rocks in the bag. While three-year-olds usually answered "rocks," four- to five-year-olds answered "crayons," indicating a beginning ability to understand the mind of another child, even when the other child's thinking is different from their own.

John Flavell has conducted research on the **appearance-reality distinction,** the understanding that appearances can be misleading. While Piaget believed that children younger than seven or eight years old had difficulty distinguishing appearance from reality, even children who are three have been found to differentiate real and pretend actions or real objects and pictures of objects. However, when three- to five-year-old children were shown objects with misleading appearances, such as an eraser that looked like a cookie, they mistakenly said that it *looked* like an eraser after learning that it was an eraser. Children at this age may have limited **mental representational** skills, having a hard time in their mind thinking of the cookie eraser as *looking* like a cookie but *being* an eraser.

Development of Memory: Creating Files and Retrieving Them

Children's memory is assessed using **recognition** tasks, correctly identifying stimuli to which they've previously been exposed, and **recall** tasks, being able to reproduce information regarding material to which they'd previously been exposed. Multiple-choice questions are examples of recognition tasks while short-answer questions are examples of recall tasks. As you might predict, preschoolers can recognize more items from a list of possible items than they can produce through recall. While younger preschool children come close in performance to older preschool children on recognition memory, the older children clearly outperform the younger ones on recall tasks.

When the content is relevant, even very young children have demonstrated amazing memory. Bauer and Mandler found that sixteen-month-olds could repeat a sequence of actions to create a "rattle" from a ball and cups after a delay of six weeks. Four-year-olds remember events that happened as long as a year and a half earlier. Katherine Nelson reported evidence that three-year-old children have **scripts**—that is, they can describe sequences of familiar events, such as what happens when they go to McDonald's. Young children also have **autobiographical memory,** memory for past events in their own lives. Autobiographical memory may be linked to children's language development; children are able to learn from others about events that have happened to them in the past.

Preschool children more easily remember activities than objects. If a series of events follows a logical order (how to make pretend cookies from Play-Doh), this sequence is more easily remembered than a series without that order (play activities in the sand). As with older children and adults, interest level and motivation also contribute to better memory. **Retrieval cues,** links with the material to be remembered, are more important for younger children than for older children.
Older children and adults use strategies such as **rehearsal,** using repetition, and organizing the information into meaningful units to help them remember. In general, preschool children are not likely to use strategies such as rehearsal and organization unless someone suggests to them that they do so. However, even young children point, look at, and touch objects when trying to remember them. In one study, eighteen- to twenty-four-month-old children watched the experimenter hide a Big Bird doll beneath a pillow. Then they were distracted with other toys and, a little while later, asked to find Big Bird. While playing with the toys, the children pointed or looked at the hiding place and, in some cases, even repeated the hidden object's name, implying that these children may be beginning to use memory prompts. When young children do not spontaneously use memory strategies, they can be encouraged to do so with marked improvement in their recall ability.

Factors in Cognitive Development: On Being in "The Zone" (for Proximal Development)

Many social and family factors influence development during preschool years. Parents and teachers may provide **scaffolding** to help children reach a higher developmental level; the assistance helps children advance further through their **zone of proximal development,** the difference between children's current level and their possible level of functioning with additional help. One study exploring mothers' interaction with three- to five-year-olds found that mothers tailored their interaction to the child's level of competence, giving more concrete and detailed suggestions to the younger, compared to older, children.

The Home Observation for the Measurement of the Environment, or HOME, was developed to evaluate children's home environments. This scale includes six subscales and has been a better predictor of later intelligence scores than social class or mothers' intelligence scores. Subscales of the HOME, assessing maternal responsiveness, maternal involvement, and the provision of a variety of experiences/appropriate play materials, were related to higher IQ scores when children were three and four years of age as well as higher achievement scores when they were seven.

A reason for starting some preschool programs in the 1960s and 1970s was to increase school readiness in children from impoverished environments. Head Start is an example of such a program. The initial impact of such programs was impressive, with increased IQ scores and better performance on school readiness and achievement tests, compared to children not participating in the programs. Long-term gains have also been found, with those children who went through preschool intervention programs' being more likely to have graduated from high school and to have attended college. Girls from preschool programs may also be less likely to become pregnant and drop out of school.

Continued intervention during early elementary school is likely to enhance the effects of preschool programs. Also, when parents are included and involved in the programs, results are more positive. Two examples of such programs are the Maryland-based Success for All program and Chicago's Child–Parent Centers, with children from these programs having higher reading scores.

Children in North America spend more time watching television than in school. Therefore, television has the potential to impact children's cognitive development. *Sesame Street* has been found to positively affect preschoolers from a variety of backgrounds. Watching the program helps children learn numbers and letters as well as develop cognitive skills such as sorting. Vocabulary was also enhanced in one study. Potential negative effects of heavy television viewing include poorer impulse control and greater restlessness. Because of children's limited perspective-taking skills, commercials may be particularly likely to mislead children. Younger children may not understand that the intent of commercials is to sell a product and have difficulty differentiating commercials from the programs. Also, children who watch more TV are even more likely to buy into commercial claims. Commercials for sugar-laden food have been especially criticized for encouraging children to choose unhealthy food.

Critical Thinking Exercises

Exercise 1

Meagan and Richard have several preschool children. They're worried about the impact of television on their children. What advice could you give them? Be sure to discuss pros and cons of television viewing as well as some suggested general guidelines.

Exercise 2

Discuss how a preschool child's thoughts differ from yours and mine, according to Piaget. Include examples and the following terms in your discussion:

- animism
- artificialism
- centration
- egocentrism
- class inclusion

Internet Activities

Activity 1

Choose one of the following terms and run an Internet search:

- language acquisition
- children's speech
- language development

Choose one of the sites that come up as a result of your search and read the information presented. Assume that you are giving a talk to a group of parents with preschool children and advising them on language development during the preschool years. Based on what you have learned from this article or site:

1. How accurately do you feel this site portrays information about your topic? Why?

2. Were there any critical pieces of information missing that you feel should have been provided? If so, what were they? If not, what were the most critical pieces conveyed?
3. What is the most important thing you learned by reading the information on this site? Why?

Activity 2

Access the Internet and go to the following URL:

http://www.sesameworkshop.org

Surf around the site, focusing your attention on the following issues:

1. What is the mission of this site?
2. What specific materials are provided that support the accomplishment of that mission?
3. What information did you find to be the most informative? Why?
4. What information do you believe would be most beneficial for a parent with a young child? Why?

Observing Children and Adolescents CD-ROM Activity

Watch the "Piaget's Preoperational Stage" video (Module 2, Section 2) and read the material on pages 69 and 70 in *Observing Children and Adolescents.* Then answer the following questions:

1. Describe symbolic play and mental representation in the play of Sarah, Jill, Jarred, and Todd.
2. Give an example of egocentrism shown on the video. Describe irreversibility and lack of conservation in the responses of Olivia, Debra, Jacob, Christopher, and Jack.
3. What aspect of the video surprised you the most, or what did you find most interesting about early childhood cognitive development?

Power Preview: Learning Objectives Sample Answers

1. Discuss whether or not children's having imaginary playmates is a sign of loneliness and psychological problems.

One study found that approximately 65 percent of children have imaginary friends. Children who have imaginary playmates actually have more friends, rather than fewer friends, and tend to be more creative, more cooperative, and less aggressive.

2. Describe how a preschooler's logic is different from your own.

Preschoolers lack certain operations that allow them to think about the world in more logical ways. The preschooler tends to be more egocentric, seeing things from his or her own point of view; lacks conservation, the understanding that quantity remains the same when simple transformations are performed; tends to believe that inanimate objects are alive; and has difficulty classifying things hierarchically (dogs and cats are both animals). Children in the preoperational stage also tend to believe that dreams are real rather than created inside their own minds.

3. Explain why two-year-olds assume their parents know everything that is happening to them, even when the parents are not present.

Two-year-olds are egocentric, meaning that they see things only from their own perspective. They believe that others see and understand the same things that they do. Therefore, if they can see something or know something, everyone else sees or knows this as well.

4. Describe why three-year-olds might believe that it gets dark outside so that they can go to sleep.

Precausal thinking refers to a child's believing that things happen for reasons other than natural causes. Not understanding the natural causes of an event can lead a child to provide another unrelated cause. This also reflects children's egocentrism, believing that darkness is related to their own needs and transductive reasoning, linking two isolated events together.

5. Why might "Because Mommy wants me to?" be a perfectly good explanation—for a three-year-old.

Children at this age lack deductive (reasoning from the general to the specific) and inductive (reasoning from the specific to the general) reasoning. For them "Because Mommy wants me to" may make just as much sense as something more logical by adult standards.

6. Discuss why a typical four-year-old might believe that dreams are real.

Typically, four-year-olds do not understand that dreams are created in their own minds. They believe that dreams are created externally and by other people; dreams are kind of like movies. This is an example of the preoperational child's confusing mental and physical activities.

7. Explain how children's levels of intelligence, not just their knowledge, are influenced by early learning experiences.

The Home Observation for the Measurement of the Environment, or HOME, was developed to evaluate children's home environments. This scale has been a better predictor of later intelligence scores than social class or mothers' intelligence scores. Maternal responsiveness and involvement with children were related to higher IQ scores when children were three and four years old, as well as higher achievement scores when they were seven.

8. Describe the advantages provided in school later on by a highly academic preschool education.

A reason for starting some preschool programs in the 1960s and 1970s was to increase school readiness in children from impoverished environments. Head Start is an example of such a program. The short-term impact of such programs were impressive, with increased IQ scores and better performance on school readiness and achievement tests, compared to children not participating in the programs. At the other end of the spectrum, middle-class parents who place children in preschool programs that are highly academic and also enroll them in various music, sports, or art lessons after school may have children who excel for a short period of time. These advantages do not seem to last long, and some research indicates that children of these "high expectation" parents may be less creative and suffer greater anxiety regarding task performance.

9. Explain why preschoolers often cannot differentiate between commercials and the TV programs themselves.

Because of children's limited perspective-taking skills, commercials may be particularly likely to mislead children. Young children may not understand that the intent of commercials is to sell a product and may have difficulty differentiating commercials from the programs. Also, children who watch more TV are even more likely to buy into commercial claims. Commercials for sugar-laden food have been especially criticized for encouraging children to choose unhealthy food.

10. Describe memory for past events in one- and two-year-olds.

Infants eleven and a half months of age were able to remember a sequence of events that had just happened. Sixteen-month-olds could remember how to make a simple rattle from a ball and cups after a six-week delay.

11. Describe three-year-old children's use of rehearsal, even without their being taught to do so.

While three-year-olds typically do not spontaneously use rehearsal, if they are told explicitly to try remembering something, they will begin to use labelling and rehearsal strategies. Even eighteen- to twenty-four-month-old children indicate the beginnings of memory strategies by pointing or looking at a hidden object.

12. Why does a three-year-old girl say, "We singed it all up" to explain that she and her mother finished singing a song?

Children demonstrate creativity in their use of language. Since the song is finished, in a sense it is all used up. "Singed," rather than "sang," demonstrates overregularization—the child applying the rule of adding "ed" to form a past tense inappropriately. Also at three years of age, prepositions such as "up" are part of their vocabulary.

13. Explain why "Daddy goed away" rather than "Daddy went away" is really a sign that three-year-olds understand rules of grammar.

While children may initially learn some of the irregular past tenses such as "went" before learning the rule of grammar for regular verb forms of adding "ed," when they acquire that rule, the rule is then applied even to the irregular forms of past tense verbs. This clearly demonstrates that they are learning rules since they usually haven't heard adults use these forms of incorrect grammar.

Chapter Review

Multiple Choice

1. Piaget's called the stage for ages two to seven:
   a. concrete operations
   b. sensorimotor
   c. formal operations
   d. preoperational
2. Preoperational thought is characterized by:
   a. the development of symbolic thought
   b. the acquisition of logical operations
   c. the ability to think abstractly
   d. the use of actions to guide thought processes
3. Which of the following is NOT true regarding imaginary friends?
   a. around 65 percent of preschoolers have imaginary friends
   b. children who have imaginary friends have more advanced language development
   c. children with imaginary friends tend to have fewer real friends
   d. children with imaginary friends are less aggressive and more cooperative

4. Piaget uses this term to refer to the preschooler's thinking about causality:
   a. pericausal
   b. precausal
   c. anticausal
   d. exicausal
5. Animism refers to:
   a. children's belief that inanimate objects are alive
   b. children's failure to understand that dreams are created inside them
   c. children's failure to understand cause-and-effect relationships
   d. children's lack of role-taking ability
6. Piaget believed that a child in the preoperational stage of cognitive development:
   a. typically had acquired irreversibility and hence the ability to conserve
   b. typically had acquired centration and hence the ability to conserve
   c. typically had not acquired centration and hence did not have the ability to conserve
   d. typically had thought characterized by irreversibility and hence did not have the ability to conserve
7. The understanding that a category can include several other subcategories or subclasses is called:
   a. class inclusion
   b. class diffusion
   c. class infusion
   d. irreversibility
8. Regarding more recent research on Piaget:
   a. some researchers have found that Piaget may have overestimated children's perspective taking ability
   b. children never seem to be able to solve conservation tasks regardless of their age
   c. demand characteristics of some tasks have kept younger children from successfully solving role-taking and conservation tasks
   d. children do not exhibit the cardinal word principle until they are approximately ten years of age
9. The understanding and awareness of how the mind works is called a:
   a. common knowledge framework
   b. theory of mind
   c. common mind framework
   d. general cognitive theory
10. In one study described in your text, three-year-olds looked at a crayon box and believed that crayons were inside. The children were then shown that the box really contained candles. When they were then asked what they had believed was in the box earlier (before the crayon box was opened), they said:
    a. crayons
    b. candles
    c. candles that were really crayons
    d. they refused to give an answer

11. Multiple choice test questions are an example of this kind of memory task:
    a. rote
    b. recall
    c. recognition
    d. reduplicated
12. According to one study, sixteen-month-olds could reenact a sequence of events to make a "rattle" after how long of a delay?
    a. the events could be reenacted only if the delay was shorter than twenty-four hours
    b. the events could be reenacted only if the delay was shorter than four days
    c. the events could be reenacted only if the delay was shorter than thirty days
    d. the events could be reenacted only if the delay was as long as six weeks
13. Children as young as three show evidence of a __________, describing what happens at an event such as a birthday party.
    a. script
    b. serial
    c. scaffolding
    d. scribe
14. Regarding children and television:
    a. preschool children typically watch very little television
    b. preschool children may not understand the distinction between commercials and other programming
    c. even children's programming such as *Sesame Street* has been found to negatively impact children's cognitive development
    d. because of their limited cognitive understanding, television programming typically has little influence on the preschool child
15. "Mommy telled me" demonstrates that young children:
    a. overregularize and hence are acquiring rules of grammar
    b. overgeneralize and hence are acquiring the rules of grammar
    c. underregularize and hence are acquiring the rules of grammar
    d. undergeneralize and hence are acquiring the rules of grammar

Matching

Match each of the items from Column A with the corresponding item from Column B. There is only one correct answer per item.

1.	______	HOME	a.	support provided while learning a task
2.	______	scaffolding	b.	memory for events like a birthday party
3.	______	preoperational	c.	one label per object
4.	______	script	d.	practical "social norms" part of language
5.	______	overregularization	e.	improves preschoolers' vocabulary
6.	______	pragmatics	f.	mistakenly applying a rule of grammar
7.	______	contrast assumption	g.	strategy for remembering
8.	______	*Sesame Street*	h.	scale to assess home environment
9.	______	rehearsal	i.	Piagetian stage for 2- to 7-year-olds
10.	______	transductive reasoning	j.	going from one isolated event to another

True–False

1. Around 65 percent of preschoolers have imaginary companions.

   TRUE or FALSE

2. Artificialism is believing that inanimate objects are alive.

   TRUE or FALSE

3. Centration facilitates performance of conservation tasks by the preoperational child.

   TRUE or FALSE

4. Scaffolding refers to support provided by others to help a child understand a cognitive task.

   TRUE or FALSE

5. The HOME inventory contains ten subscales.

   TRUE or FALSE

6. Canadian children aged two to eleven spend an average of 14.4 hours a week watching television.

   TRUE or FALSE

7. Watching *Sesame Street* has been found to enhance cognitive skills like classification and sorting.

   TRUE or FALSE

8. Hours spent watching television is correlated with increased body fat in preschool children.

   TRUE or FALSE

9. Typically, children don't spontaneously use passive sentences even when they are five or six years old.

   TRUE or FALSE

10. According to Piaget, language development precedes cognitive development.

    TRUE or FALSE

Solutions

Chapter Review

Multiple Choice

1. d (316)
2. a (316)
3. c (317)
4. b (319)
5. a (319)
6. d (321)
7. a (322)
8. c (324)
9. b (335)
10. b (336)
11. c (338)
12. d (344)
13. a (339)
14. b (348)
15. a (329)

Matching

1. h (344)
2. a (342)
3. i (316)
4. b (339)
5. f (329)
6. d (331)
7. c (324)
8. e (348)
9. g (341)
10. j (319)

True–False

1. T (317)
2. F (319)
3. F (321)
4. T (342)
5. F (344)
6. T (347)
7. T (348)
8. T (350)
9. T (331)
10. F (333)

CHAPTER **10**

Early Childhood: Social and Emotional Development

Learning Objectives

By the end of this chapter, you should be able to generate well-thought-out responses to demonstrate your understanding of the following learning objectives (sample answer comments are included at the end of this chapter):

1. Discuss whether or not parents should be restrictive or relaxed/permissive.
2. Should a parent try to reason with a two- to six-year-old child?
3. Does encouraging a child to act maturely actually result in more mature behaviour, or does it backfire?
4. Explain why firstborn children tend to be more highly motivated to achieve than later-born children.
5. Discuss whether or not children who play by themselves are more likely to develop social problems.
6. How does childhood aggression relate to aggression in adulthood?
7. Discuss the relation between physical punishment and aggression in children.
8. Describe children's television viewing and exposure to violence.
9. Describe the violence in G-rated animated films.
10. When can children usually first describe themselves in terms of their usual pattern of behaviours and feelings?
11. Describe the fears of preschool children.
12. Describe gender roles—what it means to act "like a man" or "like a woman."
13. Do boys and girls typically think their own gender is superior?
14. Explain why a two-and-a-half-year-old may know that she's a girl but think that she can grow up to be a daddy.
15. Discuss why many/most males and females act in stereotypical ways.

Chapter Summary

Influences on Development: Parents, Siblings, and Peers

Different dimensions of child rearing have been studied. Two of these dimensions are whether the parent is warm/cold and restrictive/permissive. As you might expect, warm parents give affection freely and are supportive and caring toward their children while colder parents give few such indications. In terms of child outcomes, the warm parenting style is clearly superior, relating to internalizing moral standards and healthy emotional development.

Parents who are restrictive tend to impose and enforce many rules compared to more permissive parents. If a restrictive parenting style is combined with parental warmth, the resulting parenting style is termed **authoritative** and is associated with positive outcomes for the child. However, if the restrictive style is combined with little warmth and frequent punishments, negative outcomes frequently occur. Some parents may be permissive because of disinterest and lack of involvement; others may simply believe that children should have more freedom.

Parents use different techniques to discipline their children. **Induction** refers to reasoning, explaining why a child should or should not do a certain behaviour. Power assertion is using coercive techniques; such methods could include taking away privileges or using physical punishment. Withdrawal of love, as the name implies, refers to a parent becoming, or threatening to become, cold and ignoring/isolating the child after his or her misbehaviour. The use of power assertion as the main discipline style is associated with more antisocial behaviour in children, poorer academic performance, and less peer acceptance. Use of love withdrawal may increase feelings of anxiety and guilt.

Diana Baumrind described several parenting styles. As previously mentioned, the authoritative parent combines restrictions and warmth. In many ways, this style has the best outcome, including inducing in children high self-esteem, social competence, and self-reliance. **Authoritarian** parents combine restriction with coldness, relying more on coercion. Children of authoritarian parents have been found to be more hostile/defiant (boys) and be less independent (girls). **Permissive–indulgent** parents combine permissiveness with warmth while **rejecting–neglecting** parents are permissive but low in responsiveness and warmth. The latter style is associated with children who show the least competence and lack responsibility and maturity.

Parenting style may also be influenced by the situation and may vary from child to child. Parents tend to become more power assertive in discipline style when children clearly violate rules and should have acted differently. Events such as a divorce may also increase a parent's likelihood of using coercive discipline styles. The child's temperament may also affect parenting style. Parenting practices are also influenced by cultural characteristics. People in many Western cultures tend to be **individualistic,** placing high value on personal identity and goals. Other cultures are more **collectivistic.** Collectivists tend to define themselves in terms of the group they belong to and focus on the group's priorities rather than their own.

Siblings may also influence each other, providing physical care and emotional support. Older siblings may be more dominating but also more nurturant compared to younger siblings; younger siblings may imitate their older siblings. Siblings also fight with each other; milder confrontations may help children develop their identity and social competence. As siblings grow older, their relationships tend to become more egalitarian.

Mixed feelings are common when a new brother or sister is born. Jealousy can result in a child's **regression,** or returning to more babylike behaviours, often in an attempt to gain attention from the parents. **Sibling rivalry,** competition among siblings, may be diminished by preparing the older child ahead of time for the new birth and by providing support and affection to the older child after the birth.

A child's birth order can affect his or her interactions with family members. Only children and firstborn children have been found to have be more motivated to achieve, to perform better academically, and to score higher on standardized tests. Parents may have higher expectations for only children and firstborn children than for later-born children. Firstborn children are also more likely to have imaginary playmates. Later-born children are more likely to have to compete for their parents' attention, and parents tend to be more relaxed and permissive in the rearing of later-born children.

Peers may also influence each other. Even infants as young as six months of age show interest in other babies. As children grow older, their interactions increase, and at two years of age, children may have two or three children who are preferred playmates. Even for preschoolers, friendships are relatively stable. One study of one- to six-year-old children reported that they tended to keep the same friends, in some cases even for three years. When asked about their friends, preschoolers typically mentioned they liked sharing activities and play materials. Older children (five to seven years of age) typically mention having fun with their friends.

Social Behaviours—In the World, Among Others

Besides being fun, play has a number of useful functions, including developing motor coordination and the child's social skills. For instance, through **dramatic play,** children have the opportunity to try on new roles. Mildred Parten described six types of play in preschool children. As you might guess, **unoccupied play** describes children who do not seem to be playing, while **solitary play** refers to children playing independently by themselves. **Onlooker play** is used to describe children who are watching others, perhaps making suggestions but not joining them in the play. These are all types of **nonsocial play**. Children who play near others with similar toys but with little interaction are engaged in **parallel play. Associative play** characterizes children interacting and sharing toys, but they are not necessarily working toward a group goal. **Cooperative play** involves not only interaction but also a common goal with division of labour. Pretending to be the various members of a family might exemplify this kind of play. Parallel play, associative play, and cooperative play are all considered forms of **social play,** play that involves influencing and interacting with others. Associative play and cooperative play are not common in young preschoolers but do occur more commonly in children by the age of five. Older preschoolers also still spend some time in parallel constructive play that may have educational value.

By eighteen months, children have been found to have toy preferences related to their gender. Girls, though, are more likely to vary from stereotypical toy choices than boys, perhaps because boys playing with girls' toys might be perceived as assuming an inferior role. Not only do toy preferences vary by sex, but the activities and environment do as well. On average, boys tend to prefer outdoor activities involving physical skills such as roughhousing and climbing while girls spend more time in arts and crafts activities.

Children are encouraged by parents and adults to engage in gender-stereotypical play activities, but boys are more likely than girls to be criticized for cross-stereotypical play. Also, children as young as two begin to show preferences for same-sex playmates. Perhaps boys perceive girls as inferior, and girls may not want to participate in boys' more aggressive play.

Prosocial behaviour, or altruism, involves helping others without a reward for one's self. Sharing, one type of prosocial behaviour, has been observed even during the first year of life. Being sensitive to others' feelings is **empathy.** Infants often cry when they hear other babies cry, perhaps indicating the beginnings of empathy. Children who are empathic are more likely to behave in prosocial ways, such as trying to comfort a distressed child, and less likely to behave aggressively. Girls may be more empathic than boys, perhaps because of socialization to be sensitive to the emotions of others.

Prosocial behaviour may be enhanced by increased perspective-taking skills as the child grows older. Also, children who are friendly, generous, and cooperative are likely to have others respond to them in a positive way so there in fact may be some reward for this kind of behaviour. Observing prosocial models may also help children become more cooperative and more likely to share. Parents who use inductive discipline techniques such as reasoning are also more likely to have children who engage in more prosocial behaviour.

Aggression in preschoolers is often related to possessions or has some instrumental purpose (sitting in a favourite chair, for example). Children who are more aggressive as preschoolers are more likely to be rejected by their peers, and children who are aggressive are more likely to have a variety of difficulties in adulthood. Consistency of aggression is higher for boys than girls; in other words, aggressive boys are more likely than aggressive girls to become aggressive adults. However, both aggressive boys and girls, compared to their less aggressive peers, have been found to have higher incidences of adult criminal convictions and spousal abuse.

Various factors have been proposed as contributing to the causes of varying levels of aggression. Possible biological factors include the roles of genes, levels of testosterone, and the child's temperament. Aggression in children may also be related to children's cognitive understanding. Boys who are more aggressive are more likely than nonaggressive boys to misinterpret other children's behaviour.

Social learning and social-cognitive explanations of differences in children's aggression levels look at the roles of observational learning and operant conditioning (rewards, punishments). Some children may get what they want (reinforcement) when they are aggressive; also, aggressive children may be in peer groups that value aggressive behaviour. Parents may also unintentionally reward aggressive behaviour in their children by giving in when the child throws fits or yells. Children may also learn through observing others that aggression pays if they see their peers or parents behave aggressively. Parents who physically punish their children are being models of aggression for their children; physical punishment may also increase anger in children, which can lead to increased aggression.

The role of the media in children's aggression has also been studied. Bandura found that preschool children who observed a film with an adult kicking and hitting a Bobo doll were more aggressive to the Bobo doll than children in a control group who saw a film with no aggression. In addition to modelling the specific aggressive behaviours they saw in the film, the children who saw the aggressive model showed other aggressive behaviours that were not shown. One interpretation is that witnessing the aggression of another **disinhibits** aggressive responses in general.

Children who watch television are exposed often to violence. According to one estimate, a child watching two to four hours of television a day will see about 8,000 murders as well as 100,000 other violent acts by the end of elementary school. Movies are violent as well, with an average of nine to ten minutes of violence in a G-rated film. Moreover, media violence may mislead children about consequences of aggression; often only minimal effects of violence are portrayed in children's media, with cartoon characters frequently bouncing back from a certain death. Also, the long-term negative consequences of violent behaviour are rarely shown. Media violence may contribute to children's aggression not only through observational learning and disinhibition but also through increasing the child's arousal, suggesting or "priming" aggressive thoughts, and through habituation, making violence seem mundane through repeated exposure.

Violent video games have been found to increase aggressive behaviour and thoughts in the laboratory. Playing these video games also has been found to be related to juvenile delinquency in adolescents. Males may be more affected than females by these games, and students with higher grades, compared to those with lower grades, were less likely to be aggressive after exposure to these games.

Personality and Emotional Development

Self-concept, children's sense of who they are, continues to develop during the preschool years. Children can describe their **categorical self,** based on readily observable, external traits such as sex or age, about as soon as they learn to talk. By the age of three, children can describe their internal states such as emotions and behaviours. **Self-esteem** refers to how persons value themselves. Children who have mothers who are sensitive and responsive are more likely to have higher self-esteem and behave prosocially. Around four years of age, children begin to judge their own physical and cognitive abilities as well as their social competence, but the evaluations tend to be somewhat "global," good at everything or not so good at everything.

As children enter middle childhood, personality traits become part of children's self-concepts. Their self-evaluations become more differentiated in areas such as their appearance, their behaviour, and their social relations.

In Erikson's theory, preschool children enter the stage of initiative versus guilt. As they try new things and develop a sense of self separate from their parents, they may begin to understand that not all of their efforts will turn out as they'd hoped. They may begin to feel guilt for breaking adult rules; if adults are overly critical, a child's sense of initiative may be stymied.

Fears are common in preschool children. Children between the ages of two and a half and four seem to have the most fears. While fears of strangers, falling, and loud movements may diminish during preschool years, other fears that involve imaginary creatures, animals, personal safety, and darkness may be more prominent. Children's fears at this age may be influenced by television and movies as well as stories they hear; children may be afraid to have the lights off at night because they believe they might be hurt by imaginary creatures based on media. Children also fear real objects and situations, including high places, lightning and thunder, dangerous insects, and sharp objects. As children reach middle childhood, their fears include a fear of criticism and failure in school and in relationships. Girls on average have more fears than do boys.

Participant modelling helps children overcome fears through principles of observational learning.

Development of Gender Roles and Sex Differences

The cultural expectations that are different for men and women in a society are called **gender roles.** To some extent, gender roles may be based on **stereotypes,** beliefs or ideas about a group of people such as men or women that are often distorted and oversimplified. In our society, the title woman is usually associated with being dependent, warm, submissive, gentle, and emotional while the title of man is associated with being self-confident, independent, aggressive, competitive, and mathematically and scientifically inclined.

By approximately the age of two to two and a half years, a child is able to label boys and girls and, around age three, show some understanding of which toys, activities, and clothes are appropriate for boys and for girls. After preschool, while knowledge of gender roles continues to grow, children become more flexible and can recognize similarities between boys and girls as well as recognize individual differences within boy/girl categories.

Children typically believe that their own sex is superior. Girls, for example, typically think that girls work harder, are nicer, and are less selfish than boys. Boys, though, believe that they work harder, are nicer, and are less selfish than girls.

How different are males and females? During infancy male/female differences tend to be small and somewhat inconsistent. During early childhood, boys and girls choose different toys, and boys are more likely to be aggressive and play more roughly. Girls, on average, have more fears and are more empathic toward others.

Some psychologists have argued that sex differences have evolved due to different adaptation pressures. Differences in the organization of the brain have also been hypothesized as one source of sex differences. Early prenatal exposure to sex hormones could have resulted in different organizational patterns. One study found that while males tend to use the hippocampus in both brain hemispheres when navigating mazes, females tend to primarily use the hippocampus located in the right hemisphere as well as the right prefrontal cortex.

Male sex hormones are probably involved in brain organization at the end of the embryonic period. Animal studies have supported such a role involving sex hormones; male rats do better than female rats on learning mazes unless the females have also been exposed to sex hormones prenatally or right after birth. Gender differences in aggression have also been linked to prenatal hormones.

Social-cognitive theorists emphasize the importance of observational learning and socialization processes. Children learn gender roles by imitating same-sex models and through reinforcement for gender-appropriate behaviours. Bussey and Bandura found that two- to five-year-old children were twice as likely to imitate same-sex models as other-sex models.

Parents, particularly the father, may influence gender roles. Fathers tend to be more traditional than mothers in their interactions with their children. If mothers are employed or engaged in "masculine" tasks like yardwork or assembling toys, children tend to be less gender stereotypical.

A cognitive-developmental perspective on gender-typing was described by Lawrence Kohlberg and includes the concepts of **gender identity, gender stability,** and **gender constancy.** Gender identity occurs first and includes others' labelling the child a boy or girl; by two years of age, children can indicate whether they are a boy or a girl.

According to Kohlberg, children develop gender stability, the understanding that one's gender remains the same throughout their life by four or five years of age. Gender constancy is the understanding that people's gender does not change even if they change the clothes they're wearing or their activities; a boy is a boy even if he puts on a dress or washes the dishes. Children acquire gender constancy around five to seven years of age. The ability to conserve may be cognitive "groundwork" for gender constancy; both gender constancy and conservation are based on the child's understanding that something (gender or quantity) remains the same even when appearances change.

Gender-schema theory is another cognitive approach that describes how we organize gender-related information. A schema is an organizational framework so a gender schema is grouped items or clusters of male- or female-related traits, behaviours, and characteristics. Because gender labels are so central in societies, as soon as children acquire "girl" or "boy" labels, they begin to organize information into gender schemas.

While many people think of masculinity and femininity as opposites, it is certainly possible for individuals to be **psychologically androgynous,** to have both masculine and feminine characteristics. An individual can be independent and self-confident as well as nurturant. Perhaps androgynous children and adults are better prepared to meet a wider range of situations, from fixing a flat tire to comforting a crying child. Others, including the author of your text, have criticized androgyny for continuing to define behaviour based on "masculine" and "feminine" characteristics because doing so continues to give these terms credence.

Critical Thinking Exercises

Exercise 1

Ryan and Katherine, parents of a rowdy two-year-old, were themselves raised with different discipline styles. While Ryan's parents primarily used induction, Katherine's parents were power assertive. They want to know which kind of style will result in the best outcome for their child. What advice would you give them? Discuss the research related to each kind of discipline style.

____

____

____

____

____

____

Exercise 2

Imagine that you are giving a speech about how media violence affects children. Describe the major points that you would make, and include the following terms/phrases in your speech:

- observational learning
- disinhibition
- priming
- increased arousal
- habituation

____

____

____

____

____

____

Internet Activities

Activity 1

Should parents spank their children? Do an Internet search with one or more of the following terms:

- disciplining children
- corporal punishment
- punishing children

Once you have chosen your term and conducted your search, select one of the articles that you access as a result of that search. Read the article. In order to enhance your understanding, answer the following questions about the article:

1. What content (points made) in the article did you find most informative? Why?
2. What content (points made) in the article do you think are most relevant to you, your life, and/or your career? How?
3. What is the most important thing you learned by reading this article? Why?

Activity 2

Go to the following URL:

http://www.todaysparent.com

In the right-hand search box, type in "birth order." Read some of the articles that are presented. Think about your own birth order position and the information you have read in your text. Based on what you have learned from this article or site:

1. How accurately do you feel this site portrays information about your topic? Why?
2. Were there any critical pieces of information missing that you feel should have been provided? If so, what were they? If not, what were the most critical pieces conveyed?
3. What is the most important thing you learned by reading the information on this site? Why?

Observing Children and Adolescents CD-ROM Activity

Watch the "Gender" video (Module 2, Section 3) and read the material on page 80 in *Observing Children and Adolescents.* Then answer the following questions:

1. How did the children demonstrate gender stability in the video clip?
2. What were some gender stereotypes these preschool children believed?
3. What aspect of the video surprised you the most, or what did you find most interesting about gender development in preschool children?

Power Preview: Learning Objectives Sample Answers

1. Discuss whether or not parents should be restrictive or relaxed/permissive.

Parents who are restrictive tend to impose and enforce many rules compared to more permissive parents. If a restrictive parenting style is combined with parental warmth, the resulting parenting style is termed authoritative; however, if the restrictive style is combined with little warmth and frequent punishments, negative outcomes frequently occur. Some parents may be permissive because of disinterest and lack of involvement; however, others may simply believe that children should have more freedom.

2. Should a parent try to reason with a two- to six-year-old child?

Even two-year-olds can understand simple reasoning such as "It hurts the bug when you pull off its legs. It would hurt you, too, if someone pulled off your toes."

3. Does encouraging a child to act maturely actually result in more mature behaviour, or does it backfire?

Encouraging children with praise when parents see children behaving in slightly more mature ways will gradually shape children's behaviour, resulting in more mature behaviour in the long run. However, if parents "catch children being bad" and criticize their lack of good behaviour, for some children this negative attention may in fact be reinforcing (at least they're getting some attention) and may result in children's continuing less mature behaviour.

4. Explain why firstborn children tend to be more highly motivated to achieve than later-born children.

A child's birth order can affect his or her interactions with family members. Only children and firstborn children have been found to be more motivated to achieve, to perform better academically, and to score higher on standardized tests. Parents who have only one child have more time to interact with and stimulate the child. Also, they may have higher expectations and make more demands on only children and firstborns.

5. Discuss whether or not children who play by themselves are more likely to develop social problems.

Nonsocial play, which includes unoccupied play, solitary play, and onlooker play, occurs often among two- and three-year-olds. Even older preschoolers may engage in nonsocial educational activities.

6. How does childhood aggression relate to aggression in adulthood?

Aggressive behaviour seems to be relatively stable and predicts a variety of problems in adulthood. Compared to nonaggressive children, aggressive children are more likely to be abusive to spouses, to drive under the influence of alcohol, and to have criminal convictions as adults.

7. Discuss the relation between physical punishment and aggression in children.

Parents who physically punish their children are being models of aggression for their children; physical punishment may also increase anger in children that can lead to increased aggression.

8. Describe children's television viewing and exposure to violence.

Children who watch television are exposed often to violence. According to one estimate, a child watching two to four hours of television a day will see about 8,000 murders as well as 100,000 other violent acts by the end of elementary school.

9. Describe the violence in G-rated animated films.

Movies are violent as well, with an average of nine to ten minutes of violence in G-rated films, according to research by Yokota & Thomson.

10. When can children usually first describe themselves in terms of their usual patterns of behaviour and feelings?

Self-concept, children's sense of who they are, continues to develop during the preschool years. Children use categories based on readily observable, external traits such as sex or age, to define their categorical self; they do this about as soon as they learn to talk. By the age of three, children can describe their internal states such as emotions and behaviours.

11. Describe the fears of preschool children.

While fears of strangers, falling, and loud movements may diminish during preschool years, other fears that involve animals, personal safety, darkness, and imaginary creatures may be more prominent. Children's fears at this age may be influenced by television and movies as well as stories they hear; children may be afraid to have the lights off at night because they believe they might be hurt by imaginary creatures. Children also fear real objects and situations, including high places, lightning and thunder, dangerous insects, and sharp objects. As children reach middle childhood, their fears include a fear of criticism and failure in school and in relationships. Girls, on average, have more fears than do boys.

12. Describe gender roles—what it means to act "like a man" or "like a woman."

The cultural expectations that are different for men and women in a society are called gender roles. To some extent gender roles may be based on stereotypes, beliefs, or ideas about a group of people such as men or women that are often distorted and oversimplified. In our society, being a woman is usually associated with being dependent, warm, submissive, gentle, and emotional while being a man is associated with being self-confident, independent, aggressive, competitive, and mathematically and scientifically inclined.

13. Do boys and girls typically think their own gender is superior?

Children typically believe that their own gender is superior. Girls, for example, typically think that girls work harder, are nicer, and are less selfish than boys. Boys, though, believe that they work harder, are nicer, and are less selfish than girls.

14. Explain why a two-and-a-half-year-old may know that she's a girl but think that she can grow up to be a daddy.

Two-and-a-half-year-olds typically know which sex they are, but their understanding is limited. The girl may believe she can grow up to be a daddy because she doesn't have gender stability and constancy. According to Kohlberg, children do not develop gender stability, the understanding that one's gender remains the same throughout their life, until about four or five years of age. Gender constancy is the understanding that people's gender does not change even if they change the clothes they're wearing or their activities; a boy is a boy even if he puts on a dress or washes the dishes. Children acquire gender constancy around five to seven years of age. The ability to conserve may be cognitive "groundwork" for gender constancy; both gender constancy and conservation are based on the child's understanding that something (gender or quantity) remains the same even when appearances changes.

15. Discuss why many/most males and females act in stereotypical ways.

Different theoretical approaches give somewhat different explanations. The biological approach posits genetic differences based on natural selection, different brain organization, or exposure to different prenatal sex hormones. Social-cognitive theorists emphasize the roles of reinforcement and observational learning in acquiring gender roles. Cognitive-developmental theorists believe the child's changing cognitive abilities support the acquisition of gender constancy; gender schema uses an

information-processing approach to explain the categorization of activities and characteristics into male/female categories.

Chapter Review

Multiple Choice

1. The parenting style that combines restrictiveness, enforcement of firm rules, and support and warmth is called:
   a. authoritative
   b. permissive
   c. authoritarian
   d. undifferentiated
2. Inductive methods of discipline:
   a. involve techniques such as "time-out"
   b. are associated with greater immaturity of behaviour
   c. include love withdrawal as a technique
   d. are based on reasoning with the child
3. Parental use of power assertion discipline, compared to other types of disciplines, is NOT associated with which result in children?
   a. higher levels of antisocial behaviour
   b. higher internalized standards of morality
   c. lower academic performance
   d. greater defiance
4. A study by Kobayashi-Winata and Power examined child-rearing styles in middle-class American and Japanese parents with four- to seven-year-old children. What did they find?
   a. both Japanese and American parents who used relatively little punishment and provided opportunities for appropriate behaviour had the most compliant children
   b. Japanese parents were more likely than American parents to use punishments like sending children to their rooms
   c. American parents used verbal reprimands and explanations more often than Japanese parents
   d. no cross-cultural differences were found; love withdrawal was the primary discipline used by both Japanese and American parents

5. Your text discusses a technique to help children eliminate fears in which the child experiences, with gradually greater intensity, the cause of the fear (moving a white rabbit closer and closer, for example) while engaging in a behaviour that is inconsistent with the fear (eating cookies, for example). This technique is called:
   a. participant modelling
   b. systematic deconditioning
   c. counterconditioning
   d. consistent reprogramming
6. Which statement is true regarding the effects of birth order?
   a. no birth order effects have been found
   b. usually the youngest child experiences the greatest pressure to achieve and hence usually scores higher on intelligence tests
   c. contrary to expectations, younger children are more likely to have imaginary playmates than firstborn children
   d. only and firstborn children scored higher in anxiety and were less self-reliant
7. According to cognitive-developmental theory, children acquire gender stability at what age?
   a. one to two
   b. two to three
   c. three to four
   d. four to five
8. Mildred Parten observed and classified play in preschool children. __________ play refers to play in which the children share toys and interact but do not have a common goal.
   a. Associative
   b. Parallel
   c. Cooperative
   d. Onlooker
9. According to Piaget, this kind of play is the first type of play involving repetitive actions.
   a. constructive
   b. symbolic
   c. functional
   d. formal
10. Which of the following statements is NOT true regarding empathy?
    a. empathy refers to understanding and sharing the feelings of others
    b. even infants respond to others' distress, crying when they hear another baby cry
    c. empathy seems to decrease aggression while promoting prosocial behaviour
    d. based on preliminary studies, boys are higher in empathy than girls
11. Social-cognitive theories would focus on which of the following explanations for aggression?
    a. the role of traumatic brain injuries
    b. possible genetic contributions
    c. reinforcement and observational learning
    d. the influence of testosterone

12. Regarding media and violence, which of the following statements is NOT true?
    a. children who watch between two and four hours of television every day will see 8,000 murders by the time they are out of elementary school
    b. violence on television may have a disinhibiting effect on children
    c. playing violent video games has not been related to aggression in children
    d. repeated exposure to violence may have a habituation effect on children
13. Bussey and Bandura, examining imitation of same-sex and other-sex modelling, found that:
    a. girls were equally likely to imitate men and women
    b. boys were equally likely to imitate men and women
    c. both boys and girls were twice as likely to imitate same-sex than other-sex models
    d. contrary to expectations, both boys and girls were more likely to imitate other-sex than same-sex models
14. __________ refers to a child's understanding that gender does not change even when one wears clothes or does activities of the other sex.
    a. Gender stability
    b. Gender constancy
    c. Gender identity
    d. Gender classification
15. This approach explains children's acquiring the appropriate gender roles by observing and imitating same-sex models:
    a. psychoanalytic
    b. gender schema
    c. cognitive-developmental
    d. social cognitive

Matching

Match each of the items from Column A with the corresponding item from Column B. There is only one correct answer per item.

Column A	Column B
1. ______ authoritarian	a. few demands, little support
2. ______ power assertion	b. controlling style without warmth
3. ______ rejecting–neglecting	c. understanding/sharing others' feelings
4. ______ regression	d. described six kinds of play
5. ______ Baumrind	e. return to infantile behaviours after birth of a new sibling
6. ______ Parten	f. understanding gender does not change
7. ______ empathy	g. return to babyish behaviours
8. ______ gender stability	h. based on external traits like sex, age
9. ______ categorical self	i. discipline using coercion/power
10. ______ regression	j. described parenting styles

True–False

1. Parallel play is a form of nonsocial play.

   TRUE or FALSE

2. Children's acquisition of gender constancy is described by cognitive-developmental theory.

   TRUE or FALSE

3. "Spare the rod, spoil the child" corresponds most closely to power assertive discipline.

   TRUE or FALSE

4. Inductive discipline, compared to other discipline techniques, is least likely to be associated with internalized standards of moral conduct.

   TRUE or FALSE

5. Boys who are more hostile/defiant and girls who are independent/less dominant are found in families with authoritarian parents.

   TRUE or FALSE

6. As siblings grow older, their relationships become less egalitarian.

   TRUE or FALSE

7. Firstborn children tend to have greater anxiety than later-born siblings.

   TRUE or FALSE

8. Boys who are higher in aggression are less accurate in interpreting the behaviours of others.

   TRUE or FALSE

9. Children are able to accurately label pictures of other children as boys or girls at about age two.

   TRUE or FALSE

10. Elementary school children show more stereotyping if their mothers frequently engage in traditionally "masculine" household chores.

    TRUE or FALSE

Solutions

Chapter Review

Multiple Choice

1. a (361)
2. d (360)
3. b (360)
4. a (366)
5. c (386)
6. d (369)
7. d (394)
8. a (373)
9. c (373)
10. d (377)
11. c (380)
12. c (382)
13. c (393)
14. b (394)
15. d (393)

Matching

1. b (362)
2. i (360)
3. a (362)
4. g (368)
5. j (360)
6. d (373)
7. c (377)
8. f (394)
9. h (384)
10. e (368)

True–False

1. F (373)
2. T (394)
3. T (360)
4. F (360)
5. T (362)
6. F (365)
7. T (369)
8. T (380)
9. T (388)
10. F (393)

CHAPTER **11**

Middle Childhood: Physical Development

Learning Objectives

By the end of this chapter, you should be able to generate well-thought-out responses to demonstrate your understanding of the following learning objectives:

1. When do boys begin to surpass girls in height and weight?
2. Do children tend to outgrow "baby fat," or does childhood obesity set a dangerous precedent for adolescent and adult life?
3. Discuss the role of genetic factors in obesity.
4. Are children who spend more time watching television more likely to become heavy?
5. Describe gender differences in motor activities in middle childhood.
6. In light of all of the emphasis in our society on exercise, discuss the fitness of Canadian children.
7. Is hyperactivity related to chemical food additives?
8. Explain why stimulants are used to treat children who are already hyperactive.
9. Describe why some intelligent children with stimulating home environments have difficulty learning reading and math.
10. Discuss whether or not students with disabilities fare better in classes for students with special needs or in classes with all children ("mainstreaming").

Chapter Summary

Growth Patterns

During middle childhood, children gain a little more than two inches a year in height and add around five to seven pounds to their weight every year. In general, children become more slender during this time. Individual variation tends to increase with the age of the child.

Boys are slightly taller and heavier than girls until around nine or ten years of age, when girls on average begin their adolescent **growth spurt,** a period of rapid change in height and weight. Girls then surpass boys until around age thirteen or fourteen, when boys are reaching the peak of their own growth spurt.

Boys and girls also develop increased muscular strength during middle childhood. While the ratio of muscle to fatty tissue is about the same for the sexes in early middle childhood, boys develop proportionally more muscles beginning at about age eleven.

Since children are growing regularly and expending a lot of energy, they need an average of about 2,000 calories a day when they are seven to ten years of age. Sometimes, though, children develop **obesity,** an excessive amount of body fat. One definition of obesity is a body weight that is 20% above the norm for a specific height. Using this criterion, approximately 25 percent of children in Canada are obese. The incidence of obesity has increased, in spite of our society's emphasis on health and fitness, in all races. During the past generation, obesity increased by more than 50 percent for children six to eleven years of age and by about 40 percent for children who are twelve to seventeen years of age.

Most overweight children do not "outgrow" their weight problem. Rather, most children who are overweight become overweight adults whereas a smaller proportion, 40 percent of boys and 20 percent of girls, of normal-weight children become obese as adults.

Children who are obese are more likely to be rejected by peers and, as they enter adolescence, become even less popular. Adolescents who are overweight are more likely than their normal-weight peers to be anxious and depressed.

Some children who are obese develop high blood pressure. High blood pressure in children can lead to damage to the heart, kidneys, and even the eyes. *Pediatrics* published guidelines for doctors to check blood pressure even in three-year-old children. While changes in lifestyle (diet, exercise) to reduce blood pressure are preferable, some children may need to be placed on medication to treat elevated blood pressure.

Genetic factors likely have a role in obesity. Heredity may play a role in how quickly the body burns extra calories versus turning them into fat. Genetic factors may also affect the amount of **adipose tissue,** or fat cells, individuals have. Children who have more fat cells may feel hungry sooner than those with fewer fat cells. One study supporting genetic factors found that identical twins tended to have the same body weight as adults regardless of whether they had been reared separately or together.

Environmental factors also may play a role in obesity. One longitudinal study reported that children who, during the middle childhood years, watched at least twenty-five hours of television a week were more likely to become obese in adolescence. Children who watch more television may get less exercise and consume more snacks, and, since TV programming advertises high-caloric foods, these snacks may be things like potato chips and candy. Children see around 10,000 food commercials per year, with a majority of these commercials being for fast food, candy, cereal, or soft drinks. Stresses in children's lives, such as divorce or conflict in the home, may also contribute to overeating.

Motor Development

Children continue to improve in gross motor skills during middle childhood and usually like to join group games and activities that use large muscles such as playing catch. Maturation contributes to this development, with neurons becoming more myelinated and muscles becoming stronger. Children's experiences also are very important in developing these abilities, although there are hereditary factors that contribute to individual differences as well.

Reaction time, or the time needed to respond to stimuli, is a basic skill affecting performance in activities such as batting a ball or avoiding obstacles when riding a bike. Reaction time improves, or decreases, during childhood until about eighteen years of age; during adulthood, reaction time increases, or gets worse, but older adults usually still outperform children. Fine motor skills such as buttoning clothes improve during childhood as well.

During middle childhood, boys have a slight edge in overall strength and in forearm strength, which helps with batting or throwing balls. Girls, though, have greater flexibility and limb coordination, which aids such sports as gymnastics. Gender differences become greater at puberty and favour boys. Before puberty boys may be more likely to be encouraged to participate in sports, and boys may be more involved than girls in competitive games in middle childhood. Pubertal increases in size and strength may give boys a biological advantage at that time, but environmental factors may also continue to play a role.

Exercise conveys both health and psychological benefits to children and adults. However, the Canadian Paediatric Society reports that most schools offer half of the recommended provincial requirements for physical education. Only 38 percent of acceptable-weight children and 34 percent of overweight/obese children are physically active.

Increased television viewing may contribute to a decline in fitness; also the sports emphasized by schools, such as baseball and football, may be less likely to promote fitness than bicycling, swimming laps, or jogging. Parents can encourage physical fitness in their children by reducing time in front of the TV, encouraging outdoor play, and finding time for family physical activities. Pushing children too hard too early toward excelling in team sports may lead to frustration or injury, and their becoming less likely to become involved in physical activities later.

Children with Disabilities

Some disabilities are likely to be noticed during middle childhood, when a child is required to sit still in school and learn specific academic skills. **Attention-deficit/hyperactivity disorder (AD/HD)**, characterized by the child's lack of attention, impulsiveness, and excessive movement, or **hyperactivity,** is one disability that can interfere with school performance. These characteristics apply to some extent to many children, so careful diagnosis is important, using criteria given by the American Psychiatric Association. From 1 to 5 percent of children in school are diagnosed with AD/HD, with boys being many times more likely than girls to be given this diagnosis.

AD/HD tends to recur repeatedly in a family, providing some support for physical causes. AD/HD occurs alongside other psychological disorders including depression, anxiety, and tics. AD/HD is more common in children who have had encephalitis, and brain wave frequency recordings are more likely to indicate abnormalities. For some children, an inherited defect in the thyroid hormone system may be a factor.

Some have hypothesized that chemical additives in food contribute to hyperactivity. However, studies with children on the Feingold diet, which removes food additives, have not provided support for this position.

Nigg argued that inhibitory processes related to the executive control may be involved. In other words, children with AD/HD have difficulty controlling and inhibiting their responses.

Stimulants, drugs that increase the nervous system's activity, such as Ritalin, are the most common treatment for AD/HD in children. This may seem paradoxical since these children are already overactive. These drugs, though, block the reabsorption of two of the brain's neurotransmitters, which helps to inhibit and provide control over more primitive areas in the brain. Stimulants found in coffee, cola, and chocolate also seem to help children control their behaviour. Stimulants help children increase their attention span and improve their academic performance. Critics, though, have argued that stimulants may suppress height and weight gain and may not be as effective after a period of time.

Cognitive behavioural therapy has also shown promise in treatment of AD/HD. Teaching children to "stop and think" may help them gain self-control; however, a recent study found that medication with stimulants was more effective than cognitive behavioural therapy.

Many children seem to "outgrow" AD/HD. However, some longitudinal studies have found that two-thirds of the children diagnosed with AD/HD continue to experience at least one symptom in adolescence and adulthood.

Academic performance can also be affected by **learning disabilities,** disorders that involve problems in developing specific language, speech, or academic skills. **Dyslexia,** a learning disorder affecting reading that involves reversing letters, reduced comprehension, and slower reading, is one example. If children perform below the expected level for their age and intelligence, especially when other handicaps such as sensory problems or disadvantaged environments are not present, a learning disability is frequently considered responsible for this discrepancy.

Other problems such as AD/HD or emotional problems often accompany learning disorders. Most learning disorders persist throughout an individual's life; however, recognizing the problem early and providing appropriate remediation can help the individual overcome related problems.

Dyslexia affects between 5 and 17.5 percent of children, occurring more commonly in boys. Remediation for dyslexia includes exercises that teach children blending of sounds. Accommodation, such as allowing extra time to complete tests, may be the focus as the child grows older.

Current explanations for dyslexia focus on possible neurological problems. These neurological problems may be inherited since dyslexia tends to run in families. According to various estimates, 25 to 65 percent of dyslexic children have a dyslexic parent. The neurological problems may be related to "faulty wiring" of the brain's left hemisphere; specifically, in the *angular gyrus,* an area believed to "translate" visual (written words) into auditory (sounds) information. High levels of prenatal testosterone, secreted by the fetal testes, may contribute to slower growth of the left hemisphere and may be a reason males are more likely than females to be dyslexic.

Children with a variety of disabilities, including emotional disturbance, learning disabilities, physical disabilities, and mild mental retardation have received special educational programming. A question that is debated is whether it is best to place these children in special classes or use **mainstreaming,** placing children with disabilities in regular classrooms with adaptations for their needs. If children are placed in special-needs classes, they may be stigmatized by being segregated from other children; also, teachers as well as the students themselves may have low expectations for children in these classes, expectations that become a self-fulfilling prophecy. However, mainstreaming can lead to problems for children with learning disabilities; particularly for lower-performing students, a regular classroom environment can be overwhelming.

What kinds of teaching techniques help children with learning disabilities? One study of ninety-one students with certified learning disabilities found that special instruction in "theme identification" helped them more than traditional instruction techniques. Helping children recognize themes in stories may facilitate more abstract thinking in children with learning disabilities.

Critical Thinking Exercises

Exercise 1

Jeff and Amanda are worried about a possible weight problem in their seven- and nine-year-old children. What advice might you give them based on information in Chapter 11? Include a discussion of television and physical fitness in your response.

Exercise 2

Imagine that you are talking to a friend about the causes of childhood obesity. What would you say? Include the following topics in your discussion:

- genetic factors
- adipose tissue
- television
- overeating and stress

Internet Activities

Activity 1

Should parents who have a child who seems overactive ask their doctor to prescribe Ritalin? Do an Internet search with one or more of the following terms:

- Ritalin
- attention deficit/hyperactivity disorder—diagnosis
- attention deficit/hyperactivity disorder—drug therapy

Once you have chosen your term and conducted your search, select one of the articles that is accessed as a result of that search. Read the article. In order to enhance your understanding, answer the following questions about the article:

1. What content (points made) in the article did you find most informative? Why?
2. What content (points made) in the article is most relevant for a parent who is considering Ritalin?
3. What is the most important thing you learned by reading this article? Why?

Activity 2

Access the Internet and go to the following URL:

http://www.dyslexia-teacher.com/Canada.html

On the right-hand-side menu, choose "Recognizing dyslexia." Read through the site and make notes from the material that is presented. Imagine that you are talking to a parent of a child with dyslexia. Based on what you have learned from this site:

1. How accurately do you feel this site portrays information about your topic? Why?
2. What information from the site might be helpful to parents of children with learning disabilities?
3. What is the most important thing you learned by reading the information on this site? Why?

Observing Children and Adolescents CD-ROM Activity

Watch the "Gross Motor" and "Fine Motor" videos (Module 3, Section 1) and read the material on pages 91 and 92 in *Observing Children and Adolescents.* Then answer the following questions:

1. Describe the gross motor skills of John, Sam, and Rachel in the video clip.
2. How do changes in fine motor skills affect writing ability in kindergartners, second-graders, and fourth-graders?
3. What aspect of the videos surprised you the most, or what did you find most interesting about motor development in middle childhood?

Power Preview: Learning Objectives Sample Answers

1. When do boys begin to surpass girls in height and weight?

Boys are slightly taller and heavier than girls until around nine or ten years of age, when girls on average begin their adolescent growth spurt, a period of rapid change in height and weight. Girls then surpass boys until around age thirteen or fourteen, when boys reach the peak of their own growth spurt.

2. Do children tend to outgrow "baby fat," or does childhood obesity set a dangerous precedent for adolescent and adult life?

Most overweight children do not "outgrow" their weight problem. Rather, most children who are overweight become overweight adults whereas a smaller proportion, 40 percent of boys and 20 percent of girls, of normal-weight children become obese as adults.

3. Discuss the role of genetic factors in obesity.

Genetic factors likely have a role in obesity. Heredity may play a role in how quickly the body burns extra calories versus turning them into fat. The amount of adipose tissue, or fat cells, individuals have may also be affected by genetic factors. Children who have more fat cells may feel hungry sooner than those with fewer fat cells. One study supporting genetic factors found that identical twins tended to have the same body weight as adults regardless of whether they had been reared separately or together.

4. Are children who spend more time watching television more likely to become heavy?

One longitudinal study reported that children who, during the middle childhood years, watched at least twenty-five hours of television a week were more likely to become obese in adolescence. Children who watch a lot of television may get less exercise and consume more snacks, and, since TV programming advertises high-caloric foods, these snacks may be high fat items like potato chips and candy.

5. Describe gender differences in motor activities in middle childhood.

During middle childhood, boys have a slight edge in overall strength and in forearm strength, which helps with batting or throwing balls. Girls, though, have greater flexibility and limb coordination, which aids in such sports as gymnastics. Gender differences become greater at puberty and favour boys. Before puberty, boys may be more likely to be encouraged to participate in sports, and boys may be more involved than girls in competitive games in middle childhood. Pubertal increases in size and strength may give boys a biological advantage at that time, but environmental factors may also continue to play a role.

6. In light of all of the emphasis in our society on exercise, discuss the fitness of Canadian children.

The incidence of obesity has increased, in spite of our society's emphasis on health and fitness, in all races. According to Statistics Canada, one-quarter of Canadian children are overweight and/or obese. During the past generation, obesity increased by more than 50 percent for children six to eleven years of age and by about 40 percent for children who are twelve to seventeen.

7. Is hyperactivity related to chemical food additives?

Some have hypothesized that chemical additives in food contribute to hyperactivity. However, studies with children on the Feingold diet, which removes food additives, have not provided support for this position.

8. Explain why stimulants are used to treat children who are already hyperactive.

Stimulants, drugs that increase the nervous system's activity, such as Ritalin, are the most common treatment for AD/HD in children. This may seem paradoxical since these children are already

overactive. These drugs, though, block the reabsorption of two of the brain's neurotransmitters, which helps to inhibit and provide control over more primitive areas in the brain. Stimulants found in coffee, cola, and chocolate also seem to help children control their behaviour. Stimulants help children increase their attention span and improve their academic performance. Critics, though, have argued that stimulants may suppress height and weight gain and may not be as effective after a period of time.

9. Describe why some intelligent children with stimulating home environments have difficulty learning reading and math.

Academic performance can be affected by learning disabilities, disorders that involve problems in developing specific language, speech, or academic skills. For example, dyslexia is a learning disorder affecting reading that involves reversing letters, reduced comprehension, and slower reading. If children perform below the expected level for their age and intelligence, especially when other handicaps such as sensory problems or disadvantaged environments are not present, a learning disability is frequently considered responsible for this discrepancy.

10. Discuss whether or not students with disabilities fare better in classes for students with special needs or in classes with all children ("mainstreaming").

If children are placed in special-needs classes, they may be stigmatized by being segregated from other children; also, teachers as well as the students themselves may have low expectations for children in these classes, expectations that become a self-fulfilling prophecy. However, mainstreaming can lead to problems for children with learning disabilities; particularly for lower-performing students, a regular classroom environment can be overwhelming.

Chapter Review

Multiple Choice

1. Average growth per year between six and twelve years of age is about:
   a. two inch gain in height and about five to seven pounds' weight gain
   b. one inch gain in height and about three to five pounds' weight gain
   c. three inch gain in height and about seven to nine pounds' weight gain
   d. four inch gain in height and about eleven pounds' weight gain
2. Regarding societal changes in obesity:
   a. obesity increased until about 1990, when the emphasis on fitness in schools led to a decrease in children's average weight
   b. obesity increased until about 1998, when the emphasis on fitness in schools led to a decrease in children's average weight
   c. the rates of obesity have remained relatively constant over the past two generations
   d. obesity continued to increase during the past generation

3. Regarding changes with age and obesity:
   a. most children outgrow their "baby fat"
   b. the majority of overweight children become overweight adults
   c. surprisingly, no relationship has been found between childhood obesity and obesity in adulthood
   d. contrary to researchers' expectations, individuals who are overweight during childhood tend to become underweight as adults
4. Which of the following statements describes typical gross motor skills during middle childhood?
   a. children are capable of riding a bicycle by about three or four years of age and engage in gymnastics by about seven years of age
   b. children are capable of riding a bicycle by about six or seven years of age and engage in gymnastics by about eight years of age
   c. children are capable of riding a bicycle and engaging in gymnastics by about five years of age
   d. children are first capable of riding a bicycle and engaging in gymnastics by nine years of age
5. Which statement is NOT true regarding gender and motor skills during middle childhood?
   a. girls and boys are similar in performance in most activities; gender differences are small
   b. boys have a slight advantage in overall strength
   c. girls have more limb coordination and flexibility
   d. girls have greater forearm strength
6. How many hours per week does the average Canadian child watch television?
   a. 36
   b. 10
   c. 16
   d. 26
7. Which is NOT a good suggestion for parents wanting to increase physical fitness in their children?
   a. spend time in family outdoor activities like swimming
   b. encourage children to play outside after school during daylight
   c. assume that playing a team sport will provide children with enough exercise
   d. decrease the amount of time the family watches television
8. The most common treatment for attention deficit/hyperactivity disorder is:
   a. prescription stimulants
   b. prescription depressants
   c. prescription anti-anxiety drugs
   d. prescription barbiturates
9. According to the American Psychiatric Association, a behaviour pattern must have lasted for how many months to be diagnosed as AD/HD?
   a. at least two months
   b. at least four months
   c. at least six months
   d. at least ten months

10. Dyslexia:
    a. is more common in girls than boys
    b. involves difficulty in learning to read
    c. involves a speech impediment
    d. involves abnormality in hearing
11. Children with learning disabilities:
    a. tend to be less likely than other children to be diagnosed with AD/HD
    b. communicate better with their peers than do most children
    c. are more likely to have behavioural problems in school
    d. are less likely to experience emotional problems
12. Regarding chemical additives and hyperactivity:
    a. research has supported the Feingold diet, in which foods with additives are removed from the child's diet
    b. studies on the Feingold diet have not supported claims that removing food with additives reduces hyperactivity
    c. while the Feingold diet has been found to help younger children, it does not seem to reduce hyperactivity in children over the age of eight
    d. no research has yet tested whether or not the Feingold diet helps children with hyperactivity
13. Which of the following is NOT true regarding biological approaches to dyslexia?
    a. children who are dyslexic are no more likely to have a parent who is dyslexic than other children
    b. around 40 percent of siblings of children who have dyslexia are also dyslexic
    c. people with dyslexia tend to have smaller left hemispheres in the brain
    d. prenatal exposure to testosterone may be related to dyslexia
14. Which of the following is the most accurate statement regarding children and mainstreaming?
    a. mainstreaming, compared to special-needs classes, clearly benefits children with learning disabilities
    b. special-needs classrooms have proved more beneficial to children with learning disabilities than mainstreaming
    c. mainstreaming may be more beneficial to lower-performing students with disabilities than higher-performing students with disabilities
    d. mainstreaming may be more beneficial to higher-performing students with disabilities than lower-performing students with disabilities
15. In Canada, what percentage of school-age children are diagnosed with AD/HD?
    a. 1 to 5 percent
    b. 6 to 8 percent
    c. 9 to 12 percent
    d. 14 to 19 percent

Matching

Match each of the items from Column A with the corresponding item from Column B. There is only one correct answer per item.

1. _______	angular gyrus	a.	excessive activity and impulsivity
2. _______	mainstreaming	b.	dramatic advance in growth
3. _______	adipose tissue	c.	"translates" written words to sounds
4. _______	AD/HD	d.	learning disability involving reading
5. _______	girls taller than boys	e.	taught in a regular classroom
6. _______	reaction time	f.	fat cells
7. _______	Ritalin	g.	from about 9 or 10 to 13 or 14 years of age
8. _______	growth spurt	h.	average calories needed by 7- to 10-year olds
9. _______	dyslexia	i.	stimulant used to treat AD/HD
10. _______	2,000	j.	response time to a stimulus

True–False

1. Average body weight doubles during middle childhood.

   TRUE or FALSE

2. Girls begin their adolescent growth spurt earlier than boys.

   TRUE or FALSE

3. Because of their happy personalities, obese children are less likely to be rejected by peers than normal-weight children.

   TRUE or FALSE

4. Watching television at least twenty-five hours per week has been related to obesity in children.

   TRUE or FALSE

5. Reaction time improves (decreases) from childhood to around age eighteen.

   TRUE or FALSE

6. At puberty, sex differences in motor development favouring boys tend to decrease.

   TRUE or FALSE

7. While exercise has clear physical benefits, it has not been related to psychological benefits.

   TRUE or FALSE

8. Hyperactivity is one symptom of AD/HD.

   TRUE or FALSE

9. Ritalin may help children with AD/HD by facilitating the reabsorption of dopamine and noradrenaline.

   TRUE or FALSE

10. Dyslexia has been linked to "faulty wiring" in the brain's left hemisphere.

    TRUE or FALSE

Solutions

Chapter Review

Multiple Choice

1. a (404)
2. d (407)
3. b (407)
4. b (412)
5. d (413)
6. d (417)
7. c (417)
8. a (422)
9. c (420)
10. b (423)
11. c (425)
12. b (421)
13. a (426)
14. d (428)
15. a (420)

Matching

1. c (426)
2. e (427)
3. f (408)
4. a (419)
5. g (407)
6. j (413)
7. i (422)
8. b (407)
9. d (423)
10. h (404)

True–False

1. T (404)
2. T (407)
3. F (407)
4. T (409)
5. T (413)
6. F (415)
7. F (417)
8. T (420)
9. F (422)
10. T (426)

CHAPTER 12

Middle Childhood: Cognitive Development

Learning Objectives

By the end of this chapter, you should be able to generate well-thought-out responses to demonstrate your understanding of the following learning objectives (sample answer comments are included at the end of this chapter):

1. Describe Piaget's thoughts on concrete operations.
2. What do information-processing approaches to cognitive development assume about cognitive development?
3. What are the major theories of intelligence? Discuss the major assumptions that each theory makes about intelligence.
4. How is intelligence measured?
5. What significant events in child development occur during middle childhood?
6. What is creativity?
7. What determines a person's level of intelligence?
8. How does language development occur?

Chapter Summary

Piaget: The Concrete-Operational Stage

Piaget suggested that children in middle childhood enter a cognitive stage of development characterized by **concrete operations.** These operations, as we have seen, involve the processing of information about tangible (and concrete) objects rather than ideas. A major advancement in the child's cognitive development is characterized by **reversibility.** This newfound flexibility allows the child to do mathematical operations (like subtraction) and to realize the relationships between things. This increase in flexible thinking also means the concrete-operations child is less egocentric, meaning he or she can begin to take the perspective of others and to realize that not everyone views the world in exactly the same way.

Another important cognitive advancement is **decentration.** This allows concrete operational children to focus on multiple aspects of a problem at the same time. As you might guess, this increases the speed with which they can solve complex problems. Children begin to show an understanding of conservation, which involves both reversibility and a realization that objects can have multiple properties. A tall glass, for example, may hold less than a short glass because the short glass is wider. Concrete-operational thought also involves an understanding of **transitivity** (the ability to compare multiple options and make a decision) and **seriation,** which involves setting things in order. **Class inclusion** is another ability of the concrete-operational child. This ability includes an understanding of which objects belong to which category, which represents an understanding of the principles of assimilation and accommodation. Evaluations of Piaget's theories suggest that they are too limited. Part of the concern is that he may have underestimated children's abilities. The language used in some of Piaget's tasks may have been confusing for some of the children. Nonetheless, Piaget's work has been very influential and provides a very strong foundation on which to build research on cognitive development in children.

Moral Development: The Child as Juror

Piaget was also very interested in children's moral reasoning, how they make judgments about whether something is right or wrong and their understanding of rules in children's games. Piaget gave children moral dilemmas and observed them playing games, like marbles. Based on his observations and findings, Piaget believed children experienced two stages in moral development, **moral realism** (or **objective morality**) and **autonomous morality.**

Moral reasoning begins around the age of five; at this time, children tend to regard the rules as whatever an adult authority figure tells them. Children tend to judge how wrong an action is based on the amount of damage done (breaking fifteen cups versus breaking one cup) more than intentions (purposeful cup breaking versus accidental cup breaking). Children at this age also tend to believe in **immanent justice,** the concept that a wrong behaviour and punishment are inevitably linked.

Autonomous morality tends to emerge around nine or ten years of age. Rules now are based on group consensus rather than instructions from an authority figure; more importance is given to the intentions of others. Greater role-taking ability probably facilitates these advancements.

Lawrence Kohlberg also used moral dilemmas to study children's moral development. His most famous dilemma involves a man stealing a drug to save the life of his wife. Kohlberg was very interested in the kinds of reasons children gave for whether or not the man should have stolen the drug and how these reasons tended to change with the age of the child. Kohlberg described three levels of moral development, with two stages embedded within each level. At the **preconventional level,** the child focuses on the consequences of their behaviour for themselves, avoiding punishment and reaping as many rewards as one can. Children at the **conventional level** are more concerned with pleasing others and doing their duty: obeying the law. Conventional level thinking tends to emerge during middle childhood. **Postconventional level** reasoning does not occur in a large number of adults, but it may emerge in adolescence. It involves the understanding that laws only represent agreements necessary for the survival of society and may need to be changed; in addition, individuals may have self-chosen ethical principles that take precedence over any law.

Information-Processing: Learning, Remembering, Problem-Solving

Piaget considered children to be small scientists. Those operating from the **information-processing** approach view children as computer systems. The computer metaphor may examine how children store, retrieve, and process information. Key aspects of information-processing include (1) development of selective attention, (2) development of the capacity to store and retrieve information, and (3) development of strategies for processing information. Information-processing theories focus on the capacities of three types of memory structures: **sensory memory** (sometimes called the **sensory register**), **working memory,** and **long-term memory.**

Some of the research done on information processing confirms Piaget's observations about children. Young children many not be able to conserve, for example, because they have difficulty paying attention to multiple aspects of the problem. Thoughts about how humans store and retrieve information have led to advancements in our understanding of **memory.** Research shows, for example, that auditory stimuli can be maintained longer in working memory (short-term memory) than visual information. It would be wise, then, to assist children in **encoding** information auditorially to enhance memory. As the child gets older, he or she will experience an increase in the number of chunks of information that can be held in working memory. The average adult, for example, can hold about seven chunks of information in working memory while the average five-year-old can hold only about two chunks of information in working memory.

While children can learn new material through **rote learning,** repeating something many times, a more effective **elaborative strategy** is to relate the new material to information that is already learned. Making new information meaningful, creating a **semantic code,** is the essence of this strategy. As children learn more and more, the information in their long-term memory becomes more organized into categories.

Information-processing theorists look at children's awareness of and control over their own cognitive processes and memory. Children's awareness of their cognitive processes is referred to as **metacognition** while heir understanding of how their memories work is referred to as **metamemory.** One example of how a child might use this knowledge and awareness involves selective **rehearsal** in which the child improves memory by excluding (and thereby not memorizing) unimportant information.

Intellectual Development, Creativity, and Achievement

Generally, **achievement** refers to what a child knows or has learned whereas **intelligence** refers to a child's underlying competence or learning ability. Although original theories of intelligence tended to consider intelligence something that some people had more of than others, contemporary theories look at intelligence as a set of **factors.** What this means is that people could be more intelligent than others on certain factors but less intelligent than others on other factors. In these kinds of approaches, a statistical procedure called **factor analysis** is used to try to determine the most important factors of intelligence. Many theories assume that there are primary mental abilities (such as the theory proposed by Thurstone) and differ on what other specific abilities there might be. More recently, Howard Gardner has proposed a theory of multiple intelligences. Although this theory concurs with other theories by proposing logical and problem-solving abilities, it also includes more unusual intelligences like bodily-kinesthetic (shown by gymnasts and dancers, for example), and interpersonal intelligence (defined as self-insight). A very recent theory was proposed by Robert Sternberg. This **triarchic** theory suggests that intelligence involves the three components of analytical, creative, and practical intelligences.

Although there are disagreements about how to define intelligence, psychologists administer intelligence tests every day. The Stanford–Binet Intelligence Scale and the Wechsler Scales are the most widely used tests. Despite disagreements about how to define intelligence, these tests are administered so often because important academic decisions about children depend upon these scores. Children whose scores fall below certain levels may be placed into special classes or programs that are designed to provide them different kinds of or enhanced assistance. Although these are good intentions, disagreements about the validity of the scores, and controversies surrounding the potential for racial or economic bias prompt caution in how the test scores are used. Rathus, for example, suggests that it would be wise for decisions to be made "only after a battery of tests is given by a qualified psychologist, in consultation with parents and teachers."

To provide a standard basis from which discussions about intelligence can be conducted, most tests are scored in such a way that the average score is 100. This is referred to as an **intelligence quotient,** or IQ. Typically this means that a person (be it a child or an adult) scores the same as the average person for his or her age. So, a twelve-year-old (**chronological age**) should score the same as the average twelve-year-old (**mental age**).

Intellectual development has been studied intensively. Research suggests that intellectual development is not linear and gradual. There are times of rapid intellectual development interspersed with more steady advancements. The first major spurt in intellectual development appears to occur at about age six. This spurt coincides with the child going to school and is characterized by what Piaget described as the shift from preoperational to concrete-operational thought. The second spurt occurs around age ten or eleven and may precede the multiple physical and psychological changes of adolescence.

Because of these spurts in intellectual development, IQ scores are probably less predictive for younger children. Once these spurts have occurred, one would expect there to be more consistency in how the child scores across time, and in predicting what those scores might mean. Children who score significantly lower than other children for their age may be labelled as mentally retarded. The majority of children who are mentally retarded are mildly retarded; children with Down syndrome are usually moderately retarded and can still learn to talk and take care of many daily needs such as dressing, feeding, and cleaning themselves. While some kinds of retardation are biological (Down syndrome, brain damage from various causes, genetically based conditions such as PKU), **cultural–familial delay** refers to a biologically normal child who has not received "appropriate" environmental stimulation. Gifted children are those who excel on standard tests of intelligence and/or who have outstanding capabilities in specific areas.

Socioeconomic and ethnic differences in IQ are controversial and complex topics. Poorer children tend to score lower on intelligence tests than children from more advantaged backgrounds. Since larger proportions of many minorities tend to be poorer, cultural and socioeconomic differences have at times been confused. Whether or not the traditional intelligence tests are **culturally biased** is another important issue. Recent IQ tests are designed to be **culture-free**—that is, the test items are not dependent on knowledge from a particular culture.

Sternberg defines creativity as "the ability to do things that are novel and useful." Although what constitutes "creative" may differ in the minds of different people, creative children are said to share a number of qualities. These include (1) taking chances, or doing things differently, (2) refusing to accept limitations, (3) appreciation for music and art, and (4) challenging social norms, or being nonconformists. Creative people may make associations that others do not make and may put elements together in novel ways.

Much has been made about the relationship between **creativity** and intelligence. Certainly some theorists consider creativity to be a type of intelligence (Sternberg considers it one of three types of intelligence). Others, however, suggest that the relationship between the two is modest at best. Perhaps it is best described by delineating **convergent thinking** from **divergent thinking.** Convergent thinking involves narrowing down the facts to find the best solution to a problem. This would be a necessary ability for traditional intelligence tests. But creativity involves divergent thinking. This type of thinking involves free association that is not limited to facts. A creative child appears able to make many associations from a single piece of information while less creative children see things more simply or at least within stricter limits.

Both genetics and environment influence intelligence. The question is not whether each has an influence but one of "how much?" Kinship studies look at the correlations between the IQ scores of persons differing in degree of genetic and environmental similarity. Identical twins, for example, share complete genetic similarity while other siblings share less. By looking at twins and other siblings reared together and reared apart, such studies can begin to document how much intelligence is influenced by genetics and the environment. If, for example, the correlation between IQ scores of identical twins reared together is +.85 and between identical twins reared apart it is +.67, then we can claim with some degree of certainty that genetics plays a strong role but environment does, too.

Research suggests that the **heritability** of intelligence is between 40 and 60 percent. In other words, over half of the variation in IQ scores can be explained by heredity. So about half of the difference between your IQ score and the scores of other people can be explained by genetics. But environmental influences are important, too. Even the immediate environment, such as the testing situation, can affect outcomes; when an examiner is friendly and warm, and makes sure that children understand the directions, test anxiety is reduced, and IQ scores increase. Also "stereotype vulnerability," making one's group membership such as ethnicity salient, can also affect test scores. Evidence from orphanages and adopted children studies also support the role of long-term deprivation versus stimulation.

Language Development and Literacy

It may shock the reader to discover that the typical six-year-old already has a vocabulary of 10,000 words. Children quickly learn grammar, which delineates the rules for how words can be combined. Children move from having difficulty understanding passive sentences to processing them as easily as active sentences.

Language development, of course, is a necessary precursor to the development of reading skills. Neurological maturation and experience combine to allow children to make the fine discriminations between letters necessary for reading. **Word-recognition methods** of reading teach the child to recognize what words look like and how to say them. So the child must remember what the word *cat* looks like in order to read. **Sight vocabulary** is the term used to describe the collection of words a child can immediately recognize based on familiarity with the word's overall shapes. **Phonetic methods,** on the other hand, teach the child to read by teaching how to associate certain combinations of letters (such as *ph* or *sh*) with the sounds they are meant to indicate.

Although it may seem to most of us that learning a second language is quite difficult, research appears to contradict this assumption. Most people throughout the world are **bilingual.** The exception, of course, is North Americans. Some research shows that being bilingual contributes to the complexity of the child's cognitive processes.

Critical Thinking Exercises

Exercise 1

A friend of yours has suggested that intelligence is either something you are born with or not. Based on the information presented in this chapter, how would you respond to this claim? Be sure to include a discussion of the strengths and weaknesses of at least three different views of intelligence in your answer.

____

____

____

____

____

____

Exercise 2

Consider how intelligence is measured. Also consider the relationship between intelligence and IQ scores. Given these thoughts, how would you respond to the following comment: "IQ scores tell you how intelligent someone is"?

____

____

____

____

____

____

Internet Activities

Activity 1

Choose one of the following terms and run an Internet search:

- Intelligence tests
- Memory
- Piaget

Choose one of the sites that come up as a result of your search and read the information presented. Assume that you are a parent with a school-aged child. Based on what you have learned from this article:

1. How accurately do you feel this site portrays information about your topic? Why?
2. How could you apply three pieces of information from this site to the parenting of your young child?
3. What is the most important thing you learned by reading the information on this site? Why?

Activity 2

Access the Internet and go to the following URL:
http://www.indiana.edu/~intell

Once you have accessed the site, click on several of the articles on IQ and read them. In order to enhance your understanding, answer the following questions about the articles:

1. What content (points made) in the articles did you find most informative? Why?
2. What content (points made) in the articles do you think is most relevant to you, your life, and/or your career? How?
3. Based on the content of these articles, what three pieces of advice would you give to parents of a school-aged child? Why?
4. What is the most important thing you learned by reading these articles? Why?
5. Is the information in the articles reliable? How do you know?
6. Is the information in the articles valid? How do you know?

Observing Children and Adolescents CD-ROM Activity

Watch the "Moral Development" video (Module 3, Section 3) and read the material on pages 116 and 117 in *Observing Children and Adolescents.* Then answer the following questions:

1. What reasons did the children give in the video for whether or not Heinz should have stolen the drug to save his wife? Using Kohlberg's stages, how would you classify some of these responses?
2. Did you notice any differences in the answers given by the children who appeared to be younger compared to the children who seemed to be older?
3. What aspect of the videos surprised you the most, or what did you find most interesting about moral development in middle childhood?

Power Preview: Learning Objectives Sample Answers

1. Describe Piaget's thoughts on concrete operations.

Piaget characterized the intellectual advancements of children. For school-aged children, these advancements include an understanding of reversibility, decentration, and seriation. Reversible thinking is evident in the child's increasing understanding of how to reverse his or her thought patterns, for example, if the child understands that 2+2=4 and 4-2=2. Decentration involves the

child's capacity for focusing on multiple aspects of a problem. For example, a child in this stage will understand that tall objects can be both heavy and light. Seriation involves organizing objects according to some particular property. A child might, for example, be able to take a group of toys and arrange them in order of size.

2. What do information-processing approaches to cognitive development assume about cognitive development?

The key concept for most of these approaches is to assume that the developing mind is like a computer. These approaches, therefore, focus on how children encode, store and retrieve information. When children form new memories in long-term memory, the assumption is that the information is always available. If someone tries to remember something and cannot remember it, the assumption with the information-processing approach is that the information is still in memory but that access (or retrieval) is the problem.

3. What are the major theories of intelligence? Discuss the major assumptions that each theory makes about intelligence.

Early theories of intelligence (such as that of Binet) assumed that intelligence involved multiple factors. Traditionally, these factors were assumed to correspond to traditional academic abilities (such as math and quantitative reasoning). Spearman suggested that intelligence involves a primary ability (which he called "g") and specific intelligences that could differ from person to person. Howard Gardner expanded views of intelligence to include nonacademic abilities such as body-kinesthetic intelligence (such as dancers would use) and interpersonal intelligence (reflected in how well someone has insight into the self). Sternberg suggested a triarchic theory of intelligence that assumes that people have varying levels of (1) analytical intelligence (academic ability), (2) creative intelligence (one's ability to cope with novel situations), and (3) practical intelligence (which allows people to adapt to their environment).

4. How is intelligence measured?

The first important thing to keep in mind is that intelligence and IQ are not the same. Intelligence represents one's total intellectual capacity, and IQ refers to a score on a test. Although IQ tests are designed and assumed to measure intelligence, it is unclear as to how well they do so. Most measures of IQ yield scores that are age-based. In other words, the assumption is that an average score (usually 100) means that the individual scored the same as the average person of his or her own age. Most measures of IQ focus primarily on academic abilities although some measures include problem-solving, motor skills, and more specific abilities such as interpersonal intelligence.

5. What significant events in child development occur during middle childhood?

By age nine or ten, intelligence scores begin to predict quite well scores at later ages. The major intellectual spurts occur before age ten, which may explain the increased predictability of IQ after that age. IQ scores tend to be based on an average of 100, which is age-based. In other words, scores represent the intellectual ability of the person in comparison to other persons of the same physical age. Individuals who score below 70 are considered to be mentally retarded. Controversies come up when it comes to considerations of how to deal with children who are mentally retarded. Should they be placed in special classes? Should they be mainstreamed with other students? The same questions might be asked for children who score far enough above average in IQ to be labelled "gifted."

6. What is creativity?

Creativity has been related to intelligence, but most researchers suggest that the two are, at most, modestly related. Creativity means being able to "do things that are novel and useful." Creative people are able to think in ways that are divergent rather than convergent. Divergent thinking involves the

ability to come up with multiple solutions to the same problem, and to be flexible with how one approaches the solution to problems.

7. What determines a person's level of intelligence?

Although the study of intelligence has traditionally referred to the answer to this question as the "nature–nurture debate," such is no longer the case. Researchers appear to agree that intelligence is influenced by a combination of genetic and environmental influences. Twin studies and other "kinship" studies have attempted to delineate how much of intelligence is determined by genetics and how much is influenced by intelligence. Your text estimates that about 40 to 60 percent of differences in intelligence among people is due to genetic differences; in other words, probably about an equal proportion of the intellectual differences among people are due to differences in genes and the environment.

8. How does language development occur?

Children progress very quickly from being silent and unable to speak to being quite fluent with language. Tag questions (in which a question is "tagged" onto the end of a declarative statement) begin to emerge and children have fewer and fewer problems in understanding passive sentences. The increasing ability of the child to integrate auditory and visual information allows the complex task of reading to become easier. Neurological maturation and experience combine to allow the child to make the fine visual discriminations (is that a* p *or a* q*?) that are necessary for reading. Children seem especially well-suited to develop multiple languages, an ability that appears to diminish as the child ages.

Chapter Review

Multiple-Choice

1. According to Piaget, the thinking of the concrete-operational child is characterized by:
   a. rigidity
   b. confusion
   c. reversibility
   d. centration
2. What is decentration?
   a. the ability to focus simultaneously on multiple dimensions of a problem
   b. the ability to understand that changes in appearance don't change objects
   c. the inability to reverse one's thinking, which is required for math
   d. none of these
3. The information-processing approach to cognitive development likens the mind to a:
   a. tape recorder
   b. computer
   c. videotape machine
   d. telephone

4. What is selective attention?
   a. the fact that concrete-operational children do not pay attention well
   b. an inability to ignore distraction
   c. the ability to pay attention to the relevant features of a task
   d. an automatic sensory process that assists us with memory
5. What is sensory memory?
   a. a brief, perfect memory
   b. a memory system that lasts up to thirty seconds
   c. a memory system that automatically places important sensory information into long-term memory
   d. none of these
6. What is metacognition?
   a. complex cognition
   b. cognition outside of the child's awareness
   c. a cognitive ability that does not occur until age ten
   d. a child's awareness and purposeful control of his or her cognitive abilities
7. Sternberg's triarchic theory of intelligence suggests that intelligences include:
   a. kinesthetic, interpersonal, and problem-solving
   b. analytical, creative, and practical
   c. logical, verbal, and mathematical
   d. primary mental, specific, and generalized
8. Spearman felt that:
   a. intelligence is impossible to measure
   b. the behaviours we consider intelligent have a common, underlying factor
   c. intelligence develops slowly and is influenced greatly by the environment
   d. intelligence is limited to school-related abilities
9. Which theorist suggested intelligences such as body-kinesthetic and interpersonal?
   a. Gardner
   b. Spearman
   c. Binet
   d. Thurstone
10. One of the most widely used measures of IQ is:
    a. the Sternberg Triarchic Measure
    b. the Gardner Multiple Intelligences Scale
    c. the Stanford-Binet Intelligence Scale
    d. the Thurstone Standard Scale
11. What is "mental age"?
    a. the intellectual level at which a child is functioning
    b. a concept suggesting that intelligence stays the same as we age
    c. the child's physical age
    d. the child's total intelligence score

12. How is an IQ score typically computed?
    a. by adding up the number of correct answers the child gets
    b. by calculating the ratio between correct and incorrect answers
    c. by dividing mental age by chronological age and multiplying by 100
    d. none of these
13. When is the first growth spurt in intellectual development?
    a. prenatally
    b. six months of age
    c. three years of age
    d. six years of age
14. The term "mental retardation" is generally applied when a child's IQ score is below:
    a. 100
    b. 90
    c. 70
    d. 50
15. What is the relationship between intelligence and creativity?
    a. there is none
    b. creative people are always more intelligent
    c. intelligence causes enhanced creativity
    d. they are moderately correlated

Matching

Match the following items from column A with the corresponding item from column B. There is only one correct answer per item.

A		B	
1. ______	conservation	a.	relate new material to well-known material
2. ______	decentration	b.	lining up toys based on size
3. ______	information-processing view	c.	awareness of and purposeful control over one's cognitive abilities
4. ______	selective attention	d.	the brain is like a computer
5. ______	elaboration strategy	e.	the ability to focus on multiple aspects of a problem
6. ______	recall memory	f.	primary mental abilities
7. ______	metacognition	g.	triarchic theory of intelligence
8. ______	Thurstone	h.	reversible thinking
9. ______	Sternberg	i.	ability to ignore irrelevant information
10. ______	seriation	j.	retrieval of information from memory

True–False

1. Kohlberg described two major stages of moral development, moral realism and autonomous morality.

   TRUE or FALSE

2. A child's belief in immanent justice occurs during the autonomous morality stage.

   TRUE or FALSE

3. Good-boy/good-girl moral reasoning is a stage at the conventional level of moral reasoning.

   TRUE or FALSE

4. Avoiding punishment and satisfying one's own needs are characteristic of the preconventional level of moral reasoning.

   TRUE or FALSE

5. Older children are better able than younger children to ignore irrelevant dimensions in solving a problem.

   TRUE or FALSE

6. Metamemory is a part of metacognition.

   TRUE or FALSE

7. Spearman used "g" to represent an underlying factor or generalized ability and "s" to represent more specific abilities.

   TRUE or FALSE

8. "Street smarts" corresponds to Sternberg's analytical intelligence.

   TRUE or FALSE

9. The phonetic method of learning to read has been clearly demonstrated to be superior to the word recognition method.

   TRUE or FALSE

10. In middle childhood, children learn to use connectives in language.

    TRUE or FALSE

Solutions

Chapter Review

Multiple-Choice

1. c (434)
2. a (434)
3. b (444)
4. c (444)
5. a (446)
6. d (449)
7. b (452)
8. b (452)
9. a (453)
10. c (456)
11. a (456)
12. c (456)
13. d (462)
14. c (463)
15. d (464)

Matching

1. h (434)
2. e (434)
3. d (444)
4. i (444)
5. a (448)
6. j (448)
7. c (449)
8. f (452)
9. g (452)
10. b (436)

True–False

1. F (440)
2. F (440)
3. T (443)
4. T (443)
5. T (445)
6. T (449)
7. T (452)
8. F (453)
9. F (471)
10. T (470)

CHAPTER 13

Middle Childhood: Social and Emotional Development

Learning Objectives

By the end of this chapter, you should be able to generate well-thought-out responses to demonstrate your understanding of the following learning objectives (sample answer comments are included at the end of this chapter):

1. How do children think of themselves in middle childhood? Do they focus on more superficial traits, or do they include their interests and personality traits?
2. Explain why children's self-esteem tends to decline in middle childhood.
3. Describe the importance of peer influences in middle childhood.
4. What factors contribute to popularity in middle childhood? Are children in this age group—like adolescents—pressured to conform?
5. Describe changes to power in the family during middle childhood. Do parents move toward more power sharing, or do they become more restrictive and controlling?
6. Discuss whether or not it is better for parents who are in conflict to stay together "for the sake of the children" or to separate.
7. Explain why daughters of employed women are more achievement-oriented and set higher career goals for themselves than do daughters of unemployed women.
8. Describe the kinds of challenges children face when they enter "real" school.
9. What is the "Pygmalion effect"?
10. Are teachers less likely to accept calling out from boys than from girls? Why?
11. What is meant by the term "conduct disorder"? Is this a form of mental illness?
12. Describe why some children—like some adults—blame themselves for their problems, even if they don't deserve the blame.
13. Discuss whether or not children who have school phobia should be forced to attend school.

Chapter Summary

Theories of Social and Emotional Development in Middle Childhood

While personality theories have focused less on middle childhood than on other ages, still some themes have been noted. In psychoanalytic theory, Freud described middle childhood years as the **latency stage,** during which sexual urges are repressed and children are developing social and intellectual skills. Erikson's stage for this period is **industry versus inferiority,** in which children are mastering the appropriate age-related tasks. A child who is not successful in doing so may develop feelings of inferiority.

Rewards and modelling continue to be important during middle childhood years in social cognitive theory. During this time, though, children become less dependent on external consequences and are increasingly able to use self-rewards and regulate their own behaviour.

According to cognitive-developmental theory, the child is better able to consider the perspective of others during the concrete-operations stage. **Social cognition,** children's understanding of the social world and their relationships with others, depends upon this perspective-taking ability. Based on children's responses to social dilemmas, Robert Selman developed five levels of perspective-taking.

When children respond to the question "Who am I?," their responses during middle childhood include physical traits and their competencies. During the middle childhood years, children also begin to include personality characteristics in their descriptions of themselves. In addition, membership in groups as well as relationships with others become increasingly important. Compared to boys, girls are more likely to describe themselves as members of a group. A study of children from China reported that if children have siblings, they are also more likely to describe their group membership.

Children's self-concept becomes more differentiated, and they evaluate themselves in a greater number of areas during this time. While preschool children tend to have more global self-concepts, children as young as five to seven years of age can evaluate their own performance in as many as seven different areas.

The **self-esteem** of children tends to decline during middle childhood, hitting a low at around the ages of twelve to thirteen, and then rising. Perhaps this decline is related to children's increasing perspective-taking ability. The younger, egocentric child may not realistically consider input from others while the older child includes more external information in her/his self-evaluation. Some gender differences in specific areas have been reported, with girls tending to have higher self-concepts related to reading, writing, and general academic ability while boys have higher self-concepts related to math, physical appearance, and physical ability.

Authoritative parenting seems to be linked to higher self-esteem in children. Children whose parents are warm, involved, and also strict tend to have more favourable self-images than children whose parents are authoritarian or rejecting–neglecting. Having a close relationship with parents, especially same-sex parents, has also been related to higher self-esteem, as has a closer relationship between the two parents. Being accepted by one's peers is also important to the child's self-esteem. Genetic factors may also be related to children's self-esteem.

Children with low self-esteem may develop **learned helplessness,** the belief that one's behaviour is not related to the rewards or punishments one receives. These children are more likely to give up following a failure than children who believe that effort is the key to succeeding at something.

The Family

Parents monitor children less during the middle childhood years, with children increasingly monitoring their own behaviour. While parents still have ultimate control over the child, **coregulation,** a transferring of more control gradually to the child, also is occurring. Children are beginning to internalize their parents' standards.

As they did in early childhood, children spend more time with their mothers than their fathers, with mothers' interactions including more care-giving and fathers' interactions being more recreational. As children reach the end of middle childhood, they tend to be more critical of their parents, perhaps reflecting more complex social cognitive capacities.

Some children are reared in nontraditional families. One kind of nontraditional family is one with **lesbian** or **gay** parents. Research on children with two mothers or two fathers finds that their psychological adjustment is comparable to that of children of heterosexual parents. Few differences between sexual orientation, including **transsexual** orientation, and gender roles are found, although one study found that girls reared by mothers who were lesbians tended to have a little more gender role flexibility than girls reared by mothers who were heterosexual.

Over 70,000 divorces were recorded in Canada in 2003, a slight rise from 70,155 in 2002. In the case of divorce, daily routine activities, such as meals and where the child will sleep, can no longer be taken for granted. Since two households must now be supported, the child's standard of living is also often affected. A child may move from a house to a cramped apartment and/or into a less desirable neighbourhood.

Children whose parents divorce are more likely to have problems. Children may blame themselves for the divorce and may be scared of the unknowns in their lives. In most cases, children live with their mothers; while some fathers continue to maintain strong relationships with their children after a breakup, others become less involved over time, especially if the father remarries and starts a new family.

Particularly during the first year or two following a divorce, children have higher rates of behavioural problems and substance abuse, tend to have lower self-esteem, and are more likely to receive poorer grades in school. The problems, though, may be related to a decline in parenting quality. Family life tends to become more disorganized, and divorced mothers have more difficulty enforcing restrictions on their sons' behaviour. Divorced parents tend to be less nurturant and are less likely to use an authoritative parenting style.

Children in other cultures whose parents divorce are also more likely to experience problems. Children of divorced parents in China were more likely to have somatic complaints; in a second study in China, the parent–child relationships were affected by divorce. Economic hardships following divorce, leading some children to feel inferior, were reported in a study of mothers and children in Botswana, Africa.

Boys may have a harder time adjusting to parental divorce than girls; the child's temperament may also be a factor in this. Hetherington reported that boys of divorced parents continued to have conduct, academic, and social problems as long as six years after a divorce while girls tended to adjust in two years. Interestingly, another study suggests that the negative effects may be due to indirect factors related to the mother rather than to the divorce per se. After controlling for mothers' education, socioeconomic status, and psychological adjustment, no differences were found between children from intact families and children living with separated or divorced mothers.

The majority of divorced parents remarry. About one in three children will spend part of their lives in a stepfamily. Stepfathers can serve as role models for stepsons, as can stepmothers for stepdaughters. One study found that a positive relationship between a stepmother and stepchild was related to better self-esteem in girls and less aggression in boys. On the other hand, the risk of infanticide is much higher in stepfamilies than in genetically related families; the risk of sexual abuse is also greater by a stepparent than a biological parent.

If parents have gotten a divorce, children fare best if the parents cooperate with each other in child rearing. Regarding the question of whether or not parents should stay together for their children's sake, marital conflict has been linked to problems in children just as divorce has. When children see parents fighting, even physiological measures such as heart rate, blood pressure, and skin conductance are affected. One study reported that, while separation and divorce were related to increased problem behaviours in children, families with high levels of marital conflict that remained intact had children with even more behavioural problems.

For mothers with a youngest child between the ages of six and fifteen years old, work force participation ranges from 74.4 percent in Newfoundland to 85.5 percent in Manitoba—with a Canadian average of 80.7 percent. A related question is the potential effect of maternal employment on children. The effect of paternal employment has not been examined because of the traditional assumption that the father is the breadwinner. In general, there are little data to suggest that maternal employment is significantly harmful to children. One study found that while maternal employment status per se was not related to delinquent behaviours, lack of supervision of children had a slight indirect effect on delinquency rates. Another study, using the same national data set, reported that parents' being employed more hours was related to slightly lower academic achievement and cognitive development scores in children. The same study, though, found beneficial effects for children of lower-income families and single mothers.

Maternal employment may also be related to greater independence and responsibility in school-aged children, and children of employed mothers may have less traditional gender-role stereotypes. Daughters whose mothers were employed tended to have higher career goals and were more achievement-oriented than daughters whose mothers were not employed; children may view their mothers as more competent if their mothers are employed. As one might expect, families in which the mother is employed are more egalitarian, not only in the distribution of the breadwinner role, but also in household chores. Mothers who are employed tend to be happier; this may lead to more positive interactions with their children.

Peer Relationships

Peers become increasingly important during middle childhood. Because peers are from a different generation and have different needs and interests than parents, peers broaden children's experiences. They can provide children the opportunity to practise various relationship skills and competencies. Whether or not children are accepted or rejected by their peers relates to later emotional and social adjustment.

Children who are popular tend to be physically attractive; this may be of greater importance for girls than boys. Popular children are also more likely to be nurturant, helpful, cooperative, and friendly—in general, more skilled in interactions with others. Children who are popular are likely to praise others and are likely to have higher self-esteem; the latter may be related to their academic or athletic performance. Compared to firstborns, later-born children are more popular. Children who have various kinds of problems, including learning as well as behaviour problems such as disruption and aggressiveness, tend to be rejected by their peers.

While pressure to conform to expectations of others can be powerful, in general, children who are rejected do not "shape up." They tend to remain on the outskirts of the group although another alternative is to join deviant subcultures. If children who are rejected receive training in social skills, their popularity with others tends to increase.

Friendships are somewhat superficial, with shared activities being an important component. Children from the ages of eight to eleven show greater recognition of friends' having desirable traits and meeting their needs. Children become more likely to pick friends who are similar to themselves and value loyalty, sharing of personal information, and mutual understanding. Girls' friendships are more likely to be intimate, with the sharing confidences, than are boys' friendships. Children interact differently with peers who are their friends than peers whom they do not consider friends. Children often have more than one "best" friend during middle childhood; one study found that nine-year-olds averaged four best friends.

The School

Schools influence children in many ways. Around 50 percent of children have had an arranged prekindergarten experience, but for many children, their first full-time school experience is in kindergarten or first grade. The transition from home to school may be particularly difficult for children living in poverty; parents may be less likely to provide needed emotional and economic support. One survey of 7,000 kindergarten teachers found that teachers indicated that more than one-third of students were not prepared when they began school. Language skill was a major area of concern. Many children suffer from poor nutrition and health care as well as inadequate parental support and stimulation, placing them at risk of failing even before beginning school.

Class size is an important aspect of the school environment. Children receive more attention in smaller classes; smaller class size is associated with better achievement in math and reading during the early primary grades.

Teachers who expect students to master their assignments, who spend most of the class time on academic activities, and who have an effective classroom environment enhance achievement in their students. Students do better when teachers are warm and friendly rather than when they rely on criticism and punishment.

Teachers' expectations for individual students may be important in student achievement. In *My Fair Lady*'s reworking of Pygmalion lore from Greek mythology, a society lady was fashioned from a working-class girl. Similarly, expectations of teachers can become self-fulfilling prophecies; students will be more likely to succeed or fail depending upon teachers' expectations. In a classic experiment, teachers were led to believe that a few students were "late bloomers" who would do well in the coming year. Even though these students were randomly chosen, these children made significant gains in performance on intelligence tests. Subsequent research has provided mixed support for the **Pygmalion effect,** or **self-fulfilling prophecy.** When credibility regarding the expected performance of targeted students was enhanced, the manipulation of teachers' expectations was most effective in terms of students' performance.

Sexism refers to having different attitudes toward boys than girls, resulting in discrimination. Some indicators that sexism is still a factor in schools were found in a review by the American Association of University Women; teachers give girls less attention than boys, textbooks tend to ignore or stereotype women, and some standardized tests, like the SAT, may be biased against girls. **Sexual harassment,** unwanted comments or behaviour that are of a sexual nature, from classmates may also affect girls' performance.

In a study of students from four states and Washington, DC, students in fourth, sixth, and eighth-grade classes were observed. Boys tended to dominate classroom communication and were much more likely (eight times more likely) to call out an answer without first raising their hands. Moreover, teachers were more likely to remind girls to raise their hands while they were more likely to accept the answers from boys. Perhaps boys are expected to be assertive and impetuous while girls are not.

Social and Emotional Problems

Using diagnostic criteria from the Diagnostic and Statistical Manual of the American Psychiatric Association, a number of children are diagnosed with **conduct disorders;** children must have shown evidence of a troublesome behaviour pattern for a minimum of six months to receive this diagnosis. Conduct disorders are found more commonly among boys and usually emerge by eight years of age. Children with conduct disorders often blame others for their problems and have a low frustration tolerance. Longitudinal data indicate some stability from third grade to adolescence and even adulthood; children with more problems at earlier ages are more likely to get into trouble with the police during adolescence and have problems such as antisocial behaviours and substance abuse as adults. Factors contributing to conduct disorders include kind of parental discipline, parental monitoring, and family stress.

Other children suffer from depression; symptoms of depression include feeling sad or blue, having a poor appetite, having problems sleeping, experiencing a loss of energy, having a decline in self-esteem, losing interest in people and activities, and feeling helpless and hopeless. Since younger children may not be aware of or report feelings of sadness, adults' noticing behaviour changes is especially important. Estimates for incidence of depression in children are between 5 and 9 percent.

A number of factors contributing to depression have been hypothesized or identified. These include not feeling competent in academic, social, and other areas; stressful life events; and poorer problem solving abilities. A combination of these factors may result in children's feelings of hopelessness. Cognitive factors may play larger roles as children reach middle school. As they grow older, children may blow their failures out of proportion and minimize their successes.

Attributional styles, how one explains outcomes, may be related to depression. Attributions can be internal (typically related to one's effort or ability) or external (such as task difficulty or luck). Some of these, such as effort and luck, may be less stable, or more readily changed; global explanations, compared to specific explanations, would focus on the whole person rather than a specific behaviour or trait. Children who explain negative happenings with internal, stable, and global factors are more prone to depression.

Biological factors may also play a role in depression. Examining concordance rates for depression, if one identical twin is depressed, the other is depressed about 75 percent of the time. For fraternal twins, the concordance rate is only 19 percent. Depressed adults and children may underutilize **serotonin,** a neurotransmitter in the brain. Drugs enhancing serotonin action are sometimes given to treat depression.

Some children may experience **generalized anxiety disorder,** anxiety without a specific cause, or **obsessive–compulsive disorder** (**OCD**), which is characterized by recurring thoughts and compulsions that the child cannot control such as washing their hands excessively or rechecking their belongings many times. Children can also suffer from **separation anxiety disorder,** a persistent anxiety regarding separation from the parent, which may affect the child's willingness to attend school. Children with this disorder may experience nausea and may fear losing a parent. This may develop after a significant stressor, such as death of a pet or relative, or an illness.

School phobia is a related disorder, with the child being fearful of attending school and separating from the parent. Children may believe that school is a hostile, unpleasant environment, or they may be afraid of having to perform or having to answer questions in class. About 75 percent of children with separation anxiety disorder also refuse to go to school.

The first priority in treating school phobia is getting the child back into school quickly. Even if a parent or teacher doesn't understand the origin of the phobia, in many cases symptoms will disappear once the child is attending school regularly. While trying to understand the reason for the phobia is good, this understanding does not necessarily need to precede the child's return to school. A parent should try not to give in to the child's demands to stay home but should talk about the problem with appropriate people at school (teacher, principal, school nurse). If the problem is tied to the teacher, the parent should try to help the child find ways of dealing with the situation. The child should also be rewarded for attending school. If these measures don't work, professionals can help parents and school personnel learn how to apply cognitive behavioural techniques.

Critical Thinking Exercises

Exercise 1

Was your mother employed when you were growing up? Based on information in your text, discuss pros and cons of a mother's employment. Why do you think little research has been performed examining the effects of *paternal* employment on children?

____

____

____

____

____

____

Exercise 2

Jessica and Michael are unhappily married and are considering a divorce. Based on the studies reviewed in your book, how do you think a divorce would affect their children? If they do divorce, what advice would you give them to minimize the impact of divorce on their children?

____

____

____

____

____

____

Internet Activities

Activity 1

Choose one of the following terms and run an Internet search:

- school phobia
- separation anxiety disorder
- school refusal

Choose one of the sites that come up as a result of your search and read the information presented. Imagine that you are talking with primary school teachers about children who do not want to attend school. Based on what you have learned from this article or site:

1. How accurately do you feel this site portrays information about your topic? Why?
2. What information from the site might be helpful to teachers trying to help a child who does not want to come to school?
3. What is the most important thing you learned by reading the information on this site? Why?

Activity 2

How might parents develop and/or maintain strong parenting practices with their children after a divorce? Access the Internet and go to the following site from the Public Health Agency of Canada:

http://www.phac-aspc.gc.ca/publicat/mh-sm/divorce/index.html

Based on what you read, describe how the site recommends addressing each of the following issues:

- parental conflict
- divorce and adjustment
- divorce and well-being

In order to enhance your understanding from this assignment, answer the following questions about the site:

1. What content (points made) on the site did you find most informative? Why?
2. What content (points made) on the site is most relevant for a parent who is considering divorce?
3. What is the most important thing you learned by viewing this site? Why?

Observing Children and Adolescents CD-ROM Activity

Watch the "Self-Concept" video (Module 3, Section 3) and read the material on page 106 in *Observing Children and Adolescents.* Then answer the following questions:

1. How did the preschoolers, Todd and Christopher, describe themselves?
2. Compared to the preschoolers, what differences did you notice in the way the older children, Rachel, Stephanie, Ricardo, Joseph, and Jimmy, describe themselves? How did the children's self-concepts

seem to be changing with age?

3. What aspect of the videos surprised you the most, or what did you find most interesting about the development of self-concept in middle childhood?

Power Preview: Learning Objectives Sample Answers

1. How do children think of themselves in middle childhood? Do they focus on more superficial traits, or do they include their interests and personality traits?

When children respond to the question "Who am I?," their responses during middle childhood include physical traits and their competencies. They are beginning to include rudimentary personality characteristics, such as their likes and dislikes. Girls are more likely than boys to describe themselves as members of a group. A study with children from China reported that if children have siblings, they are also more likely to describe their group membership.

2. Explain why children's self-esteem tends to decline in middle childhood.

This decline may be related to children's increasing perspective-taking ability. The younger, egocentric child may not realistically consider input from others while the older child includes more external information in his or her self-evaluations and may hence be more critical.

3. Describe the importance of peer influences in middle childhood.

Peers become increasingly important during middle childhood. Because peers are from a different generation and have different needs and interests than parents, peers broaden children's experiences. They can provide children the opportunity to practise various relationship skills and competencies. Whether or not children are accepted or rejected by their peers relates to later emotional and social adjustment.

4. What factors contribute to popularity in middle childhood? Are children in this age group—like adolescents—pressured to conform?

Physical attractiveness, especially for girls, may be a factor. Popular children are also more likely to be nurturant, helpful, cooperative, and friendly—in general, more skilled in interactions with others. They are likely to praise others and are likely to have higher self-esteem; the latter may be related to their academic or athletic performance. Compared to firstborns, later-born children are more popular. Children who have various kinds of problems, including learning as well as behaviour problems such as disruption and aggressiveness, tend to be rejected by their peers. While pressure to conform to the expectations of others can be powerful, in general, children who are rejected do not "shape up." They tend to remain on the outskirts of the group although another alternative is to join deviant subcultures. If children who are rejected receive training in social skills, their popularity with others tends to increase.

5. Describe changes to power in the family during middle childhood. Do parents move toward more power sharing, or do they become more restrictive and controlling?

Parents monitor children less during the middle childhood years, with children increasingly monitoring their own behaviour. While parents still have ultimate control over the child, coregulation, a transferring of more control gradually to the child, also is occurring. Children are beginning to internalize their parents' standards.

6. Discuss whether or not it is better for parents who are in conflict to stay together "for the sake of the children" or to separate.

Ideally, a child would live with warm, supportive parents that relate well to all family members. For a variety of reasons related to disruptions in their lives, changes in economic status, and parental discipline alterations, children clearly experience greater problems following a divorce. Usually, though, the comparison group consists of children from two-parent families in general rather than children in two-parent conflicted families. Marital conflict has been linked to problems in children just as divorce has. When children see parents fighting, even physiological measures such as heart rate, blood pressure, and skin conductance are affected. One study reported that, while separation and divorce were related to increased problem behaviours in children, families with high levels of marital conflict that remained intact had children with even more behavioural problems.

7. Explain why daughters of employed women are more achievement-oriented and set higher career goals for themselves than do daughters of unemployed women.

Daughters whose mothers were employed tended to have higher career goals and were more achievement-oriented than daughters whose mothers were not employed; children may view their mothers as more competent if their mothers are employed. As one might expect, families in which the mother is employed are more egalitarian, not only in the distribution of the breadwinner role, but also in household chores. Mothers who are employed tend to be happier and less depressed; this may lead to more positive interactions with their children.

7. Describe the kinds of challenges children face when they enter "real" school.

The transition from home to school may be particularly difficult for children living in poverty; parents may be less likely to provide needed emotional and economic support. One survey of 7,000 kindergarten teachers found that teachers indicated that more than one-third of students were not prepared when they began school. Language skill was a major area of concern. When schools have transitional activities building continuity between home and school, children's adjustment is easier.

8. What is the "Pygmalion effect"?

Teachers' expectations for individual students may be important in student achievement. In **My Fair Lady*****'s reworking of Pygmalion lore from Greek mythology, a society lady was fashioned from a working-class girl. Similarly, expectations of teachers can become self-fulfilling prophecies; students will be more likely to succeed or fail depending upon teachers' expectations. In a classic experiment, teachers were led to believe that a group of new students were "late bloomers" who would do well in the coming year. Even though these students were randomly chosen, they made significant gains in performance on intelligence tests. Subsequent research has provided mixed support for the Pygmalion effect, or self-fulfilling prophecy. When credibility regarding the expected performance of targeted students was enhanced, the manipulation of teachers' expectations was most effective in terms of students' performance.***

9. Are teachers less likely to accept calling out from boys than from girls? Why?

In a study of students from four states and Washington, DC, students in fourth, sixth, and eighth-grade classes were observed. Boys tended to dominate classroom communication and were much more likely (eight times more likely) to call out an answer without first raising their hands. Moreover, teachers were more likely to remind girls to raise their hands but more likely to accept the answers from boys. Perhaps boys' calling out responses is accepted because assertiveness and impulsiveness may be part of the male gender role; calling out responses may not fit with the ladylike behaviour expected of girls.

10. What is meant by the term "conduct disorder"? Is this a form of mental illness?

Criteria from the Diagnostic and Statistical Manual (DSM) of the American Psychiatric Association are used to diagnose children with conduct disorders. Children must have shown evidence of a

troublesome behaviour pattern for a minimum of six months to receive this diagnosis. The criteria imply that bad behaviour is considered a mental illness if it's consistent and bad enough.

11. Describe why some children--like some adults--blame themselves for their problems, even if they don't deserve the blame.

Attributional styles, how one explains outcomes, may be related to depression. Attributions can be internal (typically related to one's effort or ability) or external (such as task difficulty or luck). Some of these, such as effort and luck, may be less stable, or more readily changed; global explanations, compared to specific explanations, would focus on the whole person rather than a specific behaviour or trait. Children who explain negative happenings with internal, stable, and global factors are more prone to depression.

12. Discuss whether or not children who have school phobia should be forced to attend school.

The first priority in treating school phobia is getting the child back into school quickly. Even if a parent or teacher doesn't understand the origin of the phobia, in many cases symptoms will disappear when the child is attending school regularly. While trying to understand the reason for the phobia is good, this understanding does not necessarily need to precede the child's return to school. A parent should try not to give in to the child's demands to stay home but should talk about the problem with appropriate people at school (teacher, principal, school nurse). If the problem is tied to the teacher, the parent should try to help the child find ways of dealing with the situation. The child should also be rewarded for attending school. If these measures don't work, professionals can help parents and school personnel learn how to apply cognitive behavioural techniques.

Chapter Review

Multiple Choice

1. According to Erikson, children in middle childhood are in what stage?
   a. intimacy vs. isolation
   b. trust vs. mistrust
   c. initiative vs. guilt
   d. industry vs. inferiority

2. Children's understanding or knowledge regarding the social world is called:
   a. social cognition
   b. cognitive socialization
   c. mutual understanding
   d. relational thought

3. According to your text, which statement is true regarding the development of self-concept during middle childhood?
   a. children's self-concepts fail to include concrete, external traits such as appearance
   b. children's self-concepts primarily include abstract, internal traits
   c. children's self-concepts include concrete, external traits and begin to include more abstract internal traits
   d. children's self-concepts include concrete, external traits, and begin to include more abstract internal traits but do not include group membership
4. Children's self-esteem:
   a. increases throughout middle childhood
   b. declines during middle childhood, reaching a low point at about age twelve or thirteen
   c. varies so much from child to child that no generalization can be made regarding self-esteem in middle childhood
   d. increases for girls but declines for boys during middle childhood
5. Which of the following is NOT true regarding learned helplessness?
   a. it is a child's belief that he or she cannot gain the rewards he or she seeks
   b. children with learned helplessness tend to quit more easily after failure
   c. children with learned helplessness are more likely to believe that success is due to ability rather than effort
   d. boys demonstrate more learned helplessness than girls
6. Regarding peer acceptance and rejection:
   a. popular children tend to be less physically attractive than other children
   b. children who are popular are self-centred and less nurturant than other children
   c. popular children, contrary to expectations, actually have lower self-esteem than less popular children
   d. compared to firstborn children, later-born children are more likely to be popular
7. During middle childhood, the gradual transfer of control from parent to child, with the parent retaining ultimate control, is known as:
   a. power sharing
   b. coregulation
   c. codependency
   d. codiscipline
8. Regarding children and divorce:
   a. children's problems may be related to changes in parental discipline, with parents becoming more inconsistent in discipline and less likely to use authoritative methods
   b. approximately 80 percent of children in Canada will experience the divorce of their parents
   c. children's problems following divorce reach a peak about two years following the divorce
   d. girls have a harder time following a divorce than boys

9. Which of the following statements is NOT true regarding maternal employment?
   a. delinquency is more clearly connected with lack of supervision during preschool years than with whether or not the mother was employed
   b. data from the National Longitudinal Survey of Youth found that neither continuity nor timing of early maternal employment related consistently to children's development
   c. middle school children whose mothers are employed tend to develop less responsibility and independence than children whose mothers are not employed
   d. in one study of working class mothers, employed mothers were less likely to be depressed than were full-time homemakers

10. Regarding school environments:
    a. smaller classes are related to increased math and reading achievement during early primary grades
    b. children from larger high schools (over 400 students) have fewer behavioural problems
    c. students do best when teachers use criticism and punishment to establish strict classroom control
    d. students learn less when they are supervised and actively instructed rather than left to work on their own

11. Another name for the Pygmalion effect is:
    a. self-fulfilling prophecy
    b. self-limiting effect
    c. self-propagating effect
    d. self-defeating effect

12. Which of the following was NOT one of the findings in the report about sexism from the American Association of University Women?
    a. teachers tend to pay less attention to girls than boys
    b. girls experience sexual harassment from male classmates
    c. textbooks in schools still ignore or stereotype girls/women
    d. some standardized tests, like the SAT, are actually biased against boys

13. Conduct disorders:
    a. are more prevalent in girls than in boys
    b. are unrelated to antisocial behaviour in adults
    c. are more prevalent in biological parents of children with conduct disorders than in adoptive parents of children with conduct disorders
    d. are less prevalent when parents use coercive discipline on their children

14. What factors are thought by psychologists to lead to depression in children?
    a. genetic factors since concordance rates are higher in identical than fraternal twins
    b. gaining greater social and academic competencies
    c. boredom caused by the lack of stressful life events
    d. attributing failure to external, unstable causes

15. Which is NOT a recommendation for a child suffering from school phobia?
    a. talk about the problem with the teacher, school nurse, or principal
    b. keep the child home from school until the phobia is resolved
    c. help the child explore ways to handle a specific situation that might be causing the phobia
    d. provide a reward of some kind to the child for attending school

Matching

Match each of the items from Column A with the corresponding item from Column B. There is only one correct answer per item.

	Column A		Column B
1. ______	coregulation	a.	Freud's stage for middle childhood
2. ______	industry vs. inferiority	b.	unwanted sexual comments/behaviours
3. ______	attributional style	c.	breaking rules; violating others' rights
4. ______	serotonin	d.	Pygmalion effect
5. ______	school phobia	e.	type of explanations given
6. ______	latency	f.	believing outcomes are unrelated to effort
7. ______	learned helplessness	g.	sharing control with the child
8. ______	sexual harassment	h.	Erikson's fourth stage
9. ______	conduct disorders	i.	neurotransmitter related to depression
10. ______	self-fulfilling prophecy	j.	anxiety related to school attendance

True–False

1. Based on research with children using social dilemmas, Robert Selman developed five levels of perspective taking.

   TRUE or FALSE

2. Girls are more likely than boys to be less confident in their abilities, even when they're performing at the same level.

   TRUE or FALSE

3. Children of lesbian and gay parents are generally found to score lower on measures of psychological adjustment than children of heterosexual parents.

   TRUE or FALSE

4. Over 70,000 divorces were recorded in Canada in 2003.

   TRUE or FALSE

5. Girls usually have a harder time adjusting to divorce than do boys.

   TRUE or FALSE

6. In households with a youngest child between six and fifteen years old, the rate of maternal employment in Canada is about 80 percent.

   TRUE or FALSE

7. Families with employed mothers tend to be less egalitarian.

   TRUE or FALSE

8. Boys' friendships tend to be closer, with boys' seeking confidants more than girls.

   TRUE or FALSE

9. Teachers who expect students to excel, spend most of the class time on academics versus discipline, and ask questions and give feedback enhance learning and achievement in their students.

   TRUE or FALSE

10. Separation anxiety disorder is found in about 80 percent of the children who refuse to go to school.

   TRUE or FALSE

Solutions

Chapter Review

Multiple Choice

1. d (481)	6. d (495)	11. a (504)
2. a (481)	7. b (487)	12. d (505)
3. c (483)	8. a (489)	13. c (507)
4. b (484)	9. c (493)	14. a (509)
5. d (485)	10. a (502)	15. b (513)

Matching

1. g (487)	5. j (513)	9. c (507)
2. h (481)	6. a (481)	10. d (504)
3. e (509)	7. f (485)	
4. i (510)	8. b (505)	

True–False

1. T (482)	5. F (490)	9. T (502)
2. T (485)	6. T (492)	10. T (513)
3. F (488)	7. F (494)	
4. T (488)	8. F (496)	

CHAPTER **14**

Adolescence: Physical Development

Learning Objectives

By the end of this chapter, you should be able to generate well-thought-out responses to demonstrate your understanding of the following learning objectives (sample answer comments are included at the end of this chapter):

1. Describe current views on adolescent development. Is adolescence a time of "storm and stress"?
2. Describe the processes involved in puberty for both girls and boys. What are the implications of early maturation for girls and boys?
3. Discuss the leading causes of death in adolescence.
4. Describe adolescent problems with weight. What are the most prominent eating disorders? How common are they in adolescent girls and boys?
5. Describe substance use and abuse in adolescence. Are there gender differences? Are there cultural differences?
6. Discuss the issue of sexually transmitted diseases. What are the implications of providing students with condoms?

Chapter Summary

Adolescence is often described as a time of storm and stress. G. Stanley Hall was the first to suggest that adolescence is an important and distinct developmental stage. The child is becoming an adult, and there are social, emotional, physical, and cognitive changes that accompany this transition. Clearly, adolescence can be a challenging time for both adolescents and adults. But just assuming that it is a stressful time does little to address why the transition can be stressful and what can be done to smooth it out.

Freud believed that the adolescent was entering the **genital stage** at puberty; sexual feelings that were once focused on the parent are now transferred onto other adolescents or adults. Freud's daughter Anna, like Hall, thought that adolescence is a period of turmoil. However, some adolescents may not experience a crisis at this stage; others argue that if we believe that all adolescents experience "troubles" at adolescence, we may not take seriously the genuine problems that they are having.

Puberty: The Biological Eruption

Puberty is defined as "a stage of development characterized by reaching sexual maturity and the ability to reproduce." Adolescence and puberty coincide, but they are not one and the same. Puberty is a biological concept while adolescence involves social, emotional, and cognitive changes as well. Puberty is viewed as being controlled by a complex **feedback loop** involving (1) the **hypothalamus,** (2) the **pituitary gland,** (3) the gonads (ovaries in females and testes in males), and (4) hormones.

The sex hormones (androgens and estrogens) trigger the development of both **primary and secondary sexual characteristics.** Primary sexual characteristics are those that make reproduction possible. These include the ovaries, uterus, penis, testes, and the like. Secondary sexual characteristics are those that represent sexual maturity but do not involve the reproductive structures. Breast development in females and the appearance of facial hair in males are examples.

At some point during adolescent development, the individual will experience a growth spurt. Girls typically begin this period of rapid growth in height and weight around age ten, and boys typically begin this period around age twelve. During this time, it is common for boys to grow fourteen and a half inches and for girls to grow about thirteen inches!

Despite these averages, there is a lot of variation in the timing of the growth spurt. Adolescents are often referred to as awkward. A significant reason for this may be **asynchronous growth.** In other words, different body parts are growing at different rates, and it is difficult for the adolescent to coordinate all of these changes. Eventually, however, all body parts catch up and the awkwardness goes away. During the past century, children in the Western world have grown dramatically more rapidly and have wound up taller than children from earlier times. This historical trend toward increasing adult height, which also has been accompanied by an earlier onset of puberty, is known as the **secular trend.**

Typical pubertal changes in boys include (1) increased production of testosterone, (2) the appearance of facial, underarm, chest, and pubic hair, (3) a deepening of the voice because of growth of the **larynx,** and (for 75 to 90 percent of adolescents) the development of acne.

Nearly half of all boys experience enlargement of the breasts, or **gynecomastia.** The organs that produce **semen** grow rapidly, and boys typically ejaculate seminal fluid by age thirteen or fourteen. About a year later, they begin to have **nocturnal emissions.** At age twenty or twenty-one, men stop growing taller because testosterone causes **epiphyseal closure,** which prevents the long bones from making further gains in length.

Typical pubertal changes in girls include (1) increased production of estrogen that may stimulate the development of the breasts and **labia,** (2) increased androgens that cause the **clitoris** to develop, (3) the appearance of underarm and pubic hair, and (4) **menarche** (first menstruation). The **mammary glands** do not mature fully until a woman has a baby.

Early maturation can have some dramatic effects on those to whom it occurs. Although studies are mixed, generally it appears that early maturation in boys has its advantages. Early maturing boys are more popular and are more likely to be school leaders. On the negative side, early maturation of the body does not mean that the adolescent boy is prepared to handle the pressure from coaches or peers to put that body to use. In addition, sexual opportunities may place pressure on these boys to show "how grown up" they really are.

Early maturation in girls does not appear to have as many advantages as it does for boys. Early maturing girls outpace the growth of both girls and boys and quickly become conspicuous. Many of these girls feel awkward and even embarrassed by the growth of their breasts. Early maturing girls have been found to be more likely to have conduct problems, to violate social norms (by drinking, smoking, etc.), to have an increased risk for eating disorders, and to engage in sexual activity.

Body image is an important concept during adolescence. The typical fifteen-year-old, for example, is less satisfied with his or her body than the typical eighteen-year-old. Girls, on average, feel more negatively about their bodies and suffer more depression than boys, although body image dissatisfaction can lead to depression in both boys and girls. Boys, though, may want to build muscle and put on more weight while girls are more concerned with dieting. Girls also are more likely to have eating disorders.

Emerging Sexuality and the Risks of Sexually Transmitted Infections

Adolescence is a time of many physical as well as cognitive changes. Although the young person is not yet an adult, he or she is rapidly becoming physically mature and capable of producing children. Sexual maturity brings with it an increase in hormones that energize the sex drive, and this, coupled with peer pressure, may make it difficult for the young person to make reasoned choices about engaging in sexual relations and how to be careful in doing so. One in every six adolescents, for example, will contract a sexually transmitted infection.

The most serious STI, of course, is **HIV/AIDS.** But there are many that young persons have not heard about that can be very harmful in their own right. These include chlamydia (a bacterial infection of the vagina or urinary tract that can lead to sterility), genital warts, herpes, syphilis, and many others. It is estimated that over half of sexually active women in the United States are infected with HPV (human papilloma virus). This is the virus that causes genital warts. Although this infection, in and of itself, is not fatal, it has been linked to serious illnesses such as cervical cancer.

The four most common risk factors for sexually transmitted infections are (1) sexual activity—you cannot get an STI if you do not have sex, (2) multiple sex partners—currently about 20 percent of high school students have sex with four or more partners, (3) failure to use condoms—about 67 percent do not use condoms or do not use them regularly, and (4) substance abuse—adolescent use of drugs is associated with more risky behaviour including unprotected sex.

The primary focus of prevention programs has been education. Knowledge is power, or so the cliché goes. Adolescents need to understand that sexually transmitted diseases can be fatal, lifelong, and/or lead to sterility and other illnesses such as cervical cancer. But knowledge is not always enough to change behaviour. Males may coerce females into having sex or into having unprotected sex. Females should be empowered to say "no," to carry condoms if they plan on being sexually active, and to be aware of the increased risk of risky behaviour, coercive attempts, and peer pressure when substances such as drugs and alcohol are being consumed.

Health in Adolescence

Most Canadian adolescents are healthy. In comparison to their parents, however, Canadian teenagers may be less healthy than their parents were at the same age. The reasons, however, are external. Today's teenagers are more likely to engage in risky behaviour such as (1) excessive drinking, (2) substance abuse, (3) reckless driving, and (4) unprotected sexual activity. Adolescent males are twice as likely to die than adolescent females. This is due primarily to their tendency to engage in behaviours that end in death due to accidents, suicide, and homicide. These three causes account for 75 percent of all adolescent deaths. Alcohol is frequently implicated in fatal accidents, which include automobile accidents and drowning.

The average nutritional need of the adolescent girl is 2,200 calories per day. Adolescent boys need around 3,000 calories per day. But adolescent nutrition involves more than just the number of calories consumed. Depending on the stage of pubertal development, adolescents also have increased needs for calcium, iron, zinc, magnesium, and nitrogen. Yet many adolescents have irregular eating patterns, especially those who are "watching their weight." Calcium intake is particularly important for females to build up their bone density and help prevent a serious condition known as **osteoporosis** later in life. Osteoporosis, a progressive loss of bone, affects millions of women, particularly after **menopause.**

Many adolescent girls (and boys) are concerned about their bodies. Western culture emphasizes slimness, and this, along with the rapid body growth of adolescence, makes many adolescent girls (and some boys) at risk for developing eating disorders.

Adolescent girls are more dissatisfied with their weight than adolescent boys and are more likely to go on diets. **Anorexia nervosa** is a severe eating disorder characterized by an intense fear of gaining weight and a refusal to maintain a healthy body weight. Typically, individuals with anorexia weigh less than 85 percent of what they should weigh.

Bulimia nervosa is another life-threatening eating disorder and is characterized by binging and purging. Binges typically follow severe attempts at restricting food intake. The binge, then, is followed by extreme efforts to purge the food so that weight gain can be avoided. The individual may use laxatives and excessive dieting in an effort to compensate for the food consumed during the binge. Depression often co-occurs with bulimia.

Factors associated with the development of eating disorders include (1) childhood sexual abuse, (2) cultural idealization of slimness, (3) involvement in activities such as dancing or modelling that have weight limits, and (4) familial factors such as obsessionistic and perfectionistic personality styles.

Although eating disorders are extremely resistant to treatment, some success has been gained through the use of antidepressant medications. In addition, cognitive behavioural therapy has been used in an effort to help the individual change the perfectionism and attitudes toward the body that reinforce the disorder. These efforts are aimed at helping the individual develop a more accurate and appropriate image of his or her body.

While many adolescents use drugs for the same reasons that adults do, to relieve medical problems and to deal with tension, depression, or boredom, adolescents may also use drugs because of peer pressure or to rebel against adults in their lives. The BDOC, Big Drug on Campus, is alcohol; also, almost 50 percent of high school students have at least tried marijuana before they graduate.

Substance abuse is continuing to use a drug in spite of various physical, social, or psychological problems caused by the substance. Note that it is not really the amount of the substance that is ingested that defines it as abuse; it is the role that substance is playing in the person's life.

Substance dependence is more severe than abuse. Saying that someone is dependent upon a substance means the person has lost control over use of that substance, has developed **tolerance,** and may very well demonstrate **abstinence syndrome** when usage suddenly drops off. Abstinence syndrome for alcohol, for example, includes tremors, restlessness, anxiety, weariness, high blood pressure, and a rapid pulse rate. These physical symptoms are indicative of withdrawal. Many individuals will continue to use the substance to avoid the discomfort of withdrawal.

Drugs can be categorized into multiple classifications. These include (1) depressants such as alcohol and **sedatives**, (2) stimulants such as nicotine, cocaine, amphetamines, or caffeine and, (3) hallucinogens such as marijuana and LSD. Depressants slow down the functioning of the central nervous system.

Alcohol lowers inhibitions, resulting in adolescents' doing things they normally would resist doing. Consuming five or more drinks within a relatively short period of time is considered binge drinking and is associated with bad grades, accidents, unprotected sex, and aggression. Adolescent drinking may lead to drinking problems in adulthood and resulting physical disorders such as cirrhosis of the liver and cardiovascular problems.

Stimulants act to increase heart rate and speed up body functions; this may cause some wear and tear on the body. Nicotine, the addictive chemical in tobacco, results in adrenaline being released and sugar poured into the blood by the liver; consequently, calories are burned faster, and the appetite is lower. Besides the psychological effects of euphoria and boosted self-confidence, cocaine causes the heart to beat faster, constricts arteries in the heart, and leads to high blood pressure, a sometimes deadly combination of physical events. Amphetamines have been used to keep individuals alert, but tolerance and dependence develop rapidly.

Hallucinogenics cause perceptual distortions; users of marijuana report feeling more sensory awareness, a seeming slowdown in time, and feelings of insight and creativity. While some individuals experience relaxation and elevated moods, others report disorienting and frightening experiences at stronger levels of intoxication. Marijuana use has been associated with impairment of working memory and perceptual–motor coordination.

Although lifetime substance use increased in adolescents from 1991 to 1996, the percentage of those reporting having used illicit drugs declined in 2003. A 2001 University of Michigan survey reported that around 30 percent of seniors in high school had engaged in binge drinking, as well as 10 to 20 percent of eighth-grade students. Approximately 3 percent of students in high school report having used steroids.

Adolescent substance abuse is related to having peers using and tolerating drugs. Parents with neglecting–rejecting or permissive styles of parenting are more likely to have adolescents who use drugs than parents using an authoritative style. Genetic predispositions may also be inherited from parents.

Adolescents who use drugs more often tend to have school problems and have low academic motivation. Symptoms of maladjustment such as antisocial behaviour, low self-esteem, anxiety, and depression may occur before drug abuse begins, so determining the direction of cause–effect relationships—whether drug use results from or leads to psychological problems—can be difficult.

Treatment/prevention approaches have come from a variety of individuals and disciplines including educators, health professionals, and police. Since many adolescents dependent upon drugs do not want to discontinue their substance use, treating them can be frustrating. Their social milieu may encourage the drug use, and relapse after treatment may occur. Treatment of related psychological disorders and/or family problems may also be important if relapse is to be prevented.

Critical Thinking Exercises

Exercise 1

Yvonne and Quint Bartel are worried about their daughter. They suspect that she is suffering from an eating disorder. Based on what you have learned from this chapter, what five questions would you ask the Bartels to determine if their daughter may suffer from such an illness and, if she does, which disorder (anorexia or bulimia) she might be suffering? Based on your reading of this chapter, what would you recommend as an approach to outpatient treatment for the daughter?

Exercise 2

You have been asked to design a campaign for the local high school to try to lower the number of students contracting sexually transmitted infections. Based on this chapter, how would you design this program? Be sure to include at least five specific recommendations that you would make and explain why you think each would help in lowering the incidence of infection.

Internet Activities

Activity 1

Access the Internet and go to the following URL:

http://anthro.palomar.edu/social/soc_4.htm

After reviewing this site, write out your thoughts on rites of passage. To focus your thinking, respond to the following questions:

1. What rituals do you think we could use in Canada to mark the transition from adolescence to adulthood?
2. What problems do you think such rites of passage would help to alleviate? Why?
3. Could such rites of passage create problems? If so, how? If not, why not?

Activity 2

Run an Internet search using one or more of the following terms:

- anorexia
- bulimia
- puberty
- body image
- adolescent drug use

Once you have chosen your term and conducted your search, select one of the sites that is accessed as a result of that search. Read the material. In order to enhance your understanding, answer the following questions about the information from the site:

1. What content (points made) on this site did you find most informative? Why?
2. What content (points made) on this site is most relevant to you, your life, and/or your career? How?
3. What is the most important thing you learned by viewing this site? Why?
4. If you were working with adolescents, what one piece of advice would you give them based on the content of this site? Why?
5. How reliable is the information from this site? How do you know?
6. How valid is the information from this site? How do you know?

Observing Children and Adolescents CD-ROM Activity

Watch the "Puberty and Body Image" video (Module 4, Section 1) and read the material on pages 128 and 129 in *Observing Children and Adolescents.* Then answer the following questions:

1. How do the comments of the three adolescent girls interviewed compare with the views of the girls you knew in high school? How do those comments compare with the views of the women you know now?
2. Do you feel that body image is more of a problem for women than for men? If so, why do you think this is?
3. What aspect of the videos surprised you the most, or what did you find most interesting about the puberty and body image in adolescence?

Power Preview: Learning Objectives Sample Answers

1. Describe current views on adolescent development. Is adolescence a time of "storm and stress"?

Early psychoanalytic views considered adolescence to be stressful as children grappled with their developing sexuality. Other views (such as that of Hall) viewed adolescence as a time of storm and stress. According to this view, adolescents swing back and forth between positive and negative moods, strive for independence yet crave dependence, and move between overconfidence and self-doubt. Clearly, however, not all adolescents will experience this transition period between childhood and adulthood to be stressful. Another problem with believing that everyone experiences "troubles" at adolescence is that we may not take seriously the actual problems that adolescents do have.

2. Describe the processes involved in puberty for both girls and boys. What are the implications of early maturation for girls and boys?

Girls and boys both experience psychological and physiological changes during adolescence. The physical changes tend to be referred to as "puberty." These include the development of primary sex characteristics (those that will lead to the ability to reproduce such as maturation of the sperm or the ovaries) and secondary sex characteristics that signal the transition to adulthood but are not indicative of reproductive capacity (such as the growth of facial hair in males and the development of breasts in females). Early maturation tends to have mostly beneficial implications for boys. They are seen as more mature and, because of their physical maturity may perform better in sports and be more popular. Early maturing girls, however, do not fare as well. Early maturation brings with it an increase in pressure to engage in adult acts (such as substance use and sexual activity). Because these girls are more mature than their female peers and tend to tower above same-age boys, they are more likely to affiliate with older girls and boys. This may expose them to adultlike behaviour.

3. Discuss the leading causes of death in adolescence.

Accidents are the leading cause of death among children and youth in Canada and may be related to the adolescent tendency to engage in risky behaviour. These behaviours include use of substances, engaging in unprotected sex, and unsafe driving habits. Many adolescents experience a sense of "invulnerability" that may lead them to believe that bad things will not happen to them. People who feel invulnerable are more likely to engage in dangerous behaviours such as drinking and driving.

4. Describe adolescent problems with weight. What are the most prominent eating disorders? How common are they in adolescent girls and boys?

The two main eating disorders are anorexia nervosa and bulimia nervosa. These are considered to be predominantly "female" illnesses due to different pressures placed on males and females to maintain a particular body image. Some studies find that ten times as many females as males suffer from eating disorders. European American females from more affluent families are particularly at risk. Anorexia involves an intense fear of being overweight. This may prompt severe dieting and weight loss, and lead to a distorted body image that causes the person to continue to lose weight long after others have noticed that too much weight has been lost. Bulimia may involve a perfectionistic perception of one's body shape and weight. Individuals with bulimia tend to engage in binge eating. Such eating, however, may prompt anxiety about gaining weight and, thereby, destroy the perfect weight they struggle to achieve. This anxiety often results in efforts to purge the consumed food via vomiting, intense exercise, and even the use of diuretics.

5. Describe substance use and abuse in adolescence. Are there gender differences? Are there cultural differences?

About half of high school seniors have tried illicit drugs. Marijuana use seems to be on the rise. Most students have tried alcohol, and many use it regularly. About 50 percent of males and 35 percent of females aged fifteen to nineteen reported binge drinking at least once in a given year. Although lifetime substance use increased in adolescents from 1991 to 1996, the percentage of those reporting having used illicit drugs declined in 2003. Approximately 3 percent of students in high school report having used steroids. Males, perhaps because of involvement in athletic programs and bodybuilding, are more likely than females to use steroids. Having peer groups who use drugs is a risk factor for drug abuse as is having parents with permissive or neglecting–rejecting patterns of parenting. Genetic predispositions may also be involved in adolescent drug abuse.

6. Discuss the issue of sexually transmitted diseases. What are the implications of providing students with condoms?

Sexually transmitted infections are most likely to occur during the adolescent and early adulthood years. The primary reasons are (1) the increased tendency for adolescents to engage in risky behaviours and (2) lower rates of condom usage. The most prevalent STI appears to be chlamydia, with many not even knowing they are infected. Chlamydia infection, however, can lead to pelvic inflammatory disease that often leads to infertility. HIV/AIDS is of particular concern because of the high likelihood of death. Providing education on the correct use of condoms is related to lower incidences of infection globally.

Chapter Review

Multiple Choice

1. G. Stanley Hall described adolescence as:
   a. the transition period between childhood and adolescence
   b. a time of storm and stress
   c. a relatively peaceful transition period
   d. none of these
2. The historical trend involving earlier onset of puberty and increased adult weight is referred to as:
   a. pubertal advancement
   b. pubertal enhancement
   c. the secular trend
   d. the bioprogressive trend
3 The average adolescent boy needs to consume how many calories per day?
   a. 2,000
   b. 3,000
   c. 4,000
   d. 5,000
4. Which statement **best** reflects the research described in your text regarding early and late maturation at adolescence?
   a. early maturation has few benefits for either boys or girls
   b. early maturation in general is very beneficial to both boys and girls
   c. girls seem to benefit more from early maturation than do boys
   d. boys seem to benefit more from early maturation than do girls
5. Which of the following is a primary sex characteristic?
   a. the ability to ovulate
   b. the growth of pubic hair
   c. deepening of the voice
   d. breast development

6. Roughly how many inches per year will the typical adolescent boy grow during the adolescent growth spurt?
   a. two
   b. three
   c. four
   d. five
7. Which of the following represents "asynchronous growth"?
   a. the speed of the adolescent growth spurt
   b. the fact that girls experience the growth spurt earlier than boys
   c. different parts of the body growing at different rates
   d. the presence of cephalocaudal development
8. What is primarily responsible for the development of acne in adolescents?
   a. the hormone testosterone
   b. poor hygiene
   c. poor nutrition
   d. stress
9. Men stop growing around age twenty or twenty-one because:
   a. of the presence of testosterone
   b. of an event called epiphyseal closure
   c. the long bones will no longer grow in length
   d. all of these
10. The most common STI in adolescence is:
    a. herpes
    b. chlamydia
    c. genital warts
    d. syphilis
11. Which of the following is considered a depressant?
    a. marijuana
    b. nicotine
    c. LSD
    d. alcohol
12. What percentage of adolescent deaths is due to accidents, suicide, or homicide?
    a. 45
    b. 65
    c. 75
    d. 85
13. Which of the following is/are true about eating disorders?
    a. prevalence rates have increased dramatically in recent years
    b. they primarily affect European American females
    c. individuals suffering from them tend to be higher in socioeconomic status
    d. all of these are true

14. Which of the following is the most severe?
    a. substance use
    b. substance abuse
    c. substance dependence
    d. tolerance
15. Transmission of infection of HIV:
    a. globally is predominantly through gay male sex
    b. is rare in the non-gay population
    c. has declined in recent years
    d. globally is predominantly through male–female intercourse

Matching

Match each of the items from Column A with the corresponding item from Column B. There is only one correct answer per item.

Column A		Column B
1. _______	primary sex characteristic	a. repeated use despite problems
2. _______	anorexia nervosa	b. leading cause of adolescent deaths
3. _______	substance dependence	c. intense fear of gaining weight
4. _______	accidents	d. maturation of the ovaries
5. _______	hallucinogenics	e. person will experience withdrawal
6. _______	HPV	f. 1 million new cases per year in the U.S.
7. _______	secondary sex characteristic	g. cycles of binge eating and purging
8. _______	chlamydia	h. 4 million new cases per year in the U.S.
9. _______	bulimia nervosa	i. growth of pubic hair
10. _______	substance abuse	j. give rise to perceptual distortions

True–False

1. Viewing adolescence as a time of "storm and stress" may lead some adults to take problems of adolescence less seriously.

   TRUE or FALSE

2. Typically, nocturnal emissions occur about a year after boys first ejaculate.

   TRUE or FALSE

3. Gynecomastia refers to enlargement of boys' breasts at puberty and is experienced by almost 50 percent of boys.

   TRUE or FALSE

4. The majority of adolescent deaths are due to accidents, most of them involving motor vehicles.

   TRUE or FALSE

5. *Menopause* refers to girls' first menstruation.

   TRUE or FALSE

6. Girls who are early maturers usually adjust more easily and have fewer problems than boys who mature early.

   TRUE or FALSE

7. HPV is another name for herpes.

   TRUE or FALSE

8. Around the age of eleven, adrenal glands in girls produce androgens that stimulate pubic and underarm hair growth.

   TRUE or FALSE

9. Parents who use the authoritative parenting style are less likely to have children who abuse substances.

   TRUE or FALSE

10. Women who smoke cigarettes during pregnancy increase their risk of having miscarriages and babies with low birth weights.

    TRUE or FALSE

Solutions

Chapter Review

Multiple Choice

1. b (522)
2. c (527)
3. b (524)
4. d (532)
5. a (523)
6. c (524)
7. c (526)
8. a (527)
9. d (528)
10. b (536)
11. d (551)
12. b (544)
13. d (547)
14. c (551)
15. d (540)

Matching

1. d (523)
2. c (545)
3. e (551)
4. b (544)
5. j (553)
6. f (536)
7. i (523)
8. h (536)
9. g (548)
10. a (550)

True–False

1. T (523)
2. T (528)
3. T (528)
4. T (544)
5. F (544)
6. F (534)
7. F (536)
8. T (528)
9. T (557)
10. T (553)

CHAPTER 15

Adolescence: Cognitive Development

Learning Objectives

By the end of this chapter, you should be able to generate well-thought-out responses to demonstrate your understanding of the following learning objectives (sample answer comments are included at the end of this chapter):

1. Describe intellectual development during adolescence. Be sure to discuss adolescent concern for privacy, adolescent feelings of invulnerability, and gender differences in intellectual development.
2. How does moral thinking in adolescence differ from moral thinking in younger children? Are there gender differences in moral development? If so, what are they?
3. Discuss the adolescent transition into high school. Is this transition more difficult for boys or for girls? Why? How many adolescents drop out of school and what are the leading causes for this dropout rate?
4. Discuss career development and work experience. Are there gender differences in employment rates after high school? If so, what are they? Do female and male adolescents view life after high school differently? If so, how?

Chapter Summary

The Adolescent in Thought: My, My, How "Formal"

According to Piaget, intellectual development in adolescence is characterized by the stage of **formal operations.** In this stage, the young person has moved from the concrete thinking of the middle and late childhood years and begins moving into the abstract reasoning and logic that will be a necessary part of adulthood. Young persons are able to hypothesize (e.g., "If I do this, then that will happen"), and their cognitive capacities are reversible and flexible.

This hypothetical thinking allows adolescents to project many possible outcomes from following many different pathways; this kind of thinking allows them to transcend the present experience and fantasize about possible futures. This expansive thinking that moves beyond self brings a price along with it. Although it opens the adolescent's mind to a spectrum of future possibilities (what is often called **utopian** thinking), it also creates a sense of empathy, causing the adolescent to consider the suffering of others.

Adolescents who reach the level of formal operations (according to Piaget, not all adolescents or even all adults reach this level of cognitive development) are able to think in metaphor (figures of speech about one thing that can signify another, such as "grasping at straws") and show an ability to engage in deductive reasoning. This form of reasoning involves drawing conclusions about objects or people once the thinker has classified that information. The following example illustrates deductive reasoning: "All people are mortal. Socrates is a person. Therefore, Socrates is mortal." Prior to formal-operational thinking, this concept would be difficult, if not impossible, to comprehend.

Although the adolescent is now able to contemplate and understand the thoughts and feelings of others, they are still quite egocentric when it comes to thoughts about themselves. Teenagers often experience what is called the **imaginary audience.** This is the misperception that others are as concerned with their thoughts, feelings, looks, etc. as they are. This may lead to an intense desire for privacy that can cause many conflicts between the adolescent and the parents or caregivers. While some researchers have explained the imaginary audience in terms of adolescent cognitive changes, others think it may emerge due to increased social scrutiny that leads to more social anxiety in the adolescent.

The **personal fable,** another development related to adolescent egocentrism, is believing that one's feelings and thoughts are unique and very special. This can lead to a sense of invulnerability that may be related to risky behaviours and the belief that others, especially parents, could never understand one's feelings and experiences.

In terms of cognitive abilities, there appears to be some fairly consistent gender differences. Adolescent females tend to outperform males on verbal tasks, and males tend to outperform females on tasks requiring visual–spatial ability. It is hard to separate how much of these differences are due to actual brain differences and how much is due to socialization and the different ways in which individuals interact with male and female children. Some research is looking at prenatal sex hormones as a possible contributor to these gender differences in cognitive abilities while other research focuses on environmental factors such as parents talking more to female infants than male infants and gender differences in play activities.

Sex differences in math are even more complex. Females may have a slight advantage in computation during middle childhood, but males have a bigger advantage in more select groups (like college students) on higher-level mathematical problems.

In considering the issue of gender differences, it's important to remember that any differences are just small, average group differences. Many males score higher than the average female on verbal tasks, and many females score higher than the average male on visual–spatial or math tasks.

The Adolescent in Judgment: Moral Development

As described in Chapter 12, Lawrence Kohlberg postulated three main levels of moral development with two stages within each level. At the first level, the preconventional level, children focus on consequences for themselves, avoiding punishment and possible reinforcements. At the conventional level, moral judgments begin to be made based on concerns related to pleasing others and obeying laws. Some individuals will reach what Kohlberg termed the **postconventional level** of moral development. The individual's own personal values are now seen as being more important than a specific law; laws have value because they are based on group consensus rather than being correct in their own right. Universal ethical principles are also recognized in stage 6 though Kohlberg in his later years dropped reasoning at stage 6 from his theory. Stage 6 is also characterized by **reciprocity,** the principle that actions have mutual effects and that people depend on one another to treat each other morally. Formal-operational thinking may be a prerequisite to postconventional moral reasoning, but an adolescent's having attained formal-operational thinking doesn't mean that he or she will make moral judgments at the postconventional level.

The majority of adolescents still use lower levels of moral reasoning.

Some correspondence has been found between individuals' levels of moral reasoning and their behaviours. For example, a person who makes moral judgments at the preconventional level is more likely to steal, cheat, and behave in other problematic ways. Altruistic behaviour is more likely to be associated with higher levels of reasoning about moral dilemmas.

Perhaps Kohlberg's theory is culturally biased, or the emergence of postconventional reasoning may be dependent upon higher education. In developing societies, postconventional reasoning is essentially absent.

The Adolescent in School

Adolescents, of course, are profoundly influenced by their experiences at school. They are receiving pressure from peers and teachers to act certain ways, to think certain thoughts, and to begin thinking about "where they are going." Most children experience a transition to a new school. Beyond shifts based on zoning, parental moves, and the like, all children will experience the transition from elementary school to high school. It is not unusual for this transition to be accompanied by a decline in grades and participation in school activities.

Research appears to demonstrate that girls are more influenced by this transition than boys. Girls show a more profound decrease in self-esteem. One explanation for this considers life changes. The greater the number of life changes experienced, the more difficult it is to make transitions. Given that most girls start puberty before boys, they may be experiencing this life transition at the same time they are making the transition from elementary school to junior high or high school.

There is some good news regarding Canadian dropout rates—they are declining. The 2004–2005 dropout rate was reported to be about 10 percent. More males than females drop out of school. The reasons for dropping out vary according to sex. Most reasons drop out because of school disengagement or wanting to earn money. For females, dropout rates are highly related to teenage pregnancy. Adolescents who adopt adult roles early (marrying at a young age, becoming a teenage parent) are significantly more likely to drop out of school. Programs to prevent high school dropouts typically include intervention, even in preschool (Head Start), having small class sizes, providing individual instruction/counselling, including vocational components that link learning to work experiences, involving families and community members, providing a positive school climate, and having reasonable and clear goals and motivational systems.

The Adolescent at Work: Career Development and Work Experience

What do you want to be when you "grow up"? How many times have each of us been asked this question? Thinking about life beyond school takes on increasing importance to the adolescent (and his or her parents and caregivers!) as the individual makes the transition to high school. Career development is influenced by a variety of factors including (1) abilities, (2) life experiences, (3) job opportunities, (4) parental expectations and support, and (5) economic factors.

As more and more women have entered the labour force, traditional thoughts about career opportunities have begun to change. Although there are still strong gender differences in the numbers of individuals engaged in many occupations (there are still, for example, significantly more male truck drivers and engineers and significantly more female nurses and elementary school teachers), the differences are not nearly as dramatic as they were just a few decades ago. Children are still very likely to engage in **occupational gender-typing.** This involves a strong tendency to filter thoughts about what men and women do (jobwise) through the schemas they have developed. (Remember gender-schema theory from chapter 10?) In other words, the child is strongly likely to categorize careers into ones that boys do and ones that girls do. Girls, particularly girls with more self-confidence and intellectual ability, are more likely than boys to choose nontraditional careers. Despite advances of women in the work and career force, there are still role expectations. If a couple is to have a family, for example, there is still an overwhelming tendency for the woman to be expected to figure out how to combine career and family life.

About 15 percent of Canadian youth aged fifteen through twenty-four work and go to school. These figures differ from American data detailing that by the time adolescents are seniors in high school, almost three-fourths of them are employed. The potential benefits of adolescent employment include developing a sense of responsibility, self-reliance, and discipline; learning to appreciate the value of money and education; acquiring positive work habits and values; and enhancing occupational aspirations. Although adolescents of lower socioeconomic status work mainly to supplement the family income, most middle-class adolescents use their income for personal purchases such as clothing, CDs and DVDs, sports equipment, stereos, TVs, and car payments. The proportion of earnings devoted to future university expenses or family expenses is small.

Critical Thinking Exercises

Exercise 1

Katrina and Josef are worried about their son. He is thirteen years old. As soon as he comes home from school, he goes straight to his room. As soon as dinner is over, he goes back to his room. He seems to place a high degree of value on his privacy. Using what you have learned from this chapter, what would you say to these parents to alleviate their concerns? Provide them with at least three concepts from this chapter that will address their fears.

____

____

____

____

____

____

Exercise 2

A friend of yours says, "It's okay to cheat as long as you don't get caught." Based on this comment, where might this person be on Kohlberg's stage theory of moral development? Why do you place the person at this level? Given what you know about Kohlberg's theory, what might we be able to do to move individuals such as this person to the next level of moral development?

Internet Activities

Activity 1

What can be done about the high dropout rates in Canadian high schools? Access the Internet and go to the following URL from the Canadian Council on Learning:

http://www.ccl-cca.ca/CCL/Reports/LessonsInLearning/LiL-16Dec2005.htm

Read the information available on the site. In order to enhance your understanding, answer the following questions about the sites:

1. What content (points made) on the site did you find most informative? Why?
2. What content (points made) on the site is most relevant for a parent who is concerned about his or her child and the potential for the child to drop out of school?
3. What is the most important thing you learned by viewing this site? Why?

Activity 2

Choose one of the following terms and run an Internet search:

- formal operations
- career development
- deductive reasoning

Choose one of the sites that come up as a result of your search and read the information presented. Imagine that you are talking to a parent of an adolescent. Based on what you have learned from this article or site:

1. How accurately do you feel this site portrays information about your topic? Why?
2. What information from the site might be helpful to parents of adolescents?
3. What is the most important thing you learned by reading the information on this site? Why?

Observing Children and Adolescents CD-ROM Activity

Watch the "Abstraction and Hypothetical Propositions" and the "Risk-Taking" videos (Module 4, Section 2) and read the material on pages 132 and 133 in *Observing Children and Adolescents.* Then answer the following questions:

1. How did the preadolescents' (Julor and Jenny) reasoning differ from the reasoning of the adolescent (Alan) in response to the question "What if people had no thumbs"?
2. Describe the explanations adolescents gave for drinking and driving and having unprotected sex. Use the terms "personal fable" and "imaginary audience" in your description.
3. What aspect of the videos surprised you the most, or what did you find most interesting about the reasoning portrayed in the videos?

Power Preview: Learning Objectives Sample Answers

1. Describe intellectual development during adolescence. Be sure to discuss adolescent concern for privacy, adolescent feelings of invulnerability, and gender differences in intellectual development.

If we follow the work of Piaget, the primary change in intellectual development from childhood to adolescence is the move from concrete thinking to logical and abstract reasoning. Piaget called this stage of cognitive development, "formal operations." Adolescents become increasingly concerned about their privacy, which may reflect another challenge that adolescents face—the "imaginary audience," the belief that others around them are as concerned with their thoughts and behaviours as they are. Despite changes in adolescent egocentrism, many adolescents still feel unique and invulnerable. Finally, there are some modest gender differences in intellectual development in adolescence, including males' demonstrating higher performance on visual–spatial tasks (especially mental rotation tasks) and females' showing higher performance on tests requiring language skills.

2. How does moral thinking in adolescence differ from moral thinking in younger children? Are there gender differences in moral development? If so, what are they?

There are many ways to think about moral dilemmas. One can focus on consequence, intention, what authorities say is right or wrong, or an internalized set of values that may not always conform to societal rules. Children in middle childhood tend to be in what Kohlberg called "conventional" morality. With this level of morality, moral judgments are made based on what societal rules state is right versus wrong. Many adolescents move into a third level of moral reasoning called "postconventional." With this level of moral reasoning, judgments are made on one's own moral standards. These judgments are made based on personal values and not just on what the rules say. In some studies, males have been found to respond at higher stages of moral development; for example, in one study, men were more likely to use stage 4 reasoning, emphasizing law and order, while women typically used stage 3 reasoning, emphasizing caring for others. Gilligan argued that such findings are the result of socialization differences, with girls' being reared to be more concerned about the well-being of others. More recent research has not found a significant sex difference.

3. Discuss the adolescent transition into high school. Is this transition more difficult for boys or for girls? Why? How many adolescents drop out of school, and what are the leading causes for this dropout rate?

Many adolescents have a difficult time making the transition from elementary school to junior high or high school. Oftentimes, this transition is difficult because children are moving from smaller schools in which they know many of the students to larger schools, larger classes, and a higher percentage of people that they do not know. The transition appears to be more difficult for girls than for boys. This probably has more to do with degree of life change than anything else. Research shows that life changes make it more difficult for the young person to make the transition into junior high or high school. One such life change is puberty. Given that girls are likely to experience puberty before boys, it may be that many of them are making the transition (especially to junior high school) at the same time they are experiencing puberty. Canadian school dropout rates are declining. The 2004–2005 dropout rate was

reported to be about 10 percent (down from 17 percent in 1990–1991). More males than females drop out of school. The reasons for dropping out vary according to sex. For males, reasons most cited for dropping out are school disengagement or wanting to earn money. For females, dropout rates are highly related to teenage pregnancy. Children from lower-income households have higher dropout rates. When income levels are held constant, ethnic differences in school dropout rates are reduced.

4. Discuss career development and work experience. Are there gender differences in employment rates after high school? If so, what are they? Do female and male adolescents view life after high school differently? If so, how?

Many factors influence employment choices after high school. These include but are not limited to (1) individual ability, (2) personality characteristics, (3) gender-role expectations, (4) life experiences, (5) parental expectations, (6) job opportunities, and (7) economic factors. More and more women are entering the work force, and traditionally gender-typed careers are not as strongly gender-typed as they used to be. More men, for example, may go into nursing, and more women may be pursuing careers as doctors. Although the gender gap is lessening in many fields (nurses, physicians, teachers), in fields such as math, science, and engineering, the gap has not closed much. Girls, particularly girls with more self-confidence and intellectual ability, are more likely than boys to choose nontraditional careers. Occupational gender stereotyping is stronger among boys than among girls.

Chapter Review

Multiple Choice

1. According to Piaget, what stage of cognitive development are adolescents in?
   a. concrete operations
   b. preoperational
   c. formal operations
   d. reflective operations
2. Which of the following is a metaphor?
   a. multiplication is the same as fast addition
   b. flopping around like a fish out of water
   c. all people are human; Jake is a person; therefore Jake is human
   d. none of these
3. What is “deductive reasoning”?
   a. a form of reasoning requiring one to draw conclusions
   b. a form of concrete thinking
   c. a type of metaphor
   d. a method for forming schemas

4. Which of the following represents "imaginary audience"?
   a. "I know how you feel"
   b. "Everybody is watching what I do"
   c. "I wonder how Suzi feels about this"
   d. "You can't know how I feel; you've never been through this before"
5. "I am invulnerable." What can we assume from this statement?
   a. the person who made it is probably an adolescent
   b. it is an example of a "personal fable"
   c. it represents a form of egocentrism
   d. all of these
6. On what intellectual task are gender differences in adolescents the greatest?
   a. mental rotation tasks
   b. hidden figures tasks
   c. tasks requiring imagination
   d. tasks involving distraction
7. Kohlberg suggests that some adolescents will reach a level of moral development called postconventional morality. What does this mean?
   a. moral judgments are based on the consequences of one's actions
   b. moral judgments come from following authority figures
   c. moral judgments are based on the intention behind the action
   d. moral judgments are derived from personal values
8. Is there a relationship between moral reasoning and moral behaviour in adolescence?
   a. yes, and training in moral reasoning may decrease problem behaviour
   b. no, because situational influences are usually more powerful than internal reasoning
   c. yes, for females but not for males
   d. no, the relationship does not set in until adulthood
9. How well do adolescents make the transition from elementary to junior high or high school?
   a. girls appear to have more trouble with the transition than boys
   b. it depends on how many life changes the adolescent is experiencing
   c. it depends on how much control the adolescent feels he or she has in life
   d. all of these
10. What percentage of Canadian students drop out of school?
    a. about 5
    b. about 10
    c. about 15
    d. about 20
11. What percentage of youth aged fifteen through twenty-four work and go to school?
    a. 6
    b. 8
    c. 15
    d. 16

12. Which of the following individuals would be the most vulnerable for dropping out of school?
    a. a sixteen-year-old who is married
    b. a young female from a middle-class background
    c. a young female from an upper-class background
    d. a young male from a middle-class background
13. Which of the following represents "occupational gender-typing"?
    a. "women can't be nurses"
    b. "a man would probably make a better doctor than a teacher"
    c. "I think I would be happier doing something a lot of other men do"
    d. all of these
14. Which is NOT one of Holland's career typologies?
    a. investigative
    b. conventional
    c. enterprising
    d. formalistic
15. Which is true regarding adolescent employment?
    a. lower-income youth are more likely to be employed than middle-income youth
    b. middle-class adolescents put away large amounts of earnings for college expenses in the future
    c. adolescents working more than eleven to thirteen hours a week have higher rates of substance abuse and lower grades than adolescents working fewer hours
    d. most adolescents work in relatively stable jobs with good pay

Matching

Match each of the items from Column A with the corresponding item from Column B. There is only one correct answer per item.

1. _______ metaphor
2. _______ deductive reasoning
3. _______ formal operations
4. _______ visual–spatial tasks
5. _______ preconventional morality
6. _______ 10 percent
7. _______ occupational gender-typing
8. _______ 15 percent
9. _______ verbal tasks
10. _______ postconventional morality

a. males tend to outperform females
b. percentage of students who drop out of school
c. degree differs across cultures
d. all cats are felines; Cleo is a cat; therefore, Cleo is a feline
e. moral judgments based on own moral standards
f. moral judgments based on selfish consequences
g. females tend to outperform males
h. stalking fame like a cat after a mouse
i. percentage of youth aged 15–24 that work and go to school
j. characterized by adolescent egocentrism

True–False

1. According to Piaget, adolescents are entering the stage of concrete operations.

   TRUE or FALSE

2. Deductive reasoning, hypothetical "contrary to fact" thinking, and sophisticated symbol use are characteristics of formal-operational reasoning.

   TRUE or FALSE

3. Sex differences in cognitive abilities reflect individual differences, not group differences.

   TRUE or FALSE

4. One study found that girls did worse on a hard math test if they were told, as an experimental manipulation, that sex differences had previously been found on the test.

   TRUE or FALSE

5. Cross-cultural research indicates that adolescents in rural villages in Mexico, Turkey, the Bahamas, and Taiwan move to the postconventional level of moral reasoning in about the same numbers as do adolescents in the United States.

   TRUE or FALSE

6. Boys' self-esteem is more likely to drop than girls' self-esteem with the move from elementary school to junior high.

   TRUE or FALSE

7. John Holland described six kinds of career typologies in an attempt to match personality types to different kinds of careers.

   TRUE or FALSE

8. Over 20,000 occupations are listed in the "Dictionary of Occupational Titles."

   TRUE or FALSE

9. Girls are less likely than boys to participate in occupational stereotyping.

   TRUE or FALSE

10. Although adolescents of lower socioeconomic status work mainly to supplement the family income, most middle-class adolescents use their income for personal purchases.

    TRUE or FALSE

Solutions

Chapter Review

Multiple Choice

1. c (566)
2. b (569)
3. a (576)
4. b (571)
5. d (571)
6. a (572)
7. d (576)
8. a (579)
9. d (581)
10. b (582)
11. c (588)
12. a (583)
13. d (588)
14. d (586)
15. c (589)

Matching

1. h (569)
2. d (569)
3. j (570)
4. a (572)
5. f (576)
6. b (582)
7. c (586)
8. i (588)
9. g (572)
10. e (576)

True–False

1. F (566)
2. T (569)
3. F (575)
4. T (586)
5. F (577)
6. F (581)
7. T (575)
8. T (586)
9. T (588)
10. T (589)

CHAPTER 16

Adolescence: Social and Emotional Development

Learning Objectives

By the end of this chapter, you should be able to generate well-thought-out responses to demonstrate your understanding of the following learning objectives (sample answer comments are included at the end of this chapter):

1. Discuss adolescents' imitating their peers' clothing, speech, hairstyles, and ideals.
2. Are adolescent males more concerned about occupational choices than adolescent females?
3. What happens to children's self-esteem as they enter adolescence?
4. Do adolescents from ethnic minority groups in Canada have lower self-concepts than adolescents from the majority group?
5. Adolescence is sometimes depicted as a time of "storm and stress." Discuss whether or not adolescents are in a constant state of rebellion against their parents.
6. Do adolescents have fewer friends or more friends than younger children do?
7. Are most adolescents' friends "bad influences"? Do parents and peers tend to exert conflicting influences on adolescents?
8. Does the relationship adolescents have with their parents relate to their being sexual at an early age?
9. Discuss why 47,000 Canadian teenagers become pregnant each year.
10. Do most adolescents or just a few adolescents engage in acts of juvenile delinquency?
11. Why would an adolescent commit suicide? How many actually do?
12. How do we determine when someone has become an adult?

Chapter Summary

Development of Identity and the Self-Concept: "Who Am I?" (And Who Else?)

Erik Erikson describes the adolescent stage of psychosocial development as one of identity versus role diffusion. Adolescents are faced with developing a sense of what they believe and who they are, **ego identity.** Since adolescents are now capable of formal-operational thought, they are more capable of weighing the many options available to them when making choices about careers, ideology, sexual orientation, etc. Adolescents may experience a **psychological moratorium,** an exploratory period in which they may try out different roles. During this time, adolescents often experience an **identity crisis.** The range of choices and the worry that making a choice may reduce their future alternatives may be overwhelming to adolescents. In the process of searching for an identity, adolescents may prematurely try to resolve identity issues by joining a certain group, defining their clothing, hairstyles, speech, and values by what other group members do.

Using Erikson's framework, Marcia defined four identity statuses, representing four possible combinations of **exploration** (active searching and questioning) and **commitment** (investing in specific values and goals). The **role diffusion** status refers to the individual who has neither actively explored identity issues nor has a commitment to a specific identity; this is the least developmentally advanced status. Individuals in the **foreclosure** status have a commitment regarding their identity but have not actively explored alternatives. Individuals who are currently questioning and exploring alternatives but do not yet have a commitment are classified with a **moratorium** identity status. Finally, **identity achievement** refers to individuals who have explored identity issues and resolved them with a firm commitment regarding their identity.

Ethnicity may also be related to identity development. Sometimes values of the dominant culture may conflict with those of ethnic groups. Also, experiencing prejudice may affect the development of one's identity. Socioeconomic factors may mean that members of some ethnic minority groups have fewer opportunities in terms of education and careers. Phinney described three stages in the formation of **ethnic identity:** first is **unexamined ethnic identity,** in which the individual has not questioned his identity; second comes **ethnic identity search,** in which the individual is actively questioning; and finally is **achieved ethnic identity,** which is based on a confident self-acceptance as an ethnic group member.

Erikson's identity development, which tended to focus on values and careers, may have been more accurate in describing identity issues for males than females; Erikson's later writings suggested that women's development may be different from men's and proposed that relationships may be more central to women's identity. Women's identities may be based on their roles as wives and mothers, so they may acquire their identities at the same time as they develop intimate relationships. However, research has found that women may be more similar to men in their identity formation. Some studies have found males and females to be equally concerned about occupations and interpersonal relationships. One study, though, did find that most high school boys perceived no conflict between potential family and career plans whereas high school girls were more likely to want to integrate both careers and family. Perhaps society does not consider males as responsible as females in terms of family duties and responsibilities.

As children enter adolescence, their self-concepts become increasingly differentiated. They may perceive themselves as behaving differently with friends than with parents and add more categories in their self-descriptions. In early adolescence, around ages twelve to thirteen, **self-esteem** (how persons value themselves) tends to be lowest, following a decline from middle childhood. Growing cognitive awareness and increased recognition of discrepancies between their ideal and real selves, especially in their physical appearance, may contribute to this drop. After ages twelve or thirteen, self-esteem begins to increase during the rest of adolescence. Friends and families who offer emotional support contribute to the development of self-esteem, with peer support becoming more important than family support by late adolescence.

For minority adolescents, healthy self-esteem seems to be tied to a strong ethnic identity. Canadian researchers found that for first- and second-generation Lebanese–Canadians, there was a positive correlation between Canadian identity and depression. Also, for minority Francophones, having support from the majority group but low support from other Francophones correlated to depression. This work suggests that a strong ethnic identity may be related to higher levels of adjustment. It is argued that in Canada a multiculturalism approach allows ethnic and minority groups to maintain their ethnic identity while exploring the majority culture.

Self-esteem tends to dip during early adolescence as young people face the differences between their real self and their ideal self. However, self-esteem tends to improve with emotional support from family and peers. Compared to adolescent boys, adolescent girls tend to have lower self-esteem. The gender gap increased from grade school to high school in one national survey. One factor may be the physical changes of adolescence, which are central to the development of self-esteem in adolescence. Although physical appearance is a concern for both girls and boys, it is relatively more important for girls. Others attribute the drop in girls' self-esteem to the negative messages that girls receive in school.

Relationships with Parents and Peers

While adolescence is a period of transition, regarding it as a time of "storm and stress," suggesting conflict and rebellion from parents, may not be very accurate. For some adolescents, their relationships with their parents may be quite positive. Adolescents certainly spend less time with their parents than they did in childhood, with one study reporting that nine-year-olds spent twice as much time with the family as fifteen-year-olds. This decrease in family time perhaps reflects the increased striving for greater independence from parents and may be adaptive. Adolescents can become more independent and still continue to have much love, respect, and loyalty for parents. Those adolescents who feel closer to their parents tend to be more independent and have more self-reliance as well as better self-esteem and fewer problems. Certainly conflicts do occur, especially during early adolescence, and often involve such things as homework, household chores, personal appearance, and curfews. Adolescents may want more control in making decisions regarding their own lives while parents, particularly mothers, may want to retain control. Teenagers interact more with mothers than fathers, engaging in more conflicts with mothers but also perceiving their mothers as more supportive and knowing them better than their fathers.

Parenting styles differentially affect outcomes for adolescents. Authoritative parents, who combine warmth and behavioural limits, tend to have adolescents who have the most competent behaviour, are more self-reliant, have fewer problems, and do better at school.

The influence of peers increases during adolescence. Friendships become increasingly more central, with adolescents having more friends than do children who are younger. A typical pattern is for an adolescent to have one to two "best" friends plus several good friends. Talking online or on the phone to friends is also important to adolescents who may spend several hours a day communicating with friends. Compared to younger children, adolescents are more likely to self-disclose personal information and emphasize mutual understanding in friendships.

Friends are likely to be of the same gender, age, and ethnicity and have similar attitudes about education, achievement, drinking, drug use, and sexual activity. Friends can promote psychological adjustment and a good self-concept. Having intimate friends is also associated with more advanced stages of identity development. Girls' friendships may be more likely to be intimate than boys' friendships, and girls may be more likely to disclose problems, secrets, and feelings to friends. Boys are more likely to have larger networks of less intimate friends and are more likely to participate in group activities.

Cliques are groups of five to ten people who hang out and share activities whereas **crowds** are larger groups of people spending varying amounts of time together. Crowds may be identified by labels such as "jocks" or "nerds," which can refer to certain activities or attitudes of group members.

Not only do adolescents spend more time with their peers, but they also are less influenced by adult guidance and control. Peer groups may gather away from home and have less supervision. Peer groups also begin to include the other gender during adolescence; this can lead to dating relationships. Most adolescents have begun dating by high school graduation. Functions of dating include having fun, enhancing prestige with peers, gaining experience relating to different kinds of people, and preparation for courtship as an adult. As adolescence progresses, dating relationships move from short, casual relationships to more stable, committed relationships.

While parents may worry about the "bad influence" of peers, this may not be a valid concern. Although the amount of peer influence certainly increases from early adolescence to mid-adolescence (and then declines), many adolescents still have close relationships with their parents. The domains of influence may differ, with peers being more influential in clothing styles and music tastes and parents being more influential regarding serious issues like educational and career goals. Peer pressure may be both positive and negative, and include pressure to complete high school but also to use drugs and engage in sexual activity. One study did find that, while some adolescents were encouraged by peers to academically achieve, others were discouraged from doing well by peers. Since adolescents tend to choose friends who are similar to them, peers may reinforce attitudes and beliefs that the individual already has.

Girls may be a little more concerned with being accepted by peers. Boys, though, may be more likely than girls to give in to pressures for misconduct. Also, adolescents who experience authoritative parenting, rather than authoritarian or permissive parenting, may be more able to resist negative peer influences.

Sexuality: When? What? (How?) Who? Where? and Why?—Not to Mention, "Should I?"

Masturbation is stimulating one's self sexually and, in adolescents, is the most common mode of sexual expression. While most adolescents engage in masturbation, it is more common in males (nearly universal according to Kinsey) than in females.

The majority of individuals have a heterosexual orientation (are attracted to individuals of the other sex), but some individuals have a **homosexual** orientation (are attracted to same-sex people). *Gay males* refers to men with a homosexual orientation, and *lesbians* refers to women who have a homosexual orientation. Individuals who are bisexual are attracted to both men and women. Sexual activity is not the same as sexual orientation; one might have sexual activity with a member of one's own sex without having a homosexual orientation.

"Coming out" may be a very hard process for adolescent individuals with a homosexual orientation. Adolescents who are gay may be rejected by friends and family; gay youths have higher rates of depression and suicide. Theoretical explanations for sexual orientation are varied. Learning theorists emphasize consequences (reinforcements/punishments) of behaviours and observational learning. Biological factors such as genes and hormones have also been considered; identical twins have a higher concordance or agreement rate for a gay male orientation than fraternal twins. In lower animal species, prenatal hormones have been found to affect the sexual behaviour of offspring.

Although the numbers of high school students having sex has gradually declined since the early 1990s, 40 to 50 percent of students are still engaging in intercourse. Males are more likely than females to be sexually active in high school. Usually the first sexual experience is not planned but "just happens." Increased levels of testosterone at puberty are probably related to increased sexual interest and activity. However, testosterone levels are related to sexual behaviour in boys but only to sexual interest in girls. Perhaps socialization influences and pressures are more important in determining whether or not girls become sexually active in high school. Teenagers who are older when they become sexually active are more likely to use contraceptives.

The relationships adolescents have with their parents relates to their sexual activity; those with closer relationships and good communication tend to delaying becoming sexually active. Also, these teenagers are more likely to use contraceptives and tend to have fewer partners than teens who are not as close to their parents.

Peer pressure to have sex can be important in adolescence and may be related to teenage pregnancy. While historically many teenage girls married and became pregnant, in Canada today, adolescents are often expected to delay marriage while focusing on their education and careers. Over 47,000 Canadian adolescents (between the ages of fifteen and nineteen) become pregnant each year. The rate of teenage pregnancy between 1984 and 1994 actually increased in Canada, a trend opposite to those of other industrialized nations. Teenage pregnancy in First Nations adolescent girls is especially high, with a rate thirty-eight times the national average. Reasons teenage girls become pregnant include receiving little educational advice at home or in school regarding ways to resist sexual pressure and not having easy access to effective methods of birth control. Rebellion against parents or wanting a commitment from partners may be additional reasons for becoming pregnant. Many teenagers, though, just do not fully understand the female reproduction system and cycle, including the odds of pregnancy, or, even if they do understand, fail to consistently use contraception.

In general, the consequences of unplanned teenage pregnancy can include medical complications and premature birth as well as low birth weight in infants. The mothers themselves are less likely to finish high school and go to college, leading to less income and a greater need for financial assistance. Although few teenage fathers contribute financially or emotionally to their children, most have problems themselves such as lower grades and entering the labour market at an earlier age. The children of teenage mothers are more likely to be economically deprived, but children whose mothers returned to school and found employment tended to fare better than others.

Recently, efforts to prevent teenagers from becoming pregnant have increased. These efforts have included sex education programs; although some have feared that such programs will lead to more sexual activity, some sex education programs may actually delay teenagers becoming sexually active. High school students who are sexually active are more likely to use contraception effectively if they have participated in sex education programs.

Juvenile Delinquency

One study found that among eleven- to seventeen-year-olds, four of five admitted to engaging in a delinquent behaviour at some time. **Juvenile delinquency** refers to a wide variety of illegal behaviours that are committed by a child/adolescent. Behaviours, such as drinking, that are considered illegal when performed by minors are called **status offences.** Behaviours range from very serious such as rape to milder offences such as truancy. Many antisocial/criminal behaviours increase sharply during adolescence but then drop off in adulthood. Youth crime rates in Canada decreased throughout the 1990s, and then generally increased from 1999 to 2003, and finally declined again in 2005.

Adolescent boys are four times as likely to be arrested as adolescent girls. The nature of the crimes vary as well, with boys committing more crimes of violence while girls are more likely to be arrested for crimes such as running away.

A number of risk factors contribute to delinquency. Included among these are families characterized by ineffective discipline, high levels of conflict, severe punishment and abuse, and neglect. Individual factors include lower self-esteem, impulsivity, feeling alienated, less mature moral reasoning, and a lower verbal IQ score.

Efforts to prevent juvenile delinquency have included training in social skills, moral reasoning, and problem-solving skills. The short-term effectiveness (when assessed six months or a year later) of such programs are better than the long-term outcomes. Rather than intervening at the individual level, some approaches focus on social systems like the peer group, family, the school, or the community; these broader approaches may be more successful. Early childhood intervention programs like Head Start are another way that efforts are made to increase positive outcomes and reduce negative behaviours such as delinquency.

Suicide: When the Adolescent Has Everything to Lose

Among older teenagers, suicide ranks as the third or fourth leading cause of death. About one to two Canadian adolescents between the ages of fifteen and nineteen in 100,000 commit suicide each year. Suicide occurs five to six times more often among First Nations groups than among non–Aboriginal youth. Suicide risk factors include feeling hopeless and depressed. Psychological problems experienced by suicidal adolescents include interpersonal problems, confusion regarding the self, emotional instability, and impulsiveness. Having impossible expectations for achievement and being perfectionistic may also contribute. Stressful life events, including deaths of friends or parents and relationship breakups, can cause psychological pain. Sexuality concerns as well as substance abuse can be other risk factors. Ineffective problem-solving strategies may also be related to suicide attempts.

More adolescent females attempt suicide, but males are more likely to actually commit suicide since males are more likely to choose more lethal means such as shooting or hanging themselves while females are more likely to use drugs or poisons. The likelihood of a teenage girl committing suicide is greatest if she suffers from depression, but the best predictor of suicide for teenage boys is a prior suicide attempt.

Epilogue: Emerging Adulthood—Bridging Adolescence and the Life Beyond

Jeffrey Arnett referred to the transition period from adolescence into young adulthood as emerging adulthood. Emerging adulthood is described as spanning the ages of eighteen and twenty-five, existing only in those rich societies that allow time for extended role exploration. However, even in wealthy societies not all individuals have the luxury of such self-exploration. According to Arnett, when individuals who are in the late teens to early twenties are questioned regarding whether or not they're adults, about 60 percent say "yes" in some ways but "no" in others.

A number of factors affect whether or not one is considered an adult. Historically, being married was important in being considered an adult; today other factors include having a full-time job and living in a residence separate from one's parents. Being financially independent, responsible for one's self, having an equal relationship with parents, and choosing one's own values/beliefs are also characteristics of adulthood.

Critical Thinking Exercises

Exercise 1

Some of your friends in high school may have had problems with self-esteem. Your chapter describes a number of factors that are related to the development of self-esteem. Choose one of your friends (use only his or her first name or change the name) and discuss how the factors (including ethnicity, gender, parental and peer support) described in your text might have contributed to lower self-esteem in your friend.

____

____

____

____

____

____

Exercise 2

Lisa is a sixteen-year-old high school student who spends hours a day on the Internet. Based on material from your text, what are some of the dangers that relate to Lisa's online involvement? What are some of the steps her parents might take to protect her? In your opinion, what is a reasonable amount of time for Lisa to spend online per day? What do you think her rights to privacy and online access as a sixteen-year-old should be?

____

____

____

____

____

____

Internet Activities

Activity 1

Should parents and high schools provide adolescents information about birth control? Access the Internet and go to the following URL:

http://www.sexualityandu.ca

As you review the site, look for information on the following issues:

- sex education for youth—evaluation
- sex education for youth—moral and ethical aspects
- sex education for youth—social aspects
- unwanted pregnancy

Once you have reviewed the site, answer the following questions:

1. What content (points made) on the site did you find most informative? Why?
2. What content (points made) on the site are most relevant for parents/teachers who are considering sex education?
3. What is the most important thing you learned by reviewing this site? Why?
4. How do you feel about the content of this site? Why do you feel that way?

Activity 2

Choose one of the following terms/phrases and run an Internet search:

- suicide prevention
- suicide awareness
- suicide warning signs
- suicide in high school students

Choose one of the sites that come up as a result of your search and read the information presented. Imagine that you are talking with a group of high school students about suicide. Based on what you have learned from this article or site:

1. How accurately do you feel this site portrays information about your topic? Why?
2. What information from the site might be helpful to high school students who may have friends contemplating suicide?
3. What is the most important thing you learned by reading the information on this site? Why?

Observing Children and Adolescents CD-ROM Activity

Watch the "Self-Concept: Identity Formation" and the "Self-Concept: Slang" videos (Module 4, Section 3) and read the material on pages 136 and 137 in *Observing Children and Adolescents.* Then answer the following questions:

1. Describe the plans the adolescents had for their lives. What plan did you have for your life in high school?
2. What slang expressions did the adolescents use, and what purpose might these expressions have had?
3. What aspect of the videos surprised you the most, or what did you find most interesting about the future plans and slang portrayed in the videos?

Power Preview: Learning Objectives Sample Answers

1. Discuss adolescents' imitating their peers' clothing, speech, hairstyle, and ideals.

Adolescents may prematurely try to resolve identity issues by joining a certain group; they may blindly follow their peers, defining their clothing, hairstyle, speech, and values by what the styles and values of other group members are.

2. Are adolescent males more concerned about occupational choices than adolescent females?

Erikson's later writings suggested that women's development may be different from men's and proposed that relationships may be more central to women's identity. A woman's identity may be based on the roles of wife and mother, so she may postpone identity formation until after marriage/childbearing. However, research has found that women may be more similar to men in their identity formation. Some studies have found males and females to be equally concerned about occupations and interpersonal relationships. One study, though, did find that most high school boys perceived no conflict between potential family and career plans whereas high school girls were more likely to want to integrate both careers and family. Perhaps society does not consider males as responsible as females in terms of family duties and responsibilities. Perhaps timing is also important—whether or not women have uninterrupted careers or whether they postpone employment to have children. The latter group may delay personal identity achievement until after their children enter school.

3. What happens to children's self-esteem as they enter adolescence?

In early adolescence, around ages twelve to thirteen years of age, self-esteem tends to be lowest, following a decline from middle childhood. Growing cognitive awareness and increased recognition of discrepancies between their ideal and real selves, especially in their physical appearance, may contribute to this drop. After twelve or thirteen years of age, self-esteem begins to increase during the rest of adolescence.

4. Do adolescents from ethnic minority groups in Canada have lower self-concepts than adolescents from the majority group?

For minority adolescents, healthy self-esteem seems to be tied to a strong ethnic identity. Canadian researchers found that for first- and second-generation Lebanese–Canadians, there was a positive correlation between Canadian identity and depression. Also, for minority Francophones, having support from the majority group but low support from other Francophones correlated to depression. This work suggests that a strong ethnic identity may be related to higher levels of adjustment.

5. Adolescence is sometimes depicted as a time of "storm and stress." Discuss whether or not

adolescents are in a constant state of rebellion against their parents.

While adolescence is a period of transition, regarding it as a time of "storm and stress," suggesting conflict and rebellion from parents, may not be very accurate. For some adolescents, their relationships with their parents may be quite positive. Adolescents certainly spend less time with their parents, with one study reporting that nine-year-olds spent twice as much time with the family as fifteen-year-olds. This decrease in family time perhaps reflects the increased striving for greater independence from parents and may be adaptive. Adolescents can become more independent and still continue to have much love, respect, and loyalty for parents. Those adolescents who feel closer to their parents tend to be more independent and have more self-reliance as well as better self-esteem and fewer problems. Certainly conflicts do occur, especially during early adolescence, and often involve such things as homework, household chores, personal appearance, and curfews.

6. Do adolescents have fewer friends or more friends than younger children do?

Friendships become increasingly important to adolescents, and they will have more friends than do children who are younger. A typical pattern is for an adolescent to have one or two "best" friends plus several good friends. Talking online or on the phone to friends is also important to adolescents, who may spend several hours a day communicating with friends. Adolescents are more likely than younger children to self-disclose personal information and emphasize mutual understanding in friendships.

7. Are most adolescents' friends "bad influences"? Do parents and peers tend to exert conflicting influences on adolescents?

While parents may worry about the "bad influence" of peers, this may not be a valid concern. Although the amount of peer influence increases from early adolescence to mid-adolescence (and then declines), many adolescents still have close relationships with their parents. The domains of influence may differ, with peers being more influential in clothing styles and music tastes and parents being more influential in serious issues like educational and career goals. Peer pressure may be both positive and negative, and include pressure to complete high school but also to use drugs and engage in sexual activity. One study did find that, while some adolescents were encouraged by peers to academically achieve, others were discouraged from doing well by peers. Since adolescents tend to choose friends who are similar to them, peers may reinforce attitudes and beliefs that the individual already has.

8. Does the relationship adolescents have with their parents relate to their being sexual at an early age?

The relationship adolescents have with their parents is related to their sexual activity; closer relationships and good communication with parents are related to delaying becoming sexually active. Also, these teenagers are more likely to use contraceptives and tend to have fewer partners than teens who are not as close to their parents. The sexual double standard may also be an issue here; parents may tell girls not to be sexually active while the message to boys may be to use precautions.

9. Discuss why 47,000 Canadian teenagers become pregnant each year.

Some of the reasons teenage girls become pregnant include receiving little educational advice at home or in school regarding ways to resist sexual pressure and not having easy access to effective methods of birth control. Rebellion from parents or wanting a commitment from their partner may be additional reasons for becoming pregnant. Many teenagers, though, just do not fully understand the female reproduction system and cycle, including the odds of pregnancy, or, even if they do understand, fail to consistently use contraception.

10. Do most adolescents or just a few adolescents engage in acts of juvenile delinquency?

One study found that among eleven- to seventeen-year olds, four of five admitted to engaging in a delinquent behaviour at some time.

11. Why would an adolescent commit suicide? How many actually do?

About one to two Canadian adolescents between the ages of fifteen and nineteen in 100,000 commit suicide each year. Suicide risk factors include feeling hopeless and depressed. Psychological problems experienced by suicidal adolescents include interpersonal problems, confusion regarding the self, emotional instability, and impulsiveness. Having impossible expectations for achievement and being perfectionistic may also contribute. Stressful life events, including deaths of friends or parents and relationship breakups, can cause psychological pain. Sexuality concerns as well as substance abuse can be risk factors as well. Ineffective problem-solving strategies may also be related to suicide attempts.

12. How do we determine when someone has become an adult?

A number of factors affect whether or not one is considered an adult. Historically, being married was important in being considered an adult; today other factors include having a full-time job and living in a residence separate from one's parents. Being financially independent, responsible for one's self, having an equal relationship with parents, and choosing one's own values/beliefs are also characteristics of adulthood.

Chapter Review

Multiple Choice

1. The individual who described four "identity statuses" was:
   a. Erik Erikson
   b. Jeffrey Arnett
   c. James Marcia
   d. Sigmund Freud
2. An adolescent who has not made a commitment to an identity and is not exploring, trying to form an identity, is considered in which status?
   a. role diffusion
   b. foreclosure
   c. moratorium
   d. identity achievement
3. The ethnic identity search stage is most similar to which identity status?
   a. role diffusion
   b. foreclosure
   c. moratorium
   d. identity achievement
4. How do careers and gender affect identity development?
   a. recent studies have found no differences between male and female adolescents
   b. adolescent females tend to develop their gender identity earlier than adolescent males
   c. women who defer employment until after their children enter school develop a personal identity earlier than do women who have uninterrupted careers
   d. females are more likely than males to integrate family and occupational plans into their identity

5. Which of the following is true regarding the development of self-esteem?
   a. self-esteem hits a low point around ages twelve or thirteen and then improves during adolescence
   b. self-esteem hits a high point around ages twelve or thirteen and decreases during adolescence
   c. self-esteem does not change during the adolescent years
   d. self-esteem decreases for males but increases for females during adolescence
6. Which of the follow is NOT true regarding adolescents' relationships with parents?
   a. adolescents have more interactions with their mothers than their fathers
   b. late adolescence is more characterized by conflicts and bickering than is early adolescence
   c. adolescents and parents are similar in basic values such as social, political, and religious beliefs
   d. adolescents whose parents used authoritative parenting styles are more competent and self-reliant
7. Regarding friendships in adolescence:
   a. adolescent friendships are less likely than childhood friendships to emphasize self-disclosure
   b. younger children have more friends than do adolescents
   c. adolescent friends are usually similar in race, ethnicity, and educational aspirations
   d. boys' friendship networks are smaller and tend to be more exclusive than girls' friendship networks
8. According to the Kinsey studies published in the middle of the twentieth century:
   a. the incidence of masturbation was lower in boys than girls
   b. few males or females masturbated
   c. more males engaged in bestiality than masturbation
   d. masturbation was almost universal among adolescent males
9. Which statement is NOT true?
   a. the suicide rate is higher among gay and lesbian adolescents than among heterosexual adolescents
   b. learning theorists explain sexual orientation in terms of consequences received for behaviours (reinforcement and punishments) as well as observational learning
   c. sex hormones affect the sexual behaviours of lower animals
   d. fraternal twins have a higher agreement rate for male homosexuality than identical twins
10. Regarding the use of contraceptives:
    a. teenagers who are older when they become sexually active are more likely to use birth control than teenagers who are younger
    b. about two-thirds of adolescents use contraceptives the first time they have sex
    c. teens with lower self-esteem are more likely to use birth control
    d. adolescents who have poor communication with their parents are more likely to use contraception
11. Teenage pregnancy:
    a. rates are higher among middle-class adolescents than among lower-class adolescents
    b. increased during the last decade of the twentieth century
    c. occurs frequently despite the fact that 80 percent of sexually active girls use birth control
    d. will end in abortion almost half the time

12. According to Rathus et al., there are four areas of psychological problems that put adolescents at risk for suicide. Which of the following is NOT one of those areas:
    a. interpersonal problems
    b. emotional instability
    c. confusion about the self
    d. tendency to be reflective
13. Which statement is true?
    a. teenage boys are more likely to engage in delinquent behaviours, but girls are more likely to be arrested
    b. teenage boys are more likely to engage in delinquent behaviours than girls and are more likely to be arrested
    c. teenage girls are more likely to engage in delinquent behaviours than boys and are more likely to be arrested
    d. teenage girls are more likely to engage in delinquent behaviours, but boys are more likely to be arrested
14. Which of the following statements about suicide is true?
    a. Aboriginal youth have the lowest suicide rate
    b. Suicide tends to run in families
    c. Males attempt suicide more often than females
    d. Suicide is not related to drug and alcohol use
15. Which is NOT a warning sign of suicide?
    a. losing interest in previously enjoyed activities
    b. engagement in social relationships
    c. giving away possessions
    d. talking and or writing about death or dying

Matching

Match each of the items from Column A with the corresponding item from Column B. There is only one correct answer per item.

Column A		Column B
1.	_______ foreclosure	a. four identity statuses
2.	_______ Arnett	b. reaches lowest point at age 12 or 13
3.	_______ self-esteem	c. identity commitment with no exploration
4.	_______ Erikson's fifth stage	d. emerging adulthood
5.	_______ Marcia	e. illegal behaviour defined by age
6.	_______ authoritative parenting	f. occurs more often in males than females
7.	_______ clique	g. 5–10 teens who hang together
8.	_______ masturbation	h. suicide occurs 5 to 6 times more often
9.	_______ status offence	i. related to more self-reliance, competence
10.	_______ First Nations youth	j. identity versus role diffusion

True–False

1. The last stage of ethnic identity development is "achieved ethnic identity."

   TRUE or FALSE

2. Self-concept becomes less differentiated as children move into adolescence.

   TRUE or FALSE

3. Peers tend to be more influential than parents in the domains of educational plans and careers.

   TRUE or FALSE

4. Girls' friendships in adolescence tend to become more intimate than the friendships of boys.

   TRUE or FALSE

5. The likelihood of a girl committing suicide increases if she exhibits depression.

   TRUE or FALSE

6. Around 3 percent of males and 2 percent of females indicate they have a homosexual orientation.

   TRUE or FALSE

7. The percentage of teenagers (high school students) who are sexually active has increased since the early 1990s.

   TRUE or FALSE

8. One study reported that, in a sample of eleven- to seventeen-year-olds, four in five had participated in delinquent behaviour.

   TRUE or FALSE

9. Contrary to popular belief, adolescent girls are more likely than adolescent boys to participate in delinquent behaviour.

   TRUE or FALSE

10. Children who show aggressive, antisocial, and hyperactive behaviour at an early age are more likely to show delinquent behaviour in adolescence.

    TRUE or FALSE

Solutions

Chapter Review

Multiple Choice

1. c (597)
2. a (597)
3. c (598)
4. d (601)
5. a (603)
6. b (604)
7. c (606)
8. d (610)
9. d (612)
10. a (615)
11. d (615)
12. d (622)
13. b (620)
14. b (624)
15. b (623)

Matching

1. c (597)
2. d (625)
3. b (603)
4. j (597)
5. a (597)
6. i (605)
7. g (607)
8. f (610)
9. e (619)
10. h (624)

True–False

1. T (600)
2. F (601)
3. F (605)
4. T (606)
5. T (624)
6. T (611)
7. F (613)
8. T (619)
9. F (620)
10. T (620)